AUTHENTIC
VIETNAMESE
COOKING

FOOD FROM A FAMILY TABLE

CORINNE TRANG

FOREWORD BY MARTIN YAN

PHOTOGRAPHS BY CHRISTOPHER HIRSHEIMER

VERVE
EDITIONS

SIMON & SCHUSTER

SIMON & SCHUSTER
Rockefeller Center
1230 Avenue of the Americas
New York, NY 10020

Designed by Toby Fox

Manufactured in the United States of
    America

10 9 8 7 6 5 4 3 2 1

Library of Congress
    Cataloging-in-Publication Data
Trang, Corinne
    Authentic Vietnamese cooking:
    food from a family table/Corinne
    Trang; foreword by Martin Yan;
    photographs by Christopher
    Hirsheimer
    p. cm.
    Includes Index
    1. Cookery, Vietnamese. I. Title
TX724.5 V5T724 1999
641.59597—dc21
99-26713
        CIP

Produced by
VERVE
  EDITIONS
Burlington, Vermont
    verve@together.net

ISBN 0-684-86444-4

To my father,

NHU MINH TRANG,

and my mother,

MARIE-JEANNE "MINOU" TRANG,

for giving me the best of both worlds

◆

To my husband,

MICHAEL McDONOUGH,

who has as much passion for discovery as I do, and who

offers patience, support, and love each day

ACKNOWLEDGMENTS

I WISH TO EXPRESS my gratitude to the following persons whose support, enthusiasm, and professional insight were invaluable in creating my first cookbook: ◆ Michael McDonough, for his inspired editing and criticism; Kate Nowell-Smith for testing and editing the recipes; and Virginia Croft for copy editing. Their scrutiny proved to be invaluable in organizing my thoughts. Art Director Toby Fox, whose sensitivity and unique approach to design are felt on every page; photographer Christopher Hirsheimer for her encouragement, genuine passion for Asian foods, and beautiful photographs; and photo editor Maria Millán for her technical input. At Verve Editions, Gary Chassman for eating his first bowl of *pho* in my kitchen, and also for helping me make my dream come true. Steven West for his assistance in organizing the project. Martin Yan, a great master of Asian cuisines, for taking the time from his very busy schedule to write such kind words, and for being a great inspiration. At Simon & Schuster, Jonathon Brodman, production editor; Beth Wareham, director of publicity; Mary Ellen Briggs, publicist; and Andrea Mullins, assistant editor; for their expert assistance. A special thanks goes to Sydny Weinberg Miner, executive editor, for her clear vision and valuable input, which help set the tone of the book. ◆ My aunt Kheng Trang for helping me organize my various trips to Paris, and especially for her support and late-night conversations. My aunt Loan Vuong and my mother, Minou Trang, for sharing their cooking know-how with me (even when they least suspected!), and my father, Nhu Minh Trang, for his insights on Asian culture and for providing me with the best ingredients. ◆ To my toughest critics, the Trang clan—William, Philippe, Melinda, Christopher, William "petit frère," and Chloé—for heated but rewarding food conversation. Finally, to friends and fellow foodies with whom I have shared meals and exchanged ideas (and still do) and who have supported my work: Colman Andrews; Karen and Jean-Louis Dumonet; Steven Skov Holt, Mara Holt Skov, and their son Larson; Dorothy Kalins; Denise Lee; Elaine Louie; Françoise Magis; Louise Magis; Gérard and Pamela Maurice; Marianne McNamara; Hervé and Christopher Poron; Jacqueline Rolli; Ilene Shaw; Jane Sigal; and Anthony Walton. Every day is a feast!

Thanks a million to all, and to all a million thanks!

TABLE *of* CONTENTS

FOREWORD

ONE OF MY EARLIEST ENCOUNTERS with Vietnamese cuisine came in the form of a question. "What's Vietnamese food like?" someone in the audience of one of my cooking demonstrations asked. "Is it like Chinese? Or is it closer to Thai?" the person went on. This was two decades ago, when Vietnamese cuisine was just beginning to make an inroad into North America. I remember having to give a long pause to compose my answer, partly because I wasn't expecting such a question after a demonstration of Kung Pao Shrimp and partly because, to be perfectly honest, I had only the most fundamental knowledge of Vietnamese cooking at that time.

Since that unexpected Q&A incident, I have made it a personal mission to learn as much as I can about Vietnamese cuisine. To my delight, it has been a most enjoyable journey of discovery. It is undeniable that Chinese cuisine has influenced greatly the culinary landscapes of many of its Asian neighbors, but this road of influences runs in both directions. Many Southeast Asian cuisines have in turn introduced new herbs, spices, ingredients, and cooking methods to the Chinese kitchen. It is all part of the natural growth and evolution of any cuisine.

The rapid growth of Vietnamese communities in North America has brought on an explosion of Vietnamese food in this country, and those of us who live in California have reaped much of the benefits. In less than two decades I have witnessed dozens of Vietnamese restaurants spring up in areas where there was only one or two as recently as a decade ago. But quantity is only half the picture. The variety and the quality of food have vastly improved in a short span of time as more authentic spices and ingredients have become available to satisfy the taste of the newly settled Vietnamese population.

On a personal note, I have found a great sense of kinship with this newest group of Asian immigrants to America. Many of them are of ethnic Chinese background, and we share a common language, heritage, culture, and of course, great fondness for good food.

Corinne first came to visit me at my cooking school in northern California, and instantly I recognized a talented individual with a most unique approach to and outlook on food. Her multi-ethnic background has given her a unique perspective not only on French and Vietnamese cultures but also on Chinese and American. And on the culinary front, Corinne is most articulate in voicing the many international influences that Vietnamese cuisine has benefited from and the many contributions that Vietnamese cooking has made to the West as well as other Asian cuisines. But more than a voice, Corinne is never shy to roll up her sleeves and put her words into action. Her keen eye for food styling and her artistic flare have earned her a solid reputation in the New York mass media, and after so many insightful articles, I am glad that she is finally putting her energy into a full-length book.

I am very honored to be asked to write a few opening words for this wonderful book, *Authentic Vietnamese Cooking*. Now I am totally prepared for the next person who asks me, "What is Vietnamese food like?" I will simply recommend anybody to read this book. Through Corinne, I have gained a whole new perspective on Vietnamese cuisine.

Martin Yan

Yan Can Cook, Inc.

January 5, 1999

VIETNAMESE FAMILY FEAST

COOKING HAS ALWAYS BEEN my private passion, a part of my world I never thought I would share until I began this book—something reserved for holidays, for family gatherings, for rites of passage and other celebrations. Whether in France, where I was born and raised among my mother's family, or throughout Southeast Asia, where we lived and visited on and off for years with my father's family—food was always something held close to the heart.

My mother's mother, and her mother, and so on back for generations lived and learned cooking in the Loire Valley—the "Valley of the Kings"—where French cuisine was established when Paris was a minor provincial capital, and the center of power and culture was at Blois. I learned specialties from the many regions of France—*coq au vin, pommes dauphines, tarte Tatin*, and other classic dishes—watching my grandmother at her stove. Her sons would sometimes return from trips to Normandy with special salts—*sel de guérande* and *fleur de sel*, rich with minerals—used to enrich seafood, meat, and vegetable dishes. Or she would travel to Auvergne, where my late grandfather's family lives, returning with her prized *fromage*, the key to her *truffade*, sautéed potatoes and Cantal cheese. In France I was exposed to a culture in which the appreciation of food is as important as reading and proper manners: you are not whole or civilized if you are without it.

From the Asian side of my family, I learned that "food is the

Opposite page, left to right: My aunts Kiang, Kheng, and Chhorn in their home in Phnom Penh, Cambodia, in 1962.

My Chinese grandfather Mai resettled in Cambodia after leaving China during the Japanese occupation. Here, he poses on his balcony in Phnom Penh in 1962.

center of life." Consistent with Chinese culture, this is meant literally and revolves around the family, home, culture, social relations, health, a seat of ideas, an expression of emotion, a form of display, and so forth: it is life. For my family, food was and still is most certainly connected to life's celebrations and deprivations, sometimes to survival itself. The twentieth century's violent diaspora in China, Cambodia, and Vietnam found my family moving from place to place, country to country, and culture to culture. Like so many others during times of hardship, they looked to resettle, some fleeing in airplanes, others on foot for hundreds of miles through the jungle and its uncertainties. Some moved to different parts of Asia, some to Europe and the United States. When not cheated by death—as many were in Pol Pot's Cambodia—they adapted, learning new cultures while guarding the ones they already knew. Their cultures were portable and capable of absorbing elements around them. Like the Taoist view of water, perhaps, they part, transmute, absorb, remain static, or move on, but they remain water just the same.

Because of this resilience, these forced journeys, and a keen interest in the world around them, this side of my family has a deep knowledge of Southeast Asian cuisines, as well as dozens of classic Chinese dishes. Several of my aunts and uncles run restaurants in France and the United States. My father is still a purveyor of Asian staples, spices, and delicacies. He speaks seven languages, all of which are necessary in conducting the serious business of food.

Family trips to Southeast Asia—where my father's large Chinese family settled after leaving Hunan province in the 1930s—were also characterized by extraordinary culinary experiences.

My grandmother, who settled in Cambodia, made *hu tieu do bien*, a rice noodle or egg noodle soup with fresh shrimp, pork tenderloin, and fish balls; and spicy curries with *prahoc*, a pungent fish paste that fills the house, stings the eyes, and delights the palate. Her menus were a blend of dishes learned in her native China and her adopted Cambodia. Later on some of my aunts and uncles migrated to Vietnam, and they brought their foods to the table. Knowledge of yet more types of food came from family members who settled in Indonesia. So as much as I grew up among *les fromages* and *les charcuteries*, I also grew up among discussions of rice and ginseng, of *nuoc cham* (spicy and sweetened fermented fish dipping sauce) and *vit quay* (laqué duck). Woks and sauté pans, clay pots and baking dishes, chopsticks and cutlery hold equal sway in my childhood memories. Dinner could mean Chinese, Cambodian, Thai, Indonesian, Vietnamese, or French.

MY FRENCH GRANDMOTHER, JEANNE BARBET, AT THE FAMILY ESTATE IN LE MANS AROUND 1935. AS A LITTLE GIRL, I WATCHED HER PREPARING WONDERFUL FOODS AT HER STOVE. TODAY, AT 90, SHE CONTINUES TO BE A GREAT INSPIRATION.

A Cuisine's Evolution:
Absorption, Adaptation, Refinement in Cooking

IT WAS, however, in the great cultural mix of New York—where my passage into adulthood, marriage, and professional life took place—that I gained perspective on these experiences and understood their importance. French and Chinese culinary cultures are classic, even ideological; New York's culinary culture is diverse, fused, and admixed. A global crossroads, it reflects the daily rub of more than one hundred cultures. Vietnam, too, is a crossroads. For centuries it has been washed over by Chinese, Cambodian, Indian, French, Russian, and American political, military, and cultural

influences, all the while fiercely defending its indigenous traditions. Its cuisines are, in many senses, the quintessential "fused" cuisines. In Southeast Asia you can glean this complex process of development by careful study and analysis: by deconstructing the influences. A dish like *ech cari* (curried frog's legs), for example, incorporates spices and cooking methods taken from native Vietnamese cooking and southern Indian spicing. *Thit heo kho nuoc dua*, braised pork shank in coconut juice, is a northern dish derived from the Chinese classic braised caramelized pork. In Southeast Asia, cuisine's evolutionary mechanics occurred over thousands of years, through the force of conquest or the fortuitous paths of trade and commerce. It was essentially unobservable.

In New York (and, to a certain extent, San Francisco), however, I learned to see cuisine's evolutionary mechanics from day to day, driven by experimentation and a relaxed, nonideological attitude toward cooking. In restaurants, in informal conversations with friends, and in spirited debates with culinary professionals, I could discern and observe cuisine being constructed.

It is in New York that I learned to see my family's tradition most clearly, to respect its portability and flexibility. Food can be fused into new dishes and forms, can be evolved, or can be enjoyed as a classic. Using the city as a base, I have been able to travel back to places where my family once lived, to research and relearn its traditions, to see them in new ways. And it is out of these journeys and experience that this book comes. Vietnam is its focus because of all the cultures of Southeast Asia it most completely embodies the blend of French and Chinese culinary traditions, and so mirrors my own experiences and personal history. It also reflects my aspirations toward sharing the good news about Asian cooking in general: it is rich, sophisticated, subtle, and accessible, all at the same time. In Vietnamese cooking, especially, the tricky processes of evolution we so value in our contemporary world have been distilled into magnificent dishes, complex flavors, and unexpected combinations that can delight any palate. And all cooks can learn from the historical Vietnamese process of absorption, adaptation, refinement—of invention and discipline held in the mind simultaneously.

My father, Nhu Minh, as a young student in Blois, France, in 1960, shortly after leaving Cambodia for the first time to pursue his college studies.

Consider, for example, humble bread: *baguette* from Paris and *baguette* from Saigon. The first is made from wheat; the second is made from rice and wheat. I reflected on this for the first time when I was recently in Saigon. The shape and color of the loaves are similar; so is the way they are baked in large ovens and in bulk. Even the bakeries themselves are similar in size and configuration. The color, flavor, and texture are only slightly different. But the Vietnamese would more likely use their *baguette* to scoop up *cari ga* (chicken curry) than enjoy it with Brie or Saint André, as would the French while sipping their wine. There is Vietnamese pâté as well, and a series of sandwiches made with, essentially, "cold cuts," or *charcuterie*, on *baguette*. That crossover, that melding, which I took for granted as a child, is what I have come to appreciate in the United States. The Vietnam that is a crossroads between Europe, Asia, and the United States is the Vietnam I have experienced through my family wanderings, settlements, stories, and especially my family meals.

Multiple Traditions, Regional Cuisines

I N T H I S V O L U M E I want to share what I came to think of as the wonderfully varied regional cuisines of Vietnam: the Simple North, the Sophisticated Center, and the Spicy South. As a little girl, I remember eating all sorts of wonderful meals that I would later understand were influenced by China, India, and other neighboring countries, as well as France. While children in America and Europe were eating traditional Western foods, I ate *cua hap bia* (crab steamed in beer), *goi muc* (spicy squid salad prepared with holy basil), *banh xeo* (lacy rice flour crêpes filled with shrimp), and *cari ga* (curried chicken) served with a *baguette*. More important, I saw these meals prepared. Trips to the market, fires built for the grill, or the hot pots slow-cooked over coals—my earliest memories are of these things. Even when words were not exchanged, the offering of a meal carefully prepared spoke volumes, from wife to husband, from mother to child. Food as bond, as family, as the spiritual glue of a culture.

This book is a collection of recipes from my Vietnamese family table. Whether from relatives or family friends, these are the foods that delighted our senses, challenged our palates, and made us come running when called to table. My hope is to take you, the reader, through the ingredients and techniques of this extraordinarily refined cuisine and to bring the experience of my family table to yours. Wherever possible I have used the most accurate and traditional preparation and cooking methods —things learned at home, passed from mother to daughter. Ideally, you should eventually gain enough confidence to make these foods your own, absorbing their principles, ultimately improvising comfortably with your own cooking utensils, ranges, ovens, and grills. Whatever your heritage, let enthusiasm and love of food lead you, for Vietnamese cuisine is a special sort of "fusion" cuisine, a culinary cycle. My European mother learned by watching my Asian grandmother and aunts preparing dishes of Vietnamese origin—often with ingredients such as asparagus or condensed milk that had come to Asia from France over one hundred years ago. In this Vietnamese environment, it was her "foreignness" that made her at home.

ONE OF THE LAST FAMILY PORTRAITS WITH MY GRANDFATHER MAI AND GRANDMOTHER HUONG IN THEIR LIVING ROOM. MY FATHER HOLDS ME, WHILE MY MOTHER STANDS WITH MY BROTHER WILLIAM. IT WAS 1969 AND, TRAGICALLY, THE WAR IN SOUTHEAST ASIA WAS ABOUT TO EXPAND INTO CAMBODIA.

Some Essential History

IN ORDER TO UNDERSTAND the nature of Vietnamese cuisine, some small amount of history will be helpful. Why, for example, did I learn three cuisines, each different yet related? Why is the Center sophisticated, a kitchen of delicacy and refinement, while the North offers simple, hearty dishes? And what is the origin of the hot, complex foods of the South? To start, Vietnam, at the eastern edge of Southeast Asia, has been a crossroads of civilizations for centuries. Much of its diversity originates in this simple fact. A second basic: the Viet people are an ancient race who mixed with more than fifty other native or migratory ethnic groups. Originally from coastal China, the Viet lived in a rugged land, a spine of steep mountains that fall to plains and fall again to the sea. From the fifth century B.C.E., these people warred, intermixed, and created empires. They were, in turn, dominated by empires. Born of turmoil, twentieth-century Vietnam is united. The diversity

born of over two millennia of conflict, migration, and cultural aspiration is memorialized and celebrated in culture and, as I have known it, cuisine.

A Cornucopia of Influences

CHINA AND FRANCE—the major powers that colonized Vietnam—have also been the most influential in its cooking. The pervasive use of woks and chopsticks, as well as cooking methods such as stir-frying and deep-frying, can be traced from the Chinese north. Carried south by traders and occupying armies, these basic implements are now found throughout Vietnam. French colonial influence can be seen in the use of baked breads, certain desserts, vegetables, and coffees. Also important, the Annamese, an ancient native people who warred with the Chinese for centuries and eventually established an empire among the peoples of central Vietnam, also contributed a refined, even artistic or noble cuisine. This cuisine was known as the imperial cuisine, or cuisine of the emperors. Its primary goal was to combine the northern and southern Vietnamese cuisines and turn these into a refined cuisine more suited for the noble families of Hue. The presentation, an array of bite-size morsels, delicately styled, was unparalleled. Their wars with the Khmer, or native Cambodians, provided a conduit for other Asian influences, what we might think of as Indian. India's spicy cuisine is most purely felt in the South, however, where sea trading routes, the Gulf of Thailand, and the delta cultures of the Mekong River fused to form the third regional variation on a culinary theme. There are also minor and curiously exceptional influences from the former

American presence in the South, evident in the introduction of snack foods such as popcorn, which I came to know as an adolescent living in the United States. Birthed at a time when Rome was young, Vietnam was actively absorbing influences through conflict and conquest even as humans first set foot on the moon.

Corinne Trang
New York, 1999

VIETNAMESE CASSIA CINNAMON BARK

Essential Ingredients

I GREW UP in a family in which exotic foods were commonplace. As a child, I was exposed to the highly developed regional culinary cultures of France and learned many Eastern cuisines while traveling in Asia. In addition to what I picked up in the family kitchens of relatives and friends, my father, who has been supplying Asian foods to the markets and restaurants of New York's Chinatown for years, instilled in me a love of food and a respect for ingredients.

This chapter provides a listing of what I call the "essential ingredients" of Vietnamese cooking, items you will require in preparing the recipes in this book. For the most part, they are available in Asian markets, but increasingly you can also find them in the international food section of your local supermarket. If you cannot locate certain items, I have also listed some very good mail-order sources (page 245).

Rice and Other Starches

The Erawan "Three Elephant" brand, imported from Thailand, offers some of the finest-quality jasmine long-grain rice, as well as other rice and starch products. It is primarily sold in Asian markets and through mail-order sources.

LONG-GRAIN RICE (gao te)
For long-grain rice, I prefer jasmine-scented rice. The grains are tender, and they stay whole and separate when cooked; the scent and flavor are excellent. The grains are lightly translucent when raw but turn white when cooked.

MEDIUM-GRAIN RICE
This grain, like long-grain rice, is also good steamed. The grains are lightly translucent when raw but turn white when cooked. When cooked, the rice is tender and the grains are intact. (Japanese sushi rice is a very good type of medium-grain rice.)

SHORT-GRAIN RICE
This grain is perfect for making rice porridge. It breaks down easily and evenly. The grains are lightly translucent when raw but turn white when cooked.

GLUTINOUS RICE (gao nep) This short-grain rice is also referred to as sticky or sweet rice. It undergoes a special preparation in which the grains are soaked for several hours, drained, and then steamed. When cooked, the grains are thick, firm, and translucent.

RICE VERMICELLI (bun) Fresh rice vermicelli is slightly thicker than *banh hoai* (dried and ultra-thin), and is sometimes served with curries or with grilled meats and shredded vegetables.

RICE VERMICELLI, DRIED (banh hoai) Like all rice noodles, dried vermicelli is made of rice flour, salt, and water. Perhaps the thinnest vermicelli made, it is almost always part of the Vietnamese table salad served to wrap grilled meats, seafood, and other foods such as spring rolls. Before adding to the table salad, place the vermicelli in a dish with lukewarm water to cover. Let soak until pliable, about 20 minutes. Bring water to a boil in a pot over high heat and boil the vermicelli for 3 seconds.

RICE STICKS (banh pho) These dried rice sticks are flat and come in three sizes, "S" (small), "M" (medium), and "L" (large). Add them to soups or stir-fries.

RICE PAPER (banh trang) Rice papers are made of rice flour, salt, and water and are sun-dried on bamboo mats, giving them a distinctive crisscross pattern. They are sold as rounds, in several sizes, and in a single triangular size. For summer rolls I like to use 6-inch round papers, and when making spring rolls, I use the triangular papers.

RICE FLOUR (bot te) This is made from white short- or long-grain rice and is used for making batters, noodles, crêpes, and bread.

GLUTINOUS RICE FLOUR (bot nep) Made from glutinous rice, this is used for making sweet dumplings, which are fried or steamed. It has a chewy texture when cooked.

TOASTED RICE FLOUR (thinh) This flour is made by toasting rice grains in a dry skillet and grinding them to a powder. Its subtle, smoky flavor complements grilled shrimp on sugar cane especially well. Because it is not readily available, you'll need to make this quick recipe. Toast 1½ cups short-grain sticky rice (or any rice you prefer) in a nonstick skillet over medium heat, stirring occasionally until the grains turn a rich golden color, about 20 minutes. Allow to cool prior to grinding into a fine powder. You'll notice that your toasted rice flour will never be as fine as regular rice flour, but that is what gives food a unique texture. Although you will not get the smoky flavor, using rice flour is perfectly acceptable. Keep refrigerated for up to 6 months.

POTATO STARCH (bot khoai) Potato starch (not sweet potato starch) is used as a binder for making meatballs or fish *quenelles*, giving them a springy texture. Do not confuse potato starch with dehydrated mashed potato spuds. Potato starch looks and feels like a very fine flour. (The Japanese make excellent potato flour.)

TAPIOCA STARCH (bot nang) This flour is made from the cassava (or manioc) root and is used to thicken sauces. When making ice cream, I add it to the custard just before taking it off the heat. This prevents the ice cream from melting too quickly. It is also used in making fresh rice sheets, giving them a slightly translucent character.

TAPIOCA PEARLS (bot bang) Tapioca pearls are used primarily in sweets, often combined with coconut milk. The pearls come in various sizes, ranging from the size of BBs to the size of green peas. I prefer the smallest for a more delicate texture. Dry, they are white, and cooked, they are transparent. These can be found in all Asian markets and the international foods section of many supermarkets.

Fresh Ingredients

The most important fresh ingredients in Vietnamese cooking are chilies, cilantro, mint, shallots, garlic, and lime. The more exotic herbs, such as lemongrass, holy basil, *rau ram*, and saw leaves, can be hard to find, and unfortunately there are no substitutes. For example, holy basil is completely different from Italian basil, so the two should not be confused, and they are most certainly not interchangeable. What I have discovered, however, is that as long as you have cilantro and mint, you'll get by. This is not to say that these two herbs are substitutes for the rarer herbs but that their unique flavors are true to the spirit of the cuisine.

Hint: Store herbs rolled up in a paper towel and plastic wrap in the refrigerator to keep them fresh for several days. Do not wash them until you are ready to use them, as they will begin to rot soon after they get wet or if they are overhandled. Certain fruits and vegetables are also used consistently in Vietnamese cooking as critical components rather than accents or optional items. They include the exotic star fruit, or carambola, and earthy mung beans.

CARAMBOLA (khe) Also known as star fruit, this distinctively shaped fruit is yellow to light green in color and, as the name suggests, is shaped somewhat like a star. It is eaten as a fruit when ripe and as a vegetable when unripe. When unripe, its tangy flavor is an excellent complement to sweet grilled meat; as such, it is often part of the "table salad."

CHILIES (ot) Bird's eye and Thai chilies are the most commonly used in Southeast Asian cuisines. They should be seeded, as the seeds are overpoweringly hot and lack subtlety. The "heat" of these chilies can be overwhelming, so use them sparingly to complement a dish.

CILANTRO (rau mui) Also known as coriander (although this term refers not only to the greens but also to the seeds and plant as a whole) or Chinese parsley. Although you will most often use the leaves, the stems are also full of flavor, and you can include them when making soups or steaming rice. (Trim off the part of the stem closest to the root.) When choosing cilantro, make sure the leaves are bright green. If they are dull, they are beyond their prime.

GARLIC (toi) A fundamental building block of Vietnamese cuisine. Its presence in a dish can be increased or decreased depending on when it is harvested, its type, its freshness, and how it is "prepped." When I buy garlic, I look for spring garlic heads with small cloves because they tend to be sweeter. The larger cloves tend to have a bitter sprout inside, so remove it before using the clove. Garlic appears in almost every savory dish, especially meat dishes, in part because of its health benefits. It lowers cholesterol and cleanses the blood.

GINGER (gung) Although not used as commonly by the Vietnamese as by the Chinese, ginger is still an important flavor in braised dishes and stocks. There are several types of ginger rhizomes on the market. Young ginger has a nearly translucent thin yellow and pink skin and is incredibly tender. It can be preserved in salt brine or candied. Mature ginger, with a dull yellow, thicker skin, is more fibrous and should be cut against the grain for use in savory dishes. It is considered therapeutic for stomachaches and seafood poisoning.

HOLY BASIL (rau que) Also known as Thai basil, this herb has a very distinct lemony flavor. Its narrow green leaves have a subtle purple hue. It is usually part of the "traditional herbs" that accompany a number of Vietnamese dishes. It can be found in Southeast Asian markets. Italian basil is not a substitute.

LEMONGRASS (xa) Also known as citronella, lemongrass is used widely in Southeast Asian cuisine. Its unique tangy flavor complements a wide range of dishes, from soups to stir-fries to stews and even desserts. It is a grass and so will always look very fibrous and fairly dry. Remove the outer leaves and dark green leafy tops before using. The bulb, which is the lower creamy white part, can be crushed, ground, and sliced. Fresh or frozen lemongrass is best, as the dried versions have lost their flavor.

LIME LEAVES (la chanh) Available in Southeast Asian markets fresh, frozen, or dried, lime leaves are used to flavor stews and soups. If you cannot find them, substitute lime peel.

LOTUS ROOT AND SEEDS (sen) The small off-white seeds and fibrous root of the aquatic lotus plant are available in Asian markets fresh, canned in brine, or dried. The fresh are best, but the dried are perfectly fine. (Soak the dried seeds and roots overnight, then cook until tender.) I try to stay away from canned versions because they have the ability to absorb the flavor of the salt and the metal can. The seeds are commonly used in desserts or as stuffing for rice cakes, and both seeds and root are used in savory dishes.

MUNG BEAN SPROUTS (gia) Mung bean sprouts are sold in many Asian markets. There is no substitute for this sprout. They have yellow heads with a thin green skin and a white stem, about 1½ inches long. Available fresh.

RAU RAM This herb (also known as Vietnamese coriander) has pointy narrow leaves and a very distinctive flavor. Available seasonally in Asian markets, *rau ram* has no real substitute, so make a real effort to find it. If all else fails, use cilantro for a different but still authentic flavor.

SAW LEAF (ngo gai) Saw leaves are long and narrow with serrated edges. Similar in taste to cilantro but more pronounced, they are sold in Asian and Caribbean markets.

LA LOT *La lot* leaves are often referred to as pepper leaves, as they are closely related to the plant that produces peppercorns. Use these heart-shaped shiny green leaves to flavor soups or meats, as in *bo la lot* (beef in *la lot* leaves). They are available only in Asian markets. Grape leaves, although different in flavor, make a good substitute for wrapping, and they are more widely available.

SUGAR CANE (mia) Sugar cane has a long, green, segmented stalk. In Vietnam it is used as both a source of sugar and a source of food. A remark-

able example of its use in Vietnamese cooking is the classic grilled shrimp on sugar cane sticks. Sugar cane juice is also extracted from the stalks and consumed as a refreshing beverage. Fresh sugar cane can be found in Asian and Caribbean markets. Peel before using.

Dried Ingredients

CHINESE SWEET PORK SAUSAGE (lap xuong) If you have a Chinese butcher nearby, purchase dried, sweet pork sausages from him. They are usually strung in pairs. They are much nicer when made and hung to air-dry, as they have much less fat than the ones sold in vacuum-sealed packages. Look for sausages that are about 6 inches long and ½ inch in diameter.

DRIED CLOUD EARS (nam meo) Also known as tree ears, these mushrooms are sold dried and must be reconstituted in warm water before use. Cloud ears are flavorless and are used only for adding texture to stir-fried dishes or stuffings.

DRIED SHIITAKE MUSHROOMS (nam dong co) These are also known as Chinese dried black mushrooms, and the French call them *champignons parfumés*, perfumed mushrooms, because of their pungency. There are many different vari-

DRIED SHRIMP CHIPS AFTER DEEP-FRYING

DRIED SHRIMP (tom kho)

Used to season a variety of dishes, dried shrimp add a chewy texture and distinct flavor, so use them sparingly. Choose vibrant orangy-colored dried shrimp that are slightly springy to the touch, instead of dried flaky ones. Also look for the meaty thin-shelled ones. They come in different sizes and can be kept in the refrigerator or freezer.

DRIED SHRIMP CHIPS

(banh phong tom) Made of ground shrimp and egg whites, shrimp chips are round, hard, and translucent. Some are colored green and red for a more festive occasion. When deep-fried, they triple in volume and are crispy and as light as air. They are perfect served as a party food or served with salad, grilled meats, or steamed meat pâtés. The best come from Indonesia.

DRIED SQUID (muc kho)

Like dried shrimp, these are used to season and add texture to a variety of dishes. They are very pungent, so use them sparingly. They come in several sizes, but I prefer squid that weigh about 2 ounces, so I can use them whole. They can also be toasted over an open flame, shredded, and eaten as a snack.

TIGER LILIES (kim cham)

Also called golden needles, tiger lilies are used in stir-fries, soups,

eties, the best being thick and pale in color. Soak to rehydrate and soften them prior to stir-frying, steaming, or adding to stews or soups. Hint: Fresh shiitakes are very subtle in flavor and so do not replace the intense flavor of the dried shiitakes. In a pinch, however, they make a good substitute.

DRIED MUNG BEANS

(dau xanh) Rather than buy dried whole green mung beans (unpeeled yellow mung beans), choose peeled ones, which come either whole or split and are bright yellow. Soaked prior to cooking, they are used in both sweet and savory foods.

and stews, imparting a unique floral scent. When choosing them, make sure they are light golden rather than dark brown, as the dark ones have been sitting on the shelf for much too long. Soak to soften before using.

ANNATTO SEEDS (hot dieu) These mild-flavored tiny red seeds are added to dishes primarily to color them.

FIVE-SPICE POWDER (ngu vi huong) Adopted from the Chinese, this blend of fennel seeds, star anise, licorice root, cloves, and cinnamon is sometimes added to marinades for poultry and meat. Because its flavor is quite pungent, it is used sparingly.

STAR ANISE (hoi) Originally from China, star anise is cultivated in northern Vietnam. As the name suggests, it looks like stars. It tastes like licorice, is used in sweet and savory dishes alike, and is available through spice merchants and Asian markets. A good substitute is anise seeds.

TURMERIC (nghe) The taste of this rhizome, which resembles both ginger and galangal in shape, is so subtle in flavor that it is used primarily for its deep yellow and orange color. This natural food coloring is sold mostly in dry powder form.

Canned Goods

BAMBOO SHOOTS (mang) Two varieties of bamboo shoots are available spring and winter. The young winter shoots are best because they are the most tender. They are available whole, shredded, sliced, or chopped, but I recommend buying only the whole ones because they will absorb less tin flavor from the can. Blanch for several minutes before using. Ma Ling is a consistently good brand.

STRAW MUSHROOMS (nam rom) Available only canned, straw mushrooms are very delicate in flavor and tender in texture. They come two ways: unpeeled, which look like tiny brown eggs; and peeled, with small dark brown caps and short, stubby, creamy white stems. Peeled straw mushrooms are great for delicate soups, while the unpeeled ones are perfect for braising with heavier sauces.

Oil, Vinegar, Sauces, and Pastes

SESAME OIL (dau me) This flavorful oil is extracted from sesame seeds and is sometimes roasted. It is used sparingly, as it can be overwhelming, masking every ingredient in a dish. It is rich golden in color. An excellent Japanese brand is Kodoya.

RICE VINEGAR (giam gao) This vinegar is perfect for making any pickled vegetable or salads that require it. It imparts a mildly sweet flavor to the food that regular white vinegar does not. If you cannot find it, however, use regular white vinegar rather than white wine vinegar, which does not do the trick.

ANCHOVY SAUCE (mam nem) Pungent anchovy sauce is used in combination with sweet pineapple as a dipping sauce for beef dishes such as Vietnamese beef fondue. French anchovy paste can be substituted, or you can crush your own anchovies, although the latter version will not be as pungent.

OYSTER SAUCE (dao hao) This thick brown sauce is made from oyster extractives, sugar, water, salt, and cornstarch. Add it sparingly to stir-fries or braised dishes, as its flavor is quite pungent.

FISH SAUCE (nuoc mam) Made of special anchovies found in the waters of the Gulf of Thailand, this sauce is an indispensable seasoning in Vietnamese cooking. A meal would not be complete without it. I have explained this sauce throughout the book, and so here I will recommend a couple of brands: Oyster or Tiparos (a slightly less pungent sauce for those of you who are trying to get used to it).

HOISIN SAUCE (tuong ngot)
Made primarily of soybean paste, garlic, and sugar, hoisin is used to sweeten dishes. The best brand is Koon Chun.

MUSHROOM SOY SAUCE (nam huong) This dark brown Chinese soy sauce is a combination of fermented soybeans, wheat flour, mushrooms, and salt. The distinct mushroom flavor, reminiscent of dried black mushrooms, adds a nice aroma to any dishes this special soy sauce is used in.

THICK SOY SAUCE (xi dau) This Chinese soy sauce is used primarily for coloring dishes, as its flavor is bland. It is usually used in combination with fish sauce or thin soy sauce.

THIN SOY SAUCE (xi dau): Chinese thin soy sauce (not to be confused with Japanese *sho-yu*, such as Kikkoman) is best for Vietnamese cooking. Dark brown in color, it is made from fermented soybeans, wheat flour, and salt. Use as you would fish sauce. This is the primary seasoning for the cuisine of strict vegetarian Buddhist monks.

PRESERVED BEAN CURD (chao) Ice cube-size fermented pressed tofu pieces are preserved in salt brine for several months. Because they are strong in flavor, they are added to stir-fries in small amounts.

TAMARIND PASTE (me chua) Made from the fruit of tamarind pods, this paste, also referred to as a pulp, has become more widely available. Tamarind is most often sold in blocks of pure pulp (pods and seeds removed) for easy use. Sold in Middle-Eastern and Asian markets.

PRESERVED BEAN CURD

CHINESE FLAT STRAINER

Equipment & Techniques

T HE VIETNAMESE need very few cooking vessels and utensils to create their delightfully sophisticated cuisine. Discovering cooking equipment and techniques is, for me, like rediscovering my family culture, as they are deeply ingrained in the lives of my family and form a window on the values and pleasures of the country they left. Whenever I cook Asian foods, I try to stay as close as I can to the way the food is prepared in the country of origin. In Vietnamese cooking this is particularly important, as I am often re-creating recipes developed by my grandmother, my aunts and uncles, and my mother and father. I often listen to indigenous music as I prepare the food. It brings back memories of Vietnam and its people and reminds me of stories I heard while traveling as an adult, as well as stories I heard while growing up.

EQUIPMENT

K itchens in Vietnam are small, but the Vietnamese require only the bare essentials to create their wonderful cuisine. Cooking equipment and techniques in Vietnamese cooking are, for the most part, a direct influence of the Chinese and, to a lesser extent, of the French. Although electricity is now available, it is not always reliable, and most cooks prefer the old-fashioned wood or charcoal brazier. Chinese clay pots, or similar cooking vessels, are used everywhere. They are indispensable, cooking rice perfectly. Woks are used extensively in the North, principally for stir-frying, deep-frying, and steaming. In the South, the sauté pan is used for the same purposes, with the exception of steaming, for which a bamboo steamer set atop a wok is employed. A single cleaver takes care of slicing meats and vegetables, this supplemented perhaps with a heavier one for splitting bones. A pair of special long chopsticks, used for reaching over hot pots and pans while cooking, is an indispensable item. Short ones, which can double for eating, are also used in preparation. Whenever I cook

Asian food, I have a wok, a clay pot or two, a steamer, a nonstick pan, a strainer, a cleaver, and at least one pair of chopsticks.

CLAY POTS Also referred to as sand pots, these are made of a combination of clay and sand. They come in all sizes, small to large, with single or double handles, and are sold with lids. Beautiful to see and hold, they have glazed interiors (most often brown, but sometimes black or dark blue) and unglazed sandy white exteriors. Because they are fragile, clay pots are sometimes encased in wire frames, which protect and dissipate the heat evenly over the surface. Clay pots are used to cook rice, soups, or stews, and they make a beautiful presentation at the table.

◆ **When new, a clay pot may have an unpleasant odor.**
It is a good idea to soak it for several hours, even overnight, drain, and air-dry it. Then fill it with water and place it over a low flame, gradually increasing the heat to medium, and let the water boil until reduced by half. You can also place it, filled with water, in a 250° to 275°F oven until the water is reduced. This does get rid of some of the odor but not necessarily all of it. Do not be alarmed. It will not be imparted to the food, and once you really start cooking with the pot, the odor will eventually disappear.

◆ **Be sure never to place a cold, empty pot over heat** (it must have liquid or some ingredients in it), and never put a hot pot on a very cold surface. Either will crack the pot. Also, remember to start at a low temperature and increase the heat gradually. Although some cooks use high heat with their clay pots, I never go higher than medium. Braising, which is a common clay pot cooking method, is traditionally done over low to medium heat.

◆ **Clay pots are meant to be used over an open flame, so a gas stove is preferable.** Electric stoves are not particularly well suited to these pots, but if this is your only option, place a heat diffuser on the electric element first. As the pot is used over time, the outside will darken in color. Some hairline cracks may appear eventually, but as long as the glazed interior is not cracked, the pot can still be used. Clay pots can be used in ovens successfully, again starting with low heat and increasing it gradually. This technique is most appropriate for braised dishes.

◆ **After cooking, clean the pot with salt and hot water.** Gently rub the salt against the glazed surface, picking up any residue (without scratching the cooking surface), and rinse the pot under running hot water. If cooking residue is particularly stubborn, try boiling it out by filling the pot with water and gradually bringing it to a boil over medium heat. Hint: As an aid, always fill the pot with hot water after you have cooked in it to start degreasing the pot or removing any sticking bits.

WOKS Used for stir-frying, deep-frying, or steaming, woks are made of spun metal such as carbon steel, stainless steel, or aluminum. Extremely thin cast-iron woks are common in Asia but difficult to find in the West. The most popular wok in the United States is made of carbon steel and is available in several sizes. The most functional measures 14 inches across, wide enough to steam a whole fish. Because your stovetop is not made to accommodate round-bottomed vessels, woks usually come with a diffuser (or rim collar). The narrow side of the diffuser should sit directly over the flame, and the wider side should support the wok.

◆ **If you have an electric stove (or hot plate), you should cook in a flat-bottomed wok.** These are made by American manufacturers and are usually nonstick. You may prefer to use a sauté pan (see page 33).

◆ **When you first get your wok, you must wash it with an abrasive cleanser and hot water** to remove the factory's light machine oil. Repeat this process several times until you are satisfied that it is thoroughly clean. Then apply a thin layer of vegetable oil on the cooking surface with a paper towel prior to stir-frying.

◆ **With every use, your wok will darken.** This is normal, as it is curing, the same way a cast-iron skillet cures. The even layer of buildup not only will make the food taste better but will help conduct heat as well.

◆ **To wash your wok, simply sprinkle a layer of table salt across the cooking surface.** When the salt has picked up the cooking residue (i.e., turned dark), use a paper towel to lightly rub the wok in a circular motion, removing any unwanted residue. Then rinse under running hot water and heat the wok immediately to dry it completely and prevent rusting.

NONSTICK SKILLET
A nonstick skillet is especially good to have on hand. It can be used to make Vietnamese crêpes or fresh rice sheets. If the weather does not permit barbecuing, I lightly oil my nonstick skillet and home-grill meats and seafood. Be careful not to use metal utensils, as they will scratch and destroy the nonstick surface. Use only a wooden or plastic spatula and wooden chopsticks.

SAUTÉ PAN
This pan is perfect for sautéing (stir-frying) or pan-frying. If you have an electric stove, you will probably be better off using this pan instead of a wok. In Saigon, where the French presence is felt, I saw spring rolls being fried in sauté pans, and the results were just as successful as with any wok or deep-fryer.

STEAMERS
Bamboo steamers are usually set over woks that are filled one-third with water. They work well and require rinsing only with running hot water after each use. Food should not touch the bamboo rack directly. Traditionally, a few lettuce leaves or a plate is set on the steaming rack to receive the food. Cheesecloth is a more-than-adequate substitute. Stainless-steel deep steamer pots are perfect for steaming larger food items such as lobsters or crabs. Or you can buy a steaming basket to fit into a stockpot.

CHOPSTICKS
Chopsticks, traditionally made of bamboo, are also made of ivory, plastic, or lacquered wood for everyday use or the more expensive gold, silver, or jade for special occasions. I recommend old-fashioned bamboo chopsticks for their versatility and their heat resistance. Unlike plastic, they do not melt. The Vietnamese are perhaps the only Southeast Asian culture that has adopted the use of chopsticks. (The Thai and Cambodian cultures, for example, have adopted the use of Western utensils such as forks and spoons, while Indonesians prefer to eat with their hands.) Long chopsticks are generally used for stir-frying or deep-frying, while shorter ones are better for mixing batters, sauces, or marinades or for eating.

◆ **To use chopsticks** properly, it is important to relax your hand (left or right): (1) Rest the thicker upper part of a chopstick in the web between the thumb and forefinger of your hand, and rest the lower, thinner part on your fourth finger, which is slightly bent. (2) Hold the thicker, upper part of the second chopstick between the tip of your thumb and the inside of the second knuckle of the forefinger. (3) Move the top (second) chopstick up and down with the help of your forefinger and middle finger to pick up morsels of food.

FLAT STRAINER
Flat strainers have a long bamboo handle and are sold in Asian markets. These are useful not only for deep-frying but for blanching noodles as well, keeping them from falling into the oil or boiling water.

SPATULA & LADLE
I find that an Asian spatula, which usually comes with the

purchase of a wok, or a ladle is useful for scooping out stir-fried ingredients from a wok. I always have both on hand.

MORTAR & PESTLE

If you are going to use the mortar-and-pestle grinding method, make sure you have a mortar that is especially wide and a pestle that is heavy. This is necessary not only to accommodate ingredients but to ensure that the pestle has adequate room to grind. Electric mini grinders are also fine. The only items I do not grind in these are onions and shallots, which quickly turn into mush. You are better off mincing these with a cleaver.

CLEAVER

There are three main Asian cleaver sizes. The small one with a blade 2 inches wide is used for carving meats and slicing vegetables. The large and heavy one has a blade measuring 4 inches wide and is used for splitting bones. The medium size, 3 inches wide, cleaver is the most versatile, acting as a multi-purpose tool that is perfect for any type of slicing, chopping, and crushing, and can even chop through poultry bones.

TECHNIQUES

Like most Asian cuisines, Vietnamese cooking requires adequate preparation. Attention to detail and fresh ingredients are critical factors, as they largely determine the outcome of a dish relative to flavor, texture, and presentation.

In planning menus, always remember that the flavors—deriving from the style of cutting and proportion of ingredients—can be sharp or mild, spicy or sweet, but must always be well balanced (see "Seasonal Menus," page 242).

Take a simple condiment like *nuoc cham*, the spicy Vietnamese fish sauce used as a dipping sauce for *cha gio* (spring rolls) or *banh xeo* (lacy crêpe stuffed with pork, shrimp, and mung bean sprouts), or simply drizzled over a humble bowl of rice. This basic sauce varies in intensity of flavor as you travel from the north to the south of Vietnam. It can also vary from household to household and, as in my family, from individual to individual. These variations come from the way the ingredients are prepared, or "prepped." The ingredients—sugar, fish sauce, lime, garlic, and chili—should be experienced separately even as they come together on your palate. Like wine, Vietnamese sauces can be described as having a start, a finish, and a development of complex flavors. *Nuoc cham's* spicy finish comes from the garlic and chili undergoing different "prepping" methods, depending on how strong you want the sauce to taste. Leave the garlic whole for a less pronounced flavor, or increase its sharpness by crushing, slicing (thick to thin), chopping (coarse to thin), or mincing it. The idea is simple: the more you break down the garlic, the more pronounced its flavor will become. For the chili, either seed it or not, slice it thick or thin, diagonally or in rounds, or mince it. These measures will determine the "heat"; the thinner the slice (and the more seeds), the more exposure you give the chili, and the hotter the sauce will become. Time is also a factor: the longer you let the ingredients blend, the sharper they become.

Cutting Techniques

Before slicing anything, the single most important thing you can do is to practice holding a cleaver. The cleaver should always slice perpendicular to the cutting board, with the knuckles of the free hand guiding the blade through each cut. When slicing, make sure the sharp edge of the cleaver does not rise above your knuckles, or the blade's return could result in serious injury. If you do not feel comfortable with a cleaver, use your favorite knife.

JULIENNING (SHREDDING)

The food to be julienned must sit flat against the cutting board. For example, in the case of a carrot, cut it in half lengthwise and lay the cut side

CHINESE CLAY POTS AND CERAMIC SOUP SPOONS

on the board to stabilize the carrot. It is now safe to slice the carrot in thin planks. Collect the planks and slice them lengthwise into long thin strings or matchsticks.

DIAGONAL SLICING
Hold the food at an angle of about 60 degrees against the blade of the cleaver (or knife) and slice.

CHOPPING AND MINCING
For chopping or mincing boneless meats or vegetables, the motion is in the wrist. As you grip the handle of your cleaver, the awkwardness of the position will allow your wrist to move up and down while the blade falls naturally of its own weight onto the food. I use one cleaver, although some cooks will use two, one in each hand, to go faster. During chopping, the food will scatter around the chopping board. Just gather it back to the center by scooping it up with the side of the blade.

CHOPPING THROUGH BONES
Hold the cleaver with your thumb pressed against the side of the blade and your other fingers grasping the handle. Your thumb will steady the blade while you move your forearm up and down in clean, firm strokes. This technique will allow you to successfully and cleanly chop through fish and poultry bones. If you are uneasy

about it, hit a wooden mallet against the flat top of the blade after you have properly positioned it against whatever you are cutting. Then lifting the blade is not necessary.
Note: Never use a medium-weight cleaver to chop through heavy beef, veal, or pork bones. The blade will turn, causing you to lose control of the cleaver. Instead, use a heavier bone cleaver, or ask your butcher to take care of this task. When chopping through bones, any movement must be firm, decisive, and clean so the bones do not splinter and you do not damage the cleaver or injure yourself.

FREEZE AND SLICE
Unless you have a professional slicing machine at home, a good way to slice any meat or lemongrass paper-thin, for example, is to lightly freeze the ingredient, then use a sharp blade to thinly slice against the grain or fiber.

Miscellaneous Techniques

SKIMMING FAT OFF THE TOP
When making stock, you will need some fat in order to get a flavorful stock. At the end of the simmering process, you can skim off as much fat as you desire. Here are three techniques that work well: (1) Lower a ladle so it floats on top of the stock. Angle the ladle just enough to let only the fat

seep in, then discard it. Do this in batches rather than all at once to ensure that you do not take any of the stock along with the fat. This technique can easily be used in stews or sauces. (2) Hold a thick paper towel at each of two corners with your fingertips, then lower it so that it floats and covers the entire surface of the stock. Then lift the towel. You will notice that the fat clings to it. Discard the fat-laden paper towel and repeat as necessary. (3) Refrigerate the stock for at least 6 hours, then remove the solid mass of fat that has formed on the surface and discard it.

SEEDING CHILIES
To seed a chili without opening it completely is a simple trick, making the slicing into perfectly round or diagonal slices easy and ensuring a beautiful presentation. Slice the very top of the stem end open crosswise, then roll the chili between your index finger and thumb. The seeds will "crawl" out. When handling chilies, I never wear gloves. If you have sensitive skin, however, I suggest you wear thin surgical gloves so you can still feel what you are doing. And always keep your fingers away from your eyes.

SELECTING OFFAL OR INNARDS
When buying chicken or duck hearts and gizzards, look for a bright reddish

color and a firm texture. Whenever possible, use only fresh innards, as frozen ones, unfortunately, lose some texture, taste, and color.

CLEANING SQUID Insert your thumb and index finger into the body (mantle) of the squid to pull out the head and as much innards as you can. The innards should be discarded along with the plastic-like center bone (or cartilage). Run your fingers inside the body, pulling out any remaining tissue, or cut the body open and scrape it off. Peel off and discard the skin from the body. Cut the tentacles above the eyes, squeeze out the hard inner structure, then discard along with the eyes. Once cleaned, the tentacles are edible.

BARBECUING When barbecuing do not use too much charcoal; a little will go a long way. Rather than use lighting fluid, which has a strong smell, use a lighting chimney. It is easy to use; just place some paper at the bottom and put some charcoal on top. Light the paper with a match. When the charcoal is lit place it in the barbecue pit. Place the grill on top, and wait until the flames have subsided and the charcoal turns red with white ashes. Your grill is now ready to receive any meat or seafood. Be sure to clean your grill after each use.

THAI AND VIETNAMESE FISH SAUCE

CHAPTER ONE

CONDIMENTS

 CONDIMENTS are an integral part of nearly every Vietnamese dish. The cuisine assumes that they necessarily complete an item rather than optionally enhance it. Complex in flavors and well balanced in terms of sweet and savory as well as texture, they are never used to mask an ingredient. Suffice it to say that a Vietnamese table without its array of condiments is a table that has not yet been fully set. ◆ There are four basic groupings of condiments: dipping sauces, pickles, flavorings, and garnishes. Many incorporate the most important—in fact, defining—Vietnamese dipping sauce and seasoning, *nuoc mam*, or fish sauce. The best version is made on the island of Phu Quoc in the Gulf of Thailand in the South. It is made of a silvery, almost translucent type of anchovy called *ca com*. These anchovies are layered, salted, and left to ferment for months in wooden barrels. The first "juice" extraction happens after the first three months of fermentation, and it is poured back into the barrel on top of the layered anchovies. After another six months, the juices are extracted again, and it is this extraction that is considered the "first pressing," which is also the best quality. It is used plain, as a seasoning for the table, or as a base in dipping sauces. The second and third pressings, which follow, are weaker and are used for everyday cooking, in stir-fries and stews, for example. Fish sauce is to the Vietnamese what salt is to Westerners and soy sauce is to the Chinese. It is an integral part of the cuisine, for without it, a meal would not be considered a meal.

Vietnam's varied dipping sauces are important in all of its cuisines, and the most important of all is the indispensable *nuoc mam cham* (most often referred to as *nuoc cham*), fermented fish sauce diluted with lime juice, distilled white rice vinegar, sugar, fresh chilies, and garlic (page 42). It accompanies many, if not most, dishes, from the most elaborate meat and fish preparations to the most humble bowl of plain steamed rice. At home it is almost always on the table, and we often make batches large enough to last a few days.

Other dipping sauces are often equally interesting but are commonly served as an accompaniment to specific dishes. For example *nuoc leo*, peanut sauce (page 44) is served with *nem nuong*, grilled pork meatballs (page 200), or *goi cuon*, summer rolls (page 156); *mam nem*, pineapple and anchovy dip (page 46), complements beef dishes, specifically *bo nhung dam*, beef fondue (page 208).

Pickled and preserved vegetables comprise the second condiment category, and they are eaten almost on a daily basis. To pickle, the Vietnamese use white rice vinegar, sugar, and salt. To preserve, they use salted water. My mother used to pickle vegetables in great quantity to accompany barbecued meats and seafood, especially during the spring and summer months. Our favorites were always carrot, cucumber, and daikon, and this tradition continues today. I've also included a recipe for preserved mung bean sprouts, which are delicious served with grilled meats and seafood.

The third category includes flavorings that are generally not served at the table but are used during the preparation of various dishes. *Sate*—peanut, garlic, and chili paste (page 49)—is one of the many exotics used in Vietnam. It is often simply added to stir-fries, creating simple yet interesting meat, seafood, or vegetable dishes that can be served over steamed rice for lunch or dinner.

The fourth category is garnishes, which include fried shallots, scallion oil, and fried garlic oil. These are often drizzled over steamed pâtés, soups, and grilled meats or seafood. For example, fried shallots (page 51) are often sprinkled over a bowl of *pho ga*, rice noodle and chicken soup (page 87), to add a crunchy texture as well as sweeten the soup. Scallion oil complements *cha dum*, steamed beef pâté (page 213). Fried garlic adds a pungent, uplifting note to *canh ca nau dua*, a sweet and sour fish and pineapple soup (page 75).

Lastly, aromatic greens called traditional herbs and table salad are generally used to add texture, flavor, and freshness to cooked dishes brought to the table. Traditional herbs include such exotics as holy basil, *rau ram*, saw leaves, *la lot* leaves, cilantro, and mint, which are among the most commonly used. The table salad can include cooked rice vermicelli, lettuce leaves, sliced cucumber, unripe star fruit, fresh chilies, shredded carrot, and lime or lemon wedges. Traditional herbs are served generally with the table salad to complement *cha gio*, spring rolls (page 198), and *nem nuong*, grilled pork meatballs (page 200), for example, and specifically with *pho*, rice noodle and chicken, beef, or pork soups.

When preparing the table salad, make individual piles of each ingredient on one platter; traditional herbs are similarly arranged. With regard to the herbs, be sure to leave the stems intact, as it is up to each diner to pick the leaves off and use them as they prefer. The leaves are always freshly torn. You can find most of the exotics in Asian markets. If not, do not be discouraged. I always find that the problem goes away as long as you have cilantro, an herb that today is available in any supermarket.

NUOC CHAM
Fish Dipping Sauce

Makes about 2 cups

5 tablespoons sugar

3 tablespoons water

⅓ cup fish sauce

½ cup lime or lemon juice
(about 3 limes or 2 lemons)

1 large clove garlic, crushed,
peeled, and sliced or
minced

1 or more bird's eye or Thai
chilies, seeded, and sliced or
minced

1 shallot, peeled, thinly
sliced, rinsed, and drained
(optional)

A MEAL WITHOUT NUOC CHAM is no meal at all. Served as a dipping sauce with many dishes such as *cha gio*, spring rolls (page 198); *banh xeo*, sizzling "sound" crêpes (page 114); and grilled meats and seafood; it is perhaps the most important sauce you will learn to make. There are several variations on this recipe. If you like your sauce spicier, mince rather than slice the chilies and garlic. Sometimes distilled rice wine vinegar is used to round out the flavor. My aunt Loan likes to slice and add shallots, saying they make the sauce sweeter. Try it different ways, mild or hot, more sweet or sour, with or without shallots. All are interesting. Following is my favorite version, which balances the sweet, sour, and spicy levels. I suggest you make 2 cups, as it goes quickly. Any left over can be refrigerated for up to 2 weeks.

1. Whisk together the sugar, water, fish sauce, and lime or lemon juice in a bowl until the sugar is completely dissolved. Add the garlic, chili, and shallot (if using), and let stand for 30 minutes before serving.

I've been making *nuoc cham* ever since I can remember. In fact, it was perhaps the first Vietnamese recipe I learned to make as a child. Nobody liked chopping the garlic, so I was stuck doing it. I became such an expert at making this sauce that every time we cooked, my mother would ask me to make it. The one difficult thing was to please both my mother and father simultaneously. She liked it sour, while he preferred it sweet. I resolved this quandary by creating a finely balanced version that allowed all of the various flavors to come out, and I continue to use it to this day.

NUOC CHANH OT
Sweet and Spicy Lemon Dipping Sauce

Makes about 1 cup

¼ cup sugar
½ cup lemon juice and pulp
¼ cup fish sauce
1 large clove garlic, crushed,
  peeled, and minced
3 bird's eye or Thai chilies,
  seeded and minced

MY AUNT HUOY, who lived in Saigon, showed me how to make this dipping sauce. The ingredients are basically the same as for *nuoc cham* (page 42), but this very spicy sauce is undiluted with water and therefore is much more concentrated. It is best eaten with steamed lobsters and crabs (page 159).

1. Use a mortar and pestle to pound the sugar, lemon juice and pulp, fish sauce, garlic, and chilies into a thick sauce.

Nuoc Leo
Peanut Dipping Sauce

Makes about 2 cups

1 tablespoon vegetable oil

1 large clove garlic, peeled and minced

1 or more bird's eye or Thai chilies, seeded and minced

3 ounces unsalted roasted peanuts, 1 tablespoon chopped, the rest finely ground (but not butter)

1 cup chicken stock (page 61)

⅓ cup canned unsweetened coconut milk

1 tablespoon hoisin sauce

1 tablespoon fish sauce

1 tablespoon sugar

Throughout Southeast Asia, there are many recipes for peanut sauce, but the Vietnamese version is the lightest one I have ever tasted. It seems that you can have the authentic one only in Vietnam or at home. Most of the time in Vietnamese restaurants, peanut butter is mixed with hoisin sauce and some ground peanuts are tossed in. The result is very pasty and not very refined. This peanut sauce is true to the original in Vietnam, being fluid and light. The secret is the chicken stock, which lightens the sauce and allows you to taste all the ingredients.

1. Heat the oil in a small saucepan over medium heat. Stir-fry the garlic and chilies until fragrant, about 5 minutes. Add the ground peanuts and stir until they give up some of their natural oil, about 5 minutes more.

2. Add the chicken stock, coconut milk, hoisin sauce, fish sauce, and sugar, and bring just to a boil over medium heat. Reduce the heat to low and cook until the oil from the peanuts starts surfacing, about 15 minutes. Transfer sauce to a heatproof serving bowl, garnish with chopped peanuts, and serve.

Nuoc Xa Ot
Spicy Lemongrass Soy Dipping Sauce

Makes about 1 cup

⅓ cup thin soy sauce
½ cup vegetable oil
1 stalk lemongrass, outer
   leaves and tough green tops
   removed, root end
   trimmed, and stalk finely
   ground
2 scallions, trimmed and
   julienned into 1-inch-long
   thin strips
2 bird's eye or Thai chilies,
   seeded and thinly sliced
   diagonally

THIS IS A WONDERFUL sauce to accompany *canh nam don thit*, stuffed mushroom soup (page 76); or *ca nhoi*, stuffed fish (page 142). The Vietnamese have adopted soy sauce from the Chinese, but they most often cook with it rather than make dipping sauces. Vietnamese fried tofu is usually served with this soy sauce dip, a combination inspired by Chinese cuisine. Lemongrass, however, is most definitely a Vietnamese addition, as the Chinese do not use it.

1. Place the soy sauce in a heatproof serving bowl. Heat the oil in a saucepan over medium heat. When hot, add the lemongrass, scallions, and chilies and fry until fragrant and the lemongrass turns a golden color, about 5 minutes. Remove from the heat and immediately pour into the soy sauce.

MAM NEM
Pineapple and Anchovy Dipping Sauce

Makes about 1 cup

1 tablespoon white rice
    vinegar
Juice of 1 lemon
1 teaspoon sugar
One 2-ounce can anchovy
    fillets packed in oil, drained
1 clove garlic, peeled and
    minced
2 bird's eye or Thai chilies,
    seeded and minced
½ cup minced ripe pineapple

SWEET RIPENED PINEAPPLE mixed with salty anchovies is an acquired taste. But as strange as it may sound, this combination is quite complementing to beef dishes, especially *bo nhung dam*, beef fondue (page 208). Finding a sweet ripened pineapple is not always easy. Canned pineapple should be your last resort. If you do use it, be sure it is canned in juice, not syrup.

1. Combine the vinegar, lemon juice, and sugar in a bowl and whisk until the sugar is completely dissolved.

2. Crush the anchovy fillets with a mortar and pestle. Add the garlic, chilies, and pineapple and crush until well combined. With a spoon, stir in the vinegar mixture.

NUOC MAM GUNG
Ginger Dipping Sauce

Makes about 1 cup

1 tablespoon fish sauce
½ teaspoon sugar
Juice of 1 lime
3 ounces fresh ginger, peeled
  and finely ground
1 scallion, root end and tough
  green tops removed,
  minced
2 bird's eye or Thai chilies,
  seeded and minced
½ cup vegetable oil

THIS GINGER SAUCE is perfect for the steamed or simmered chicken for which it was developed. Whenever we serve *com ga*, ginger and garlic rice with chicken (page 103), this sauce always accompanies it.

1. Combine the fish sauce, sugar, and lime juice in a bowl, and whisk until the sugar is completely dissolved. Add the ginger, scallion, chilies, and oil and mix well. Allow to stand for 30 minutes prior to serving.

DUA GIA
Preserved Mung Bean Sprouts

Serves 4

2 tablespoons coarse sea salt
2 pounds mung bean sprouts,
  root ends trimmed
1 scallion, root end and tough
  green tops removed, cut
  into 1-inch-long pieces
  and quartered lengthwise
  (optional)

MUNG BEAN SPROUTS are eaten a lot in Vietnamese cuisine. They're stir-fried with meats, used as stuffing, and preserved in salt brine as a condiment. A great combination, if you would like to experiment, is to preserve the mung bean sprouts with scallions. Refrigerate for up to a week.

1. Bring 2 cups water and the salt to a boil in a saucepan over high heat. Remove from the heat and let cool until warm. Mix the sprouts and scallion (if using) and pack into a jar with the salted water to cover. Allow to cool, close with the lid, and refrigerate for 48 hours prior to serving.

RAU CAI CHUA
Pickled Vegetables

Serves 8

1 pound carrots, peeled, cut
   into 2-inch-long matchsticks
3 tablespoons coarse sea salt
1 pound daikon, peeled, cut
   into 2-inch-long by ½-inch-
   wide thin planks
6 tablespoons sugar
1 cup white rice vinegar
1½ pounds cucumber, peeled,
   halved lengthwise, and sliced
   diagonally ⅛-inch thick

PICKLED VEGETABLES have long been condiments at the Vietnamese table. Their crunchiness and sweet, salty, and sour flavor especially complement grilled or fried fish, seafood, poultry, and meat. Whereas the daikon and carrot need at least 24 hours to absorb the flavor of the rice vinegar marinade, the more delicate cucumber needs only 4 to 6 hours. In Vietnamese restaurants pickled daikon is often served with *laqué* duck (page 189). In my family we like to serve a combination of the three with it.

1. Put the carrots in a sieve set over a bowl. Toss carrots with 1 tablespoon of the salt and let stand to get rid of water content, about 45 minutes. Gently press the carrots against the sieve to remove any remaining moisture. Rinse and drain. Place the carrots in a clean kitchen towel, then twist the towel to squeeze out any excess water.

2. Repeat the process using the daikon.

3. Whisk together the sugar and vinegar until sugar is completely dissolved. Divide this pickling mixture among 3 quart-size plastic bags and set 1 bag aside to use in step 4. Add the carrots and daikon separately to the other 2 bags, seal, and toss to coat evenly. Lay bags flat on a plate and refrigerate at least 24 hours, turn-

ing the bags over every hour as possible.

4. After about 20 hours, repeat step 1 using the cucumbers. After draining, place the cucumbers in the third plastic bag of pickling mixture, seal, and toss to coat evenly. Lay the bag flat on a plate and refrigerate for 4 to 6 hours, turning bag over every hour as possible.

5. Drain the carrots, daikon, and cucumbers well at room temperature for 30 to 45 minutes before serving.

SATE
Peanut, Garlic, and Chili Paste

Makes about ½ cup

¼ cup vegetable oil
4 cloves garlic, peeled and
  minced
1 teaspoon curry powder
3 to 4 dried red chilies, seeded
  and ground
¼ cup finely ground unsalted
  roasted peanuts

IN SOUTHEAST ASIA, *sate* paste differs from country to country. This combination of garlic, curry powder, chilies, and peanuts is a simple Vietnamese *sate* I make at home. Although I use it mostly to stir-fry meat, seafood, and even rice or egg noodle dishes, sometimes I like to add it to marinades. If you plan on grilling marinated meats, the spiciness of *sate* is delicious, but use it in moderate quantities, as it can be very spicy if you're not careful.

1. Heat the oil in a saucepan over medium heat. Stir-fry the garlic until fragrant, about 5 minutes. Add the curry powder, chilies, and peanuts and stir until the mixture forms a paste, 10 to 15 minutes. Remove from the heat and allow to cool. Transfer to a jar and refrigerate until ready to use.

When my family first moved to the United States, we had to make many adjustments in addition to learning a new language. We were used to shopping in the Quartier Chinois, the Chinese quarter, located in the 13th district of Paris. Although it bore a Chinese name, the shops were owned principally by Vietnamese people of Chinese descent who sold a broad cross-section of Asian products. In New York's Chinatown we found that many vendors were from Hong Kong and Canton rather than Southeast Asia, and so did not have some of the ingredients we were used to finding, such as Vietnamese *sate* paste. This is a family recipe developed over 20 years ago. With it, you will never have to go without.

HANH LA PHI
Scallion Oil

Makes about 1 cup

¾ cup vegetable oil

**6 scallions, root ends and
tough green tops removed,
thinly sliced**

SCALLION OIL, made with thinly sliced scallions and vegetable oil, is commonly brushed over grilled meats, seafood, and steamed meat pâtés, or drizzled over rice or noodles. There are several ways of making it. For example, you can heat the oil first, turn it off, and then add the scallions. Or you can add the scallions to the hot oil and keep the combined ingredients over the flame for just a minute or so. Feel free to experiment. Scallion oil can be kept refrigerated for up to a week.

1. Heat the oil in a small saucepan over medium heat. Add the scallions and fry until fragrant, about 2 minutes. Remove from the heat and allow to cool, then transfer to a heatproof jar.

VARIATION: *Toi phi dau*, fried garlic oil, is especially complementary to seafood soups such as *canh ca nau dua*, pineapple and fish soup (page 75), and *hu tieu do bien*, noodle with seafood soup (page 92). Reminiscent of roasted garlic in flavor and aroma, it should be used sparingly, as a little will go a long way. Heat ¾ cup vegetable oil in a small saucepan over medium heat. Add 8 peeled and minced large cloves of garlic and fry until light golden brown, 3 to 4 minutes. Allow to cool briefly and transfer the fried garlic and oil to a heat-resistant jar. Allow to cool completely before sealing with a lid. Fried garlic oil will keep about a week refrigerated.

Hanh Phi
Fried Shallots

Makes about 1 cup

¾ cup vegetable oil
8 shallots, peeled, sliced thinly
    crosswise, and separated
    into rings

FRIED SHALLOTS complement many dishes with their sweet flavor and crisp texture. It is important not to over-fry the shallots or let them become dark brown because they will become bitter. A light golden color is preferable, as it will give you the sweet flavor you're looking for. If you are sensitive to strong flavors in general, or to shallots and other onions specifically, and want a more subtle flavor, soak the sliced shallots in cold water for 30 minutes. Then drain them on a paper towel until completely dry prior to frying them. Properly drained, they can be refrigerated for up to a month in an airtight jar.

1. Heat the oil in a small saucepan over medium heat. Working in batches, add the shallots and fry, stirring frequently, until golden, about 4 minutes. Remove with a slotted spoon and transfer to a paper towel to drain. Repeat the process until you have fried all the shallots. Allow to cool completely and transfer to a jar.

SA LACH DIA
Table Salad

Serves 4 to 6

1 head Boston lettuce,
leaves separated, or
12 small round or triangle
rice papers, soaked

½ cucumber, peeled, halved,
seeds removed, and thinly
sliced

2 to 3 carrots, peeled and
julienned or shredded

1 unripe star fruit, thinly
sliced into stars

1 cup rice vermicelli (optional)

TRADITIONALLY, a table salad—traditional herbs (page 53), cucumbers, carrots, star fruit, and rice vermicelli—is served with finger foods such as *cha gio*, spring rolls (page 198), *nem nuong*, grilled pork meatballs (page 200), or *banh xeo*, sizzling "sound" crêpes (page 114). Often a bit of each ingredient is wrapped around a cooked morsel with a lettuce leaf. The table salad and wrapper, however, can vary according to the dish you serve. For example, if you were to serve *nem nuong*, you would use a softened rice paper rather than a lettuce leaf as a wrapper in order to add starch to the meal. If you wanted to serve *banh xeo*, stuffed rice flour crêpe, the rice vermicelli would be omitted because the crêpe provides the starch. It can be a little confusing, but one thing to remember is that your meal must be balanced with vegetable, protein, and starch.

1. Arrange the lettuce (if using) or rice papers, cucumber, carrots, and star fruit on a large serving platter or several plates.

2. Place vermicelli (if using) in a dish with lukewarm water to cover. Let soak until pliable, about 20 minutes. Bring a pot filled with water to a boil over high heat. Drain the vermicelli and, working in batches, place them in a sieve and lower into the boiling water. Untangle the noodles with chopsticks and boil until tender but firm, about 3 seconds. Drain and set on the plate with the other ingredients.

NOTE: Rice papers are traditionally used to wrap grilled meats. First, however, they must be soaked in lukewarm water to cover, about 10 minutes, and drained on paper towels. A combination of lettuce leaves and a small amount of rice vermicelli is also acceptable.

RAU
Traditional Herbs

Serves 4 to 6

1 bunch cilantro
1 bunch mint
1 bunch holy (Thai) basil
1 bunch saw leaf (*ngo gai*)

SOME OF THESE HERBS are hard to get unless you live near a Southeast Asian food market. Mint and cilantro, however, are available in most markets, lessening the problem of not finding the more exotic herbs. Italian basil is not a substitute for holy, or Thai, basil, as its flavor is much different. This traditional herb garnish is used in soups or served alongside the "table salad" to complement grilled or fried meats and seafood dishes.

1. Keeping the stems and leaves intact, clean the cilantro, mint, holy basil, and saw leaves thoroughly, drain on paper towels, and arrange on a plate in individual piles.

CONDIMENTS

HANOI CHICKEN AND RICE NOODLE SOUP

STOCKS & SOUPS

 SOUPS ARE AT THE HEART of Vietnamese cuisine. Although they are rooted in Chinese tradition, a fragrant complexity distinguishes Vietnamese soups
from those of their Asian neighbors. They are further distinguished by their French
influence. There are four basic categories of these soups: *canh, sup, chao,* and *pho.*
Canh, a palate-cleansing clear broth with bits of vegetable and meat served from a large communal bowl and shared by everyone at the table throughout the meal, is as clear as French *consommé*
and similarly complements a meal. *Sup* is a hearty combination of slightly thickened broth, which
can be similar in texture to the French *velouté*; rather than accompanying a meal, *sup* is served in
individual portions as a starter. *Chao* is a rice porridge (much like Chinese *congee*) served in individual bowls and generally enjoyed throughout the day. *Pho* is a combination of rice noodles and beef,
chicken, pork, or seafood served in large individual bowls of clear steaming broth; hearty and filling,
it is considered a meal in itself. Although originally eaten principally for breakfast, *pho* is now conve-
niently offered throughout the day. In Vietnam soup stalls seem to be everywhere, each offering

variations on these fragrant and colorful bowls. Like *chao*, *pho* is considered a full meal.

Although my family is most influenced by southern Vietnamese traditions—originally from Hunan, China, they migrated to Phnom Penh, Cambodia, in the late 1930s, and to Saigon in the 1960s—they eagerly embraced these fragrant soups from the North. *Canh* and *sup* became part of our meals whenever we prepared Asian food. Whether below freezing or scorching-hot outside, we enjoyed soups all year round. Growing up, I remember my father, Nhu Minh, often asking my mother, Minou, to make *pho*—meat and rice noodles served in steaming broth and garnished with fresh herbs—during the hottest summer days. Other times, around midnight while relaxing in front of the television, he would call out my mother's name and ask her to make *chao*, rice porridge.

My father is not a cook, but after working in the food industry for decades, it is fair to say he knows food well. I remember one day, when I was young, he asked me to make a soup. The timing could not have been worse. He had not eaten all day, I did not have time to shop for proper ingredients, and I had to ferret around in the kitchen for whatever I could find. We chatted, but all the while he watched as I nervously did my best. In the freezer I found two air-cured Cantonese duck legs. In the pot of water they went to boil. When the broth had reduced in volume, I removed the legs and shredded the meat. Hoping to make a beautiful presentation, I carefully "styled" a serving in a soup bowl, placing lightly boiled egg noodles in the center, a few leaves of blanched baby bok choy (Asian leafy greens) and the shredded duck meat on top. A good amount of broth went into the bowl. When I had garnished the whole thing with fresh cilantro leaves, fried garlic oil, and a few chili slices, I was ready to serve it to my father. After a first bite and a hearty slurp, he paused and said in his authoritative voice, "I appreciate that you took so much effort to cook and present this soup to me. But, my daughter, chicken is best for making stock, not preserved duck. Do not use just anything; it is not the way to cook. Your preserved duck meat has lost its flavor. No matter how nice it looks, the soup can never succeed." I was embarrassed to offer seconds, and he saw it. "Do not be discouraged," he said, "but remember that without a good broth, you will not get a flavorful soup." He was right, of course, and the lesson for me as a cook was always to emphasize the broth and its quality above all else in preparing soup. So I never use canned stocks. I start with a few pieces of chicken, pork, or beef on the bone, add all sorts of aromatics, and simmer them for hours. Now I do not have to offer my father seconds; he asks for them before he has finished the first bowl.

BASIC STOCKS

STOCK IS A COOKING LIQUID made by simmering chicken, beef, pork, fish, seafood, or vegetables in water for several hours. Stocks are essential to Vietnamese cooking, as they form the basis for all soups and dozens of braised dishes. The complex and classic chicken curry called *cari ga* (page 184), for example, uses chicken stock flavored with lemongrass.

A stock's quality is determined by the freshness of its ingredients, proper simmering, and clarity when done. In this chapter, I give you recipes for the stocks that are most popular in Vietnamese cooking: chicken, pork, beef, and vegetable. To make these stocks (except for the vegetable stock), I start with what I call the three elements—meat, bone, and fat. Using just one element will not yield the well-rounded stock you are looking for, but using a combination of the three will, as each adds its own layer of flavor. Do not fear fat. It is as necessary as the other two elements, adding richness and balance during the cooking and reducing process of the liquid. At the end you can always skim it off.

A beautiful stock is easy to make, as long as you take your time. It is critical not to rush—by this I mean boil—a stock. If boiled, your stock will not have the time to absorb the combined flavor of your ingredients as it reduces. Also, if the ingredients are vigorously shaken in the pot by boiling, the end result is cloudy. This makes for a poor presentation, especially if you mean to serve a clear soup. Slow simmering ensures that the stock will be clear.

Exotic aromatics such as ginger, lemongrass, star anise, cinnamon, and cloves are key to the taste of traditional Vietnamese stocks. Like complex wines, Vietnamese soups have layers of intertwined flavors that develop fully on the palate. Some layers are analogous to a dominant—foreground—flavor; others to a subtle undercurrent—background—flavor. Derived in large part from Chinese soups, which use aromatically infused stocks, rice or noodles, and complementary morsels of meat, seafood, and vegetables, Vietnamese soups are similar in the logic of their basic construction. Chinese cuisine demands a balance of taste and health considerations in food preparation. Bitter flavors are therefore masked by sweet, and strong flavors are subsumed by subtle ones. Aromatic herbs are selected for their flavors as well as for their potency as curatives or preventatives. To please only the mouth or sense of taste may deprive other organs of essential nutrients. This profound balance, which took centuries to evolve, is central to all Vietnamese cuisines, particularly to their soups.

The Vietnamese have developed their own unique herbal blends, distinguishing their soups from those of not only the Chinese but from all their Asian neighbors. This is due in no small part to French colonial and other non-Asian influences. Certain Vietnamese soups have thicker, French textures and serving variations, as well as European ingredients. *Sup cua mang tay*, crab and asparagus soup (page 80), is a classic example of this.

While these fusions have produced a cuisine that is at times brilliant, they have also resulted in what I see as inappropriate substitutions. Some Vietnamese cooks, for example, have adopted the French way of making stocks, using aromatics like parsley, bay leaf, and thyme—the traditional *bouquet garni*—as flavorings. Others put sugar in their soups, a kind of poorly conceived "instant" approach to flavor. Still others use additives such as MSG (monosodium glutamate) as flavor enhancers. Sugar and MSG are unnecessary shortcuts or quick fixes.

When I compare these variations to slow-cooked and well-balanced classic stocks, I find them lacking. They certainly destroy the signature subtlety of Vietnamese soups, which is, for me, their essence. No matter how good and flavorful French stocks are as a foundation for French soups, they are much too sweet, concentrated, and overwhelming for any Asian cuisine. (Perhaps the richness of foreign influences inevitably included their corruptions, mirroring bargains made in historical confrontations and conquests in Vietnam for centuries.) I have eliminated recipes using these shortcuts, relying instead on the natural sweetness, flavors, and freshness of traditional ingredients.

One note: While the older generation in my family occasionally uses MSG and would argue that it is acceptable in their cooking, some people experience negative reactions to it, including headaches, palpitations, and severe thirst. Therefore I have omitted MSG entirely in this book.

Many cooks are comfortable using canned stocks. While I do not recommend their use, if you must rely on them, be sure you select those that are low in salt and contain only chicken or beef and water. You should at least have the freedom to flavor your stock according to the recipes in this book, or with the herbs you prefer. I encourage you, however, to make your own. Remember, aside from some minor preparation, it does not take much effort. Think of stock as a background activity, simmering quietly while you work on other things. When you have a little extra time, you can make it in bulk and freeze it so that you always have homemade stock on hand.

Chicken stock is widely used as a base for vegetable, fish, and seafood dishes of all kinds. Its delicate flavor and ability to absorb aromatics make it nearly perfect for the task. In Vietnam vegetable stock is used primarily in exceptional dishes such as the vegetarian cuisine of monks from certain Buddhist sects. I have included a simple vegetable stock for those of you who may prefer it. Fish stocks and seafood stocks—made from fish heads and bones or shrimp heads and shells—are also used occasionally, particularly in fishing villages. In general, however, my family prefers chicken stock for fish and seafood dishes because it is consistent in flavor and less obtrusive. The exception is fish and seafood soups, such as *canh ca nau dua*, fish and pineapple soup (page 75), or *canh chua tom*, sour shrimp soup (page 74), for which it is better to use a quick stock made with a fish head or shrimp heads and shells. By a quick stock, I mean one that takes less than an hour to develop a subtle flavor.

NUOC LEO GA
Chicken Stock

3 to 3½ pounds meaty chicken
 bones, including heads,
 feet, wings, necks, backs,
 and carcasses, or whole
 chicken, skinned (innards
 such as gizzard and heart
 are optional)
1 large yellow onion, peeled
3 scallions, trimmed, halved
 crosswise, and lightly
 crushed
4 ounces fresh ginger, peeled,
 cut into 4 slices, and lightly
 crushed
2 tablespoons fish sauce
1 teaspoon white or black
 peppercorns
Coarse sea salt

THERE ARE TWO basic approaches to creating a successful chicken stock. The first is to use meaty bones such as wings, necks, carcasses, or any other small parts. The second is to use a skinned whole chicken that has adequate fat. The cooked meat is reserved for other recipes such as *chao xa ga*, rice porridge with chicken and lemongrass (page 86), in which the meat is shredded. Innards can be included in making a stock, but be sure to exclude the liver, as it will cloud your stock.

1. If using meaty bones, put them in a large stockpot. Add the onion, scallions, ginger, fish sauce, and peppercorns, cover with 5 quarts water, and bring to a boil over high heat. Skim off the foam, reduce the heat to low, and season with salt. Simmer, uncovered, occasionally skimming off any foam, until the stock is reduced by 2 quarts, about 3 hours.

2. If using a whole chicken, use a cleaver to carefully separate the legs from the body of the chicken, then the wings. Cutting through the rib cage, separate the back from the breast. Halve the breast lengthwise through the bone. You now have 7 pieces in addition to the optional innards, neck, and head. Proceed with step 1, but after the first hour of simmering, remove the breast halves and legs

and debone them. (Reserve the meat for use in another dish.) Return the bones to the stock and continue simmering, uncovered and undisturbed, until the stock reduces further, about 2 hours more. At this time, skim off as much fat as you desire.

3. Strain the stock, discard the solids, and use according to the recipe of your choice. The stock can be kept up to 3 days in the refrigerator or 3 months in the freezer.

STOCKS & SOUPS

Nuoc Leo Heo
Pork Stock

Makes about 3 quarts

2 ounces dried squid or dried
 shrimp
3 pounds lean pork ribs,
 separated
1 pound daikon, peeled and
 quartered, or 3 to 4 white
 turnips, peeled and halved
1 large yellow onion, peeled
2 ounces preserved daikon or
 tien sin cabbage
2 tablespoons fish sauce
1 tablespoon thick soy sauce
 (optional)
1 teaspoon white or black
 peppercorns
Coarse sea salt

RICH PORK STOCK made with dried seafood is a perfect combination for the thinly sliced pork tenderloin and seafood soup, *hu tieu do bien* (page 92). Its smoky and sweet aroma comes from dried squid, available in Asian markets. Because this stock has many salty ingredients, including dried squid and preserved daikon, fresh turnips or fresh daikon are used to absorb the salt during the simmering process. This allows the stock to be cleansed, preserving each of its complex flavors. The thick soy sauce, which adds a golden hue to the stock, is my aunt Loan's contribution.

1. Soak the squid or shrimp in water for 15 minutes, then drain, rinse, and drain again.

2. Put the pork ribs in a stockpot with 5 quarts water and bring to a boil over high heat. Reduce the heat to low, add the dried squid or shrimp, fresh daikon, onion, preserved daikon, fish sauce, thick soy sauce (if using), and peppercorns, and season with salt. Simmer, uncovered and undisturbed, occasionally skimming off foam, until the stock is reduced by 2 quarts, about 3 hours. At this time, skim off as much fat as you desire.

3. Strain the stock, discard the solids, and use according to the recipe of your choice. Stock can be kept up to 3 days in the refrigerator or 3 months in the freezer.

VARIATION: For a more straightforward pork stock, omit dried squid or shrimp, preserved daikon or *tien sin* cabbage, and thick soy sauce. Put pork ribs, onion, fresh daikon, 2 tablespoons fish sauce, peppercorns, and 2 ounces ginger, sliced and lightly crushed, in a stockpot filled with 5 quarts water and bring to a boil, then reduce to low, season with salt, and simmer until reduced by 2 quarts, about 3 hours.

(CLOCKWISE FROM TOP LEFT) PRESERVED DAIKON, DRIED SQUID, AND DRIED SHRIMP

Nuoc Leo Bo
Beef Stock

Makes about 3 quarts

2 pounds oxtail, cut in 1-inch-
thick pieces (double amount
if not using optional meats)
8 ounces beef brisket
(optional)
8 ounces beef tendon
(optional)
1 large yellow onion, peeled
5 whole cloves
4 ounces fresh ginger, peeled,
cut into 4 slices and lightly
crushed
5 star anise
1 cinnamon stick, about 2½ to
3 inches long
1 teaspoon white or black
peppercorns
Coarse sea salt

I USE OXTAIL to create what I consider the best beef stock. Although less readily available, it is worth the extra effort to find. Oxtail contains the three elements I look for in a complex, fragrant stock: meat, bone, and fat. Some cooks blanch the meaty bones before they start making the stock. "It gets rid of the impurities," says my aunt Loan. The "impurities" she refers to are bone chips, fat, and mostly blood particles that form a floating grayish foam. "You can get rid of most of this foam by blanching beforehand," explains Loan. Throughout the stock's long simmering process, however, you will need to skim off the little amount of foam that builds up.

1. Trim some of the fat off the oxtail pieces. Put the oxtail with water to cover in a stockpot and bring to a boil over high heat. Blanch for 15 minutes, then drain and rinse both meat and pot.

2. Place the oxtail back in the stockpot, add the brisket and tendon (if using), cover with 5 quarts water, and bring to a boil over high heat. Reduce the heat to low, add the onion studded with cloves, the ginger, star anise, cinnamon stick, and peppercorns, and season with salt. Simmer, uncovered and undisturbed, occasionally skimming off foam, until the stock is reduced by 2 quarts, about 3

hours. Remove the brisket and tendon from stock, and reserve for use in another dish. At this time, skim off as much fat as you desire.

3. Strain the stock, discard the solids, and use according to the recipe of your choice. The stock can be kept up to 3 days in the refrigerator or 3 months in the freezer.

NOTE: Beef tendons are not only used in making this stock or eaten in *pho*, but they are sometimes braised in soy sauce, a great delicacy. Tendons are the white fibrous connective tissue that holds together muscle (or meat) to bone. This part of the cow is not used in

Western cooking, and so you will need to purchase it from a Chinese butcher in Chinatown.

My mother is not a fan of cinnamon, and her "cinnamon radar" is so sensitive that she can smell the stuff a mile away and detect the smallest amounts in food. But here's a paradox: although she routinely refuses anything containing cinnamon, this beef stock is one of her favorites. Perhaps it is because the spices—cloves, ginger, star anise, and cinnamon—steep together for hours, metamorphosing into complex new flavors, the cinnamon becoming a pleasant background note.

NUOC LEO CAI
Vegetable Stock

Makes about 3 quarts

1 pound daikon, peeled and cut in large chunks, or white turnips, peeled and halved

5 carrots, peeled and halved crosswise

2 leeks, trimmed

1 bunch cilantro, root ends trimmed

3 stalks lemongrass, outer leaves and tough green tops removed, root ends trimmed, and stalks halved crosswise and lightly crushed

4 ounces fresh ginger, peeled, cut into 4 slices, and lightly crushed

1 teaspoon white or black peppercorns

Coarse sea salt

I AM INCLUDING this stock for those readers who may, for health or other reasons, prefer not to use meat or poultry in their cooking. The entire stalk of the lemongrass—green fibrous part and white bulb—is used in this recipe. Since lemongrass is used for its fragrance, there is no reason why the green part, which is also fragrant, should not be included. This stock can be used as a substitute for chicken, beef, or pork stock in rice dishes and soups, and drunk as a palate cleanser at meals. It is particularly recommended as a base for *canh dau hu*, tofu soup (page 72), or any dish requiring a stock in the vegetable chapter of this book.

1. Put the daikon or turnips, carrots, leeks, cilantro, lemongrass, ginger, and peppercorns in a stockpot with 5 quarts water and bring to a boil over high heat. Reduce the heat to low and season with salt. Simmer, uncovered and undisturbed, until the stock is reduced by 2 quarts, about 3 hours.

2. Strain the stock, discard the solids, and use according to the recipe of your choice. The stock can be kept up to 3 days in the refrigerator or 3 months in the freezer.

Soups as Palate Cleansers

I N T H E U N I T E D S T A T E S, you often hear that beer is the best complement to Asian foods. Although it can be a good one, I have never believed it to be the best. Traditionally, tea, or a clear soup, is drunk with meals. This type of soup, known as *canh*, light and infused with fresh herbs, is a "palate cleanser." Similar to wine—or perhaps the sorbet served between courses during a formal French meal—it can be rich, spicy, and flavorful, in turn cleansing, lifting, and refreshing the palate. It is most likely that these soups were a direct influence from the Chinese, who also serve a light communal soup as part of the meal.

One of my favorite childhood memories involves enjoying *canh* as a palate cleanser during family meals. When we came to the table, it would be full of varied and wonderful foods for everyone to share. At each of our individual place settings—rice bowl and chopsticks aside—it was the Chinese soup spoon that was closest to the communal heart of our family feast. The spoon was used for dipping into the large bowl of steaming fragrant broth—our palate cleanser—set at the center of the table. Sometimes the soup would be a simple chicken broth with tofu and Asian greens—called *canh dau hu* (page 72). Sometimes it was *canh ca nau dua* (page 75), the classic sour-sweet and spicy fish and pineapple soup made with the biggest white fish head my mother could find. Today when I return home, every meal still includes a different bowl of my mother's palate-cleansing soup, which is replenished intermittently. I do the same at home. Whether I make dinner for two or eight, there is always the great bowl of soup at center stage.

And if the meal is a culinary stage, from the actors comes the sound of enthusiastic slurping! Between bites of whatever else was served, you would fill your ceramic soup spoon with the broth and slurp it, the louder the better—a sign in Asian culture of great satisfaction and a compliment to the cook. The first time my mother sat with grandmother Huong, grandfather Mai, and the rest of her new, extended family, she found the slurping disturbing. Having been brought up with strict French table manners—which discourages the close association of loud noises and eating—she was mildly abashed, to put it nicely. Today when my father slurps, she knows he appreciates her soup, but still she would prefer something along the lines of "Honey, it's a wonderful soup."

CANH BI DAO
Winter Melon Soup

Serves 4 to 6

1 ounce dried tiger lilies
6 cups pork stock made with
    dried shrimp (page 62) or
    chicken stock (page 61)
12 ounces winter melon or
    cucumber, seeded, peeled,
    and sliced thinly or cut into
    1-inch cubes
1 cup shredded cooked pork
    or chicken from stock
Coarse sea salt
Freshly ground white pepper
½ cup cilantro leaves
1 scallion, trimmed and thinly
    sliced diagonally

WINTER MELONS are large, mild-flavored gourds that absorb other flavors exceptionally well, especially in pork or chicken stock. Available in Asian markets, they can weigh as much as 12 pounds, but vendors usually sell them cut into wedges. Sometimes, for special occasions, if I can find a small melon (about 4 pounds), I use it as an edible cooking tureen. To do this, slice off the very top of the gourd and remove all the seeds, as you would for a pumpkin on Thanksgiving. Then carve out some of the edible melon to make the soup. The gourd should be about half an inch thick all over, and the bottom should be sliced off just enough so it sits flat on your serving platter. Pour the hot soup in it, then place the top of the gourd on top to keep the soup warm until you serve it.

1. Put the tiger lilies in a bowl with hot water to cover, and set a plate over the bowl to prevent the steam from escaping. Let stand until the lilies rehydrate and soften, about 20 minutes. Squeeze the lilies between the palms of your hands to get rid of the excess water. With a paring knife, remove any hard stems and tie each lily in a knot.

2. Pour the pork or chicken stock into a pot and bring it to a gentle boil over medium heat. Reduce the heat to medium-low, add the winter melon and shredded pork or chicken, and season to taste with salt and pepper. Simmer partially covered, until the melon is cooked, about 15 to 20 minutes. Serve hot— in communal bowl or individual soup bowls—garnished with fresh cilantro leaves and scallion.

CANH BAP CUON
Cabbage Roll Soup

Serves 4 to 6

6 dried cloud ear mushrooms

12 large cabbage leaves, halved lengthwise and ribs removed

2 scallions, trimmed, white parts minced and green tops left intact

4 ounces lean ground pork (double if not using shrimp)

6 ounces shrimp, shelled, deveined, and finely chopped

2 tablespoons fish sauce

Coarse sea salt

Freshly ground white pepper

6 cups pork stock variation (page 62) or chicken stock (page 61)

½ cup cilantro leaves

THIS CLASSIC SOUP has sweet green cabbage leaves stuffed with a pork and shrimp filling. They are virtual spring rolls floating in a delicate broth. *Canh bap cuon* is often served at special occasions such as Tet, the Lunar New Year. This recipe reminds me of the French *chou farci*, Savoy cabbage stuffed with ground pork. The Vietnamese version removes the ribs from each cabbage leaf, blanches them, then rolls them into bite-size bundles tightened with a delicate scallion knot.

1. Put the cloud ear mushrooms in a bowl with hot water to cover, then set a plate over the bowl to prevent steam from escaping. Let stand until the mushrooms rehydrate and soften, about 10 minutes. Squeeze the mushrooms between the palms of your hands to get rid of the excess water. Using a paring knife, remove any hard stems. Mince the cloud ears and place in a mixing bowl.

2. Bring a pot of salted water to a boil over high heat and blanch the cabbage leaves until just tender, 2 to 3 minutes. With a slotted spoon, remove the cabbage leaves, rinse under cold water, and drain thoroughly. Blanch the scallion tops in the same pot until just tender, about 1 minute. Rinse under cold water, drain, then tear into 20 long strips. Set both aside.

3. To the cloud ears, add the pork, shrimp, minced scallion, and fish sauce. Season with salt and pepper and mix well. Place about 1 teaspoon of filling at 1 inch from the wide edge (opposite of the pointy tip) of a cabbage leaf. Roll the cabbage leaf over the filling once, fold in the sides, and roll all the way to enclose the filling. Take a green scallion strip and tie it around the bundle to secure the filling. Repeat the process until you have 24 cabbage rolls.

4. Pour the stock into a pot and bring it to a gentle boil over medium heat. Reduce heat to medium-low, add cabbage rolls, and cook until the cabbage is tender and the filling is cooked, about 10 minutes. Serve hot—in a communal bowl or individual soup bowls—garnished with cilantro leaves.

CANH BO SEN
Beef and Lotus Root Soup

Serves 4 to 6

6 cups beef stock (page 64)
**1 pound fresh lotus root,
    peeled and cut into thin
    rounds**
Coarse sea salt
Freshly ground white pepper
**1 cup shredded cooked oxtail
    meat (from making stock)**
**¼ cup julienned holy basil
    leaves**

THE LOTUS, or water lily, is widely known in the West as a beautiful single-blossom flower, but it is actually an edible food. In central Vietnam, where the lotus is a popular vegetable, the fresh seeds are used in desserts, stews, or rice dishes such as *Hue com sen* (page 106), often decorated with its water-lily flower. The stems or tuberous roots are candied, stir-fried, or served in soups like this one. Lotus roots and seeds are available in Asian markets, dried or fresh. I much prefer using the fresh kind, so when I choose lotus roots, like all vegetables, I always look for the ones that are the least bruised. Uncut, they can be refrigerated for a couple of weeks.

1. Pour the beef stock into a pot and bring to a gentle boil over medium heat. Reduce the heat to medium-low and add the lotus root. Season to taste with salt and pepper and simmer, partially covered, until the lotus root is tender, about 35 minutes. Add shredded meat and simmer until it is heated through, about 10 minutes more. Serve hot—in a communal bowl or individual soup bowls—garnished with holy basil.

(COUNTER CLOCKWISE; FROM RIGHT) LOTUS ROOT: WHOLE, PEELED, AND SLICED

Canh Dau Hu
Tofu Soup

Serves 4 to 6

3 large dried shiitake
  mushrooms
6 cups chicken stock (page 61)
  or vegetable stock (page 66)
20 *rau ram* leaves, plus extra
  for garnish, or 10 sprigs
  cilantro, plus extra leaves
  for garnish
6 ounces baby bok choy, root
  ends trimmed, and leaves
  separated, or spinach
10 ounces medium-firm tofu,
  rinsed, drained, and cut
  into ½-inch cubes
Coarse sea salt
Freshly ground white pepper
1 scallion, trimmed and thinly
  sliced diagonally

I LIKE TO PREPARE this light and refreshing tofu soup with ginger-infused chicken stock, infusing it further with *rau ram (Vietnamese coriander)*, small, narrow, pointy, silky leaves available in Asian markets. Made from simmered soybean milk and firming agents, tofu is sold in four different textures—silken, soft, medium-firm, and firm. All are moist but differ in texture from smooth to slightly grainy. I purchase homemade tofu from a local Chinatown street vendor who makes it fresh every day, because I find hers has a more pronounced flavor than the packaged kind. If you do not have such a vendor or an Asian market near you, however, you can find a good selection of packaged tofu in health food stores or the refrigerated section of many supermarkets. If not used all at once, tofu can be kept refrigerated for up to 3 days in a water bath changed daily.

1. Put the mushrooms in a bowl with hot water to cover, and set a plate over the bowl to prevent steam from escaping. Let stand until the mushrooms rehydrate, about 20 minutes. Squeeze the mushrooms between the palms of your hands to get rid of the excess water. Using a paring knife, remove any stems from the mushrooms and julienne the caps.

2. Pour the stock into a pot and bring it to a gentle boil over medium heat. Reduce the heat to medium-low, add the *rau ram* leaves, and simmer partially covered until ready to use.

3. Meanwhile, bring a pot of salted water to a boil. Wash the bok choy under cold running water, then drain. Blanch the leaves in the boiling salted water until cooked but still firm, about 1 minute. With a slotted spoon, remove the bok choy, drain, and add to the stock along with the tofu. Season to taste with salt and pepper, and simmer over low heat until the

RAU RAM (ALSO KNOWN AS VIETNAMESE CORIANDER)

tofu is heated through, about 2 minutes. Serve hot—in a communal bowl or individual soup bowls—garnished with fresh *rau ram* leaves and scallion.

Tofu, also known as soybean curd, was introduced to the Vietnamese by the Chinese, who have been using it since approximately 164 B.C.E.. Tofu contains little fat, much calcium, and is a great source of protein. Although not all sects in Buddhism require that you be vegetarian, at certain times of the year and during special celebrations or funerals, vegetarian meals are eaten. The vegetarian cuisine of Buddhist monks has replaced some meat, poultry, seafood, and fish with tofu, turning each dish into a "mock-something-or-other," such as mock chicken, mock beef, or mock fish, reminding them of their sacrifice on the road to becoming better beings.

CANH CHUA TOM
Sour Shrimp Soup

Serves 4 to 6

1 cup canned straw
    mushrooms
1 pound medium shrimp,
    shelled and deveined,
    heads and shells reserved
3 stalks lemongrass, outer
    leaves and tough green
    tops removed, root ends
    trimmed, and stalks lightly
    crushed
3 dried red chilies
3 lime leaves or peel
2 tablespoons lime juice
3 tablespoons fish sauce
Coarse sea salt
Freshly ground white pepper
1 medium ripe tomato, cut
    into 8 equal wedges
2 scallions, trimmed and
    thinly sliced
1 cup mung bean sprouts,
    trimmed
⅓ cup julienned holy basil
¼ cup fried garlic oil, variation
    (page 50)

THIS SOUTHERN SPECIALTY is very light, but intense with all sorts of lemony flavors from lime leaves, lime juice, and lemongrass. The stock, which is made from the shrimp shells and heads, cooks just long enough to flavor it lightly. There is a similar Thai version of this soup, which gets its sourness from tamarind pulp. Straw mushrooms are available canned, with skin or without, in Asian markets.

1. Bring a pot of water to a boil over high heat. Drain and rinse the mushrooms, then blanch them in the boiling water for 3 minutes. Drain once again.

2. Place the shrimp heads and shells in a pot with 7 cups water and bring to a gentle boil over medium heat. Reduce the heat to medium-low and simmer until the liquid is reduced by 1 cup, about 30 minutes.

3. Strain the shrimp stock through a sieve over a pot, pressing the shells to extract any juices. Discard the shells and add the lemongrass, chilies, lime leaves, lime juice, and fish sauce to the stock. Season to taste with salt and pepper and simmer the stock, partially covered, over low heat for 15 minutes. Add the straw mushrooms and tomato wedges and simmer for an additional 5 minutes. Add the shrimp and cook until opaque, about 2 minutes. Remove from the heat. Serve hot—in a communal bowl or individual soup bowls—garnished with scallion, mung bean sprouts, holy basil, and fried garlic oil.

CANH CA NAU DUA
Fish and Pineapple Soup

Serves 4 to 6

12 ounces cod steaks, skinned
  and cut into bite-size
  chunks
Coarse sea salt
Freshly ground black or white
  pepper
1 white fish head, such as cod
3 to 4 tablespoons tamarind
  pulp
7 ounces ripe pineapple, cut
  into ¼-inch-thick slices,
  cored, and cut into bite-size
  chunks
1 medium ripe tomato,
  peeled, halved, seeded, and
  cut into 8 equal wedges
2 or more fresh bird's eye or
  Thai chilies, seeded and
  sliced thin diagonally
10 leaves holy basil, julienned
4 saw leaves, julienned, or
  ¼ cup cilantro leaves
¼ cup fried garlic oil, variation
  (page 50)

THIS SOUP is as much Cambodian as it is Vietnamese. At its roots it is a traditional Southeast Asian fish and tamarind soup, updated in this century with the addition of pineapple, a fruit imported from Latin America. Taking to the pineapple, the Vietnamese have made it one of their own. Today it is the second most cultivated fruit in Vietnam, after the native banana. I use fresh cod because it is readily available, flavorful but not "fishy," and stays tender and pleasantly firm when cooked. Tamarind gives the soup a sour accent, while pineapple provides the sweetness. There are several species of pineapple, but any ripe type will do. The balance between sour, sweet, and spicy is the fundamental character of this soup, although the use of chilies is at your discretion.

1. Season the fish chunks with salt and pepper and let stand in a cool place.

2. Put the fish head in a pot with 7 cups water and bring to a gentle boil over medium heat. Reduce the heat to medium-low and simmer until the liquid is reduced by 1 cup, about 30 minutes. At this time you may discard the fish head if you wish.

3. Add the tamarind pulp, pineapple, tomato, and chilies and simmer for 5 minutes. Add the fish chunks, adjust the seasoning, and simmer until the fish is cooked, 3 to 5 minutes. Serve hot—in a communal bowl or individual soup bowls—garnished with holy basil, saw leaves (or cilantro), and fried garlic oil as desired.

CANH NAM DON THIT
Stuffed Mushroom Soup

Serves 4 to 6

24 small dried shiitake
   mushrooms
¼ cup dried cloud ear
   mushrooms
6 cups pork stock variation
   (page 62) or chicken stock
   (page 61)
2 stalks lemongrass, outer
   leaves and tough green tops
   removed, root ends
   trimmed, and stalks halved
   and lightly crushed
4 ounces lean ground pork
   (double if not using shrimp)
6 ounces shrimp, shelled,
   deveined, and finely
   chopped
2 scallions, trimmed and
   minced
1 clove garlic, peeled and
   minced
1 large egg
Coarse sea salt
Freshly ground white pepper
⅓ cup cilantro leaves
Fried shallots (page 51)

THIS UNUSUAL SOUP uses stuffed dried shiitake mushrooms in a light pork stock. There are many varieties of dried shiitakes, or Chinese dried black mushrooms. Some are bite-size, some are very large and meaty, and the rest come in a full range of sizes in between. Whole mushrooms—a sign of prosperity—are customarily used in this soup, and bite-size ones (about ¾ inch in diameter when dry) are used here. Traditionally, lean ground pork is used as the stuffing, and it should be about 70 percent lean to 30 percent fat. A minimum amount of fat is needed to keep the stuffing moist. If the meat is too lean, add ground fat. If the ground pork is too fatty, then use less of it and substitute shrimp for the missing amount. In this recipe, somewhat unconventionally, I use a lot of shrimp. In Vietnam this recipe would be reserved for holidays or other celebrations.

1. Put the shiitakes and cloud ears in separate bowls with hot water to cover, then set a plate over each bowl to prevent steam from escaping. Let stand until each rehydrates and softens, about 10 minutes for cloud ears, 20 minutes for the shiitakes. Squeeze the mushrooms between the palms of your hands to get rid of the excess water. Using a paring knife, remove any hard knobs from the cloud ears and the stems from the shiitakes.

2. Pour the stock into a pot and bring it to a gentle boil over medium heat. Reduce the heat to medium-low, add the lemongrass, and simmer, partially covered, until ready to use.

3. Finely chop the cloud ears and place them in a mixing bowl with the ground pork, shrimp, scallions, garlic, and egg. Season with salt and pepper and mix well. Firmly press about 1 rounded teaspoon of filling into each shiitake mushroom cap and smooth the surface evenly.

through, 5 to 7 minutes. Serve the steamed mushroom caps in the bamboo steamer with *nuoc xa ot* on the side.

I discovered this soup while celebrating Tet—the Lunar New Year—in Vietnam in February 1996. Since then I have served it to my family. It reminded some of times past. For others—the new generation—it was a pleasant discovery. While entertaining friends, I once steamed these stuffed mushroom treats and presented them as hors d'œuvres with *nuoc xa ot* (see Variation). Served for birthdays and other celebrations, both versions of this recipe are now Trang family "classics."

BITE-SIZE DRIED SHIITAKE MUSHROOMS

4. Carefully lower the stuffed mushrooms into the stock, cap side down. Cover and cook for 5 to 7 minutes. Serve hot—in a communal bowl or individual soup bowls—garnished with cilantro leaves and sprinkled with some fried shallots.

NOTE: The stuffed mushrooms can be prepared in advance and refrigerated overnight if you wish.

VARIATION: Try these stuffed shiitakes steamed with *nuoc xa ot,* spicy lemongrass soy dipping sauce (page 45). Set a bamboo steamer with lid over a wok filled halfway with water and bring the water to a boil over high heat. When the steamer is filled with hot steam, place iceberg lettuce leaves over the bamboo rack and set the stuffed mushrooms on top. Steam until the filling is cooked

SOUPS AS STARTERS

DURING THEIR COLONIZATION of Vietnam, the French brought some of their food and table traditions with them. The Vietnamese often reinterpreted them, creating new dishes in the bargain. *Sup*, thick soups reminiscent of French *veloutés*, were introduced by the French, most likely as homage to the cream-thickened soup of their native land. *Sup cua mang tay*, crab and asparagus soup (page 80), is similar to the French *velouté d'asperges*, which has a velvety texture and cooked-down chunks of asparagus. The important difference is that traditional *veloutés* are thickened with butter, flour, egg yolk, and cream, and *sup* are thickened with cornstarch, giving the soups not only the velvety texture but a glistening effect. The Vietnamese have also added delicate bits of fresh crabmeat, transforming a borrowed concept into their very own classic dish.

Another type of starter soup is *mien ga*, chicken and cellophane noodle soup (page 79). It is not a velvety thick soup like the other but nonetheless is served individually at the start of a meal. Cellophane noodles are made of mung bean starch and so are considered a vegetable.

Sup are less rich, much lighter on the palate, and so do not fill up the stomach as quickly as *veloutés*. A menu suggestion, following the French table tradition, would have individual servings of *sup* as starters, ginger and garlic rice with chicken (page 103) as an entrée with pickled vegetables (page 48) on the side. *Banh gan*, coconut crème caramel (page 232) could follow as dessert.

Mien Ga
Glass Noodle and Chicken Soup

Serves 4

6 small dried cloud ear
   mushrooms
2 ounces dried cellophane
   noodles
6 cups chicken stock (page 61)
8 ounces boneless, skinless
   chicken breast, thinly sliced
   against the grain
Traditional herbs (page 53)
2 scallions, trimmed and
   thinly sliced
2 or more red bird's eye or
   Thai chilies, stemmed,
   seeded, and thinly sliced
¼ cup fried shallots (page 51)
Fish sauce

CELLOPHANE NOODLES, also known as glass noodles or crystal noodles, are made of mung bean starch. In fact, sometimes they are called green bean thread or vermicelli. The Vietnamese refer to them as Chinese noodles and use them in the same manner as their former rulers did. When cooked, they are tender, slippery, and translucent. They are added to soups, braised dishes, and fillings purely for texture. These noodles are considered a vegetable rather than a starch, and so this soup would be served as a starter to a meal.

1. Put the cloud ear mushrooms and cellophane noodles in a bowl with hot water to cover, then set a plate over the bowl to prevent steam from escaping. Let stand until the mushrooms and noodles rehydrate and soften, about 15 minutes. Squeeze the mushrooms and noodles between the palms of your hands to get rid of the excess water. Using a paring knife, remove any hard stems from the mushrooms, then halve them.

2. Meanwhile, pour the chicken stock into a pot and bring it to a gentle boil over medium heat. Reduce the heat to medium-low, add the mushrooms, noodles, and chicken breast, and cook until the noodles become transparent, about 10 minutes. Divide soup among 4 soup bowls and garnish with some traditional herbs, scallions, chilies, and fried shallots. Add fish sauce to taste.

CELLOPHANE NOODLES
AND CLOUD EAR MUSHROOMS
SOAKING IN WATER

SUP CUA MANG TAY
Crab and Asparagus Soup

Serves 4 to 6

6 cups chicken stock (page 61)
**1 cup cooked Dungeness
    crabmeat in bite-size chunks**
**2 cups cooked white or green
    asparagus, drained and
    coarsely chopped**
Coarse sea salt
Freshly ground white pepper
2 egg whites, lightly beaten
1 tablespoon cornstarch
½ cup cilantro leaves

THIS ASPARAGUS SOUP, rich with crabmeat, is a family favorite, especially on my mother's French side of the family. No doubt theirs is a passion similar to that of the French colonials who made such efforts to re-create asparagus soup in Vietnam. In France, whenever we made this soup, we used stone crabmeat. In the United States, I use the more available Dungeness crab. Often sold already cooked, these crabs are sweet in flavor, and it is easy to pick out the meat. So as not to waste the cooked tomalley and roe from the crab (not used in the soup), we sprinkle it with some *nuoc cham* (page 42) and eat it with steamed jasmine rice. I use asparagus packed in brine from jars. Canned asparagus tends to absorb that nasty tin flavor. If the canned version is your only choice, drain, rinse, and blanch the asparagus in salted water for a few minutes, then rinse and drain again before adding to the stock. Fresh asparagus can also be used. You must first peel them, then cook them for about 30 minutes in the chicken stock to get them incredibly tender like the ones packed in jars.

1. Pour the chicken stock into a pot and bring to a gentle boil over medium heat. Reduce the heat to medium-low, add the crabmeat and asparagus, and season to taste with salt and pepper. Partially cover and simmer until the crabmeat and asparagus are heated through and flavor the stock further, about 15 minutes.

2. Slowly, in a steady stream, pour the egg whites into the soup, stir a few times, and let simmer until cooked, about 1 minute. Mix the cornstarch with 2 tablespoons cold water and stir into the soup. Continue simmering until the soup thickens, about 1 minute more. Divide among 4 to 6 soup bowls and garnish with cilantro.

NOTE: Do not use frozen crab-meat as it has lost its soft texture and rich flavor. If using a live 1½-pound Dungeness crab, either steam it for 15 to 20 minutes or cook it in boiling water for 8 to 10 minutes. If using ¾-pound stone crabs, steam them for 10 to 15 minutes or boil them for 5 to 8 minutes. Remove the crabs from the steamer or boiling water. When cool enough to handle, sep-arate the shell from the body. Re-move and discard the spongy and inedible gills. Remove the meat from the body, claws, and legs and add to the soup in bite-size chunks.

The colonial French made sever-al failed attempts to cultivate their prized fresh asparagus during the mid-1800s. Succumbing to some-what desperate cravings, they fell to using a canned version import-ed from France. Because it is tall, thin, and has a similar growing pattern, the Vietnamese saw as-paragus as "Western bamboo." They used it to create an entirely new version of *velouté d'asperges* to please their French rulers.

SOUPS AS MEALS

IN ASIA rice is central to cuisine, and a meal without rice is not a true meal. Perhaps this is why both *chao* and *pho*, two popular rice- and rice noodle-based soups, are considered full meals. Traditionally eaten for breakfast, today *chao* and *pho* are offered throughout the day and throughout Vietnam. Soup bowls are large by Western standards, and the amount of broth may surprise you. Asian broths are used to moisten ingredients, unify flavors, and in some cases cook the ingredients in the bowl. And, of course, they are for sipping.

Chao is any rice porridge, served plain with a few condiments on the side to pick from at your leisure, or garnished with other ingredients such as poultry, meat, fish, or seafood. Originating in China, these soups are referred to as *congee* on the menus of authentic Chinese and Vietnamese restaurants. Historically, rice porridge came about because it was a way to make a bag of rice last longer and feed more mouths. One cup of raw rice, cooked only until the grains are puffed, can feed 3 to 4 mouths. The same cup of dry rice, boiled in a lot of water and served as porridge, can feed 6 to 8. There are numerous variations on rice soup, ranging from plain porridge to more elaborate preparations with meat or fish, seasoned with fresh herbs, fried garlic oil, and fresh sliced scallions and ginger. Rice soups are generally made from short-grain rice because it contains more starch than the long-grain varieties and gives a preferred thicker texture. If you do not have short-grain, however, medium- or long-grain rice is acceptable.

Surprisingly, a successful *chao* can also be made with leftover roast meats and preserved vegetables, which give up their flavors, enhancing the plain rice porridge.

Because plain *chao* is often used as a dry rice bowl substitute, I have placed it in Chapter 3, Rice, Noodles, & Bread. The soup-like *chao,* made with more water and served as a liquid base for dozens of possible ingredients, is discussed here. My favorite Vietnamese version is made with beef, *chao bo* (page 85). Topped with fried garlic oil, the soup has a wonderful smoky flavor and a delightful texture. Eaten with cups of hot pungent tea, it is one of my most cherished memories of breakfast on a cold winter's morning.

Pho is a soup with roots going back to the Mongolians. A dysphemism, its name comes from the French word *feu,* as in *pot-au-feu,* meaning "pot on the fire." Originating in the northern city of Hanoi, *pho* is essentially broth with healthy portions of thin, flat rice noodles called *banh pho*; meat, seafood, or poultry; fresh herb aromatics; and seasonings. *Banh pho* are made with rice flour, water, and salt. They are available dry, bundled like the sticks from which they derive their name, or fresh in one-pound packages.

Today, from Hanoi to Saigon, *pho* is sold in noodle shops or by sidewalk peddlers. The most traditional is beef. In fact, when people call out for *pho* in a busy restaurant, it is assumed they are referring to the beef version. Always presented in a large bowl, the noodles are set in the center, typically with paper-thin slices of raw beef atop, plenty of steaming fragrant broth ladled over, and freshly torn herbs such as holy basil and cilantro, fried shallots, and thinly sliced chilies as garnishes. The seasoning is adjusted to taste with fish sauce; the broth sweetened with hoisin, a Chinese sauce made of sugar cane extract, fermented beans, and garlic; then a lime wedge is squeezed over the whole thing before the ingredients are tossed to ensure the soup is balanced with every bite. In this way, what might seem a modest bowl of soup becomes a complete culinary experience.

CHAO BO
Rice Porridge with Beef

Serves 4 to 6

1 tablespoon vegetable oil
1 small shallot, peeled and
    minced
¾ cup short-grain rice
8 ounces ground beef (70% lean)
    or ground pork (70% lean)
½ cup finely chopped roasted
    peanuts
1 cup cilantro leaves
2 scallions, trimmed and
    sliced into thin rounds
¼ cup fried garlic oil, variation
    (page 50)
Fish sauce
Freshly ground black pepper

THIS WONDERFUL rice porridge with ground beef not only is eaten as a breakfast or snack but is also the last course eaten during a *bo bay mon*, beef seven ways, meal. After the first six intensely flavored beef dishes, this rice porridge calms the stomach with its warm, gruel-textured character. This porridge can also be made with ground pork, which is equally delicious.

1. Heat the vegetable oil in a sand pot or heavy-bottomed pot over medium heat. Add the shallot and rice and stir-fry until they become translucent, about 5 minutes. Add 8 cups water and bring it to a gentle boil over medium heat. Reduce the heat to medium-low and cook, uncovered, stirring occasionally, for 1½ hours.

2. Add the ground beef a bit at a time so the beef stays separated; stir for 3 to 5 minutes, or until the beef is completely cooked. Divide the soup among 4 to 6 soup bowls. Garnish each serving with some peanuts, cilantro, scallions, and garlic oil. Season with fish sauce and pepper.

Chao Xa Ga
Rice Porridge with Chicken and Lemongrass

Serves 4 to 6

9 cups chicken stock (page 61)
    made with whole chicken
    and without ginger

2 stalks lemongrass, outer
    leaves and tough green
    tops removed, root ends
    trimmed, and stalks cut into
    1-inch pieces and lightly
    crushed

2 to 3 red bird's eye or Thai
    chilies, stemmed

2 tablespoons fish sauce

1 cup jasmine rice or similar rice

2 cooked chicken legs, boned,
    skinned, and shredded
    (from making stock)

Coarse sea salt

½ cup julienned saw leaves, or
    cilantro leaves

1 lemon, sliced in wedges

UNLIKE OTHER rice soups, *chao xa ga* is perfumed with tangy lemon flavors. Its chicken stock is infused with lemongrass early in the cooking process. When served, the porridge is garnished with julienned *ngo gai*, or saw leaf, an herb similar in taste to cilantro but stronger. Then freshly squeezed lemon juice is drizzled over, rounding out the three lemony flavors of this unique soup. It is worth the extra effort if you can find *ngo gai*—a long, narrow, pointy, dark green leaf with a tooth-like edge all around. It is sold in Asian and Caribbean produce markets. *Chao xa ga* is an excellent warm-weather treat.

1. Pour the chicken stock into a pot and bring it to a gentle boil over medium heat. Reduce the heat to medium-low, add the lemongrass, chilies, and fish sauce, and simmer for 30 minutes. Add the rice and cook, uncovered, for 1 hour more.

2. Add the shredded chicken, season to taste with salt, and cook until heated through, about 15 minutes. Divide among 4 to 6 large soup bowls, garnish with saw leaves, and squeeze 1 wedge of lemon over each serving.

PHO GA
Hanoi Chicken and Rice Noodle Soup

Serves 4

8 ounces small or medium
    dried rice sticks
8 cups chicken stock (page 61)
8 ounces chicken breast, thinly
    sliced against the grain
Traditional herbs (page 53)
1 cup mung bean sprouts,
    root ends trimmed
2 or more bird's eye or Thai
    chilies, stemmed, seeded,
    and thinly sliced
½ cup fried shallots (page 51)
1 lime, quartered
Fish sauce

PHO GA is the ultimate "chicken noodle soup" of the East. Lighter than *pho bo*, the classic beef noodle soup (page 88), it makes a perfect breakfast or afternoon snack or supper. Chicken breast is sliced thinly on the diagonal for a delicate appearance and against the grain to ensure tenderness. This soup is particularly suited to white meat because it is blanched quickly so it does not cloud the stock. Kept moist in the steaming broth, it is complemented nicely by the soup's condiments and seasonings.

1. Place the rice sticks in a dish with lukewarm water to cover. Let stand until pliable, about 20 minutes.

2. Meanwhile, pour the chicken stock into a pot and bring to a gentle boil over medium heat. Reduce the heat to medium-low and partially cover until ready to use.

3. Bring a pot filled with water to a boil over high heat. Drain and divide the rice stick noodles into 4 equal portions. Place noodles, one portion at a time, in a sieve and lower it into the boiling water. Untangle the noodles with chopsticks and boil until tender but firm, about 7 seconds. Remove and drain the noodles, then place them in a large soup bowl. Repeat this step until you have 4 individual servings.

4. Blanch the chicken pieces in the same boiling water for about 2 minutes per batch. Divide and place atop each noodle serving. Pour a generous amount of hot broth over each serving and garnish with some traditional herbs, mung bean sprouts, chilies, and fried shallots. Squeeze a wedge of lime over each serving and adjust the seasoning with fish sauce.

Pho Bo
Hanoi Beef and Rice Noodle Soup

Serves 4

8 ounces small or medium
    dried rice sticks
8 cups beef stock (page 64)
1 small yellow onion, peeled,
    halved, and thinly sliced
8 ounces beef eye of round,
    slightly frozen, sliced paper-
    thin (if serving special meats
    from stock recipe, only use
    4 ounces eye of round)
4 ounces cooked special beef
    cuts (from making stock),
    thinly sliced (optional)
Traditional herbs (page 53)
1 cup mung bean sprouts,
    root ends trimmed
2 or more red bird's eye or
    Thai chilies, stemmed,
    seeded, and thinly sliced
½ cup fried shallots (page 51)
1 lime, quartered
Hoisin sauce
Fish sauce

PHO BO, the beef and rice noodle soup made famous in Hanoi, is distinguished by its many layers of flavors and textures. The sweet and spicy broth flavored with star anise, cloves, and cinnamon and the fresh lemony herbs are what give this soup its curiously rich character. It is this tender beef version that the Vietnamese really want when they call out, in an abbreviated manner, for a bowl of *pho*. There are numerous ways of serving *pho bo*. It can be served simply with thinly sliced lean beef in a flavorful broth with oxtail as its base. When I am in the mood to eat more exotic cuts of beef, I add beef tendon and brisket and even the wonderfully tender navel to the stock. I can then remove them, slice a few pieces of each, and add them as I wish to my bowl of *pho*.

1. Place the rice sticks in a dish with lukewarm water to cover. Let soak until pliable, about 20 minutes.

2. Meanwhile, pour the beef stock into a pot and bring to a gentle boil over medium heat. Reduce the heat to medium-low, add the onion, and partially cover until ready to use.

3. Bring a pot filled with water to a boil over high heat. Drain and divide the rice stick noodles into 4 equal portions. Place them, one portion at a time, in a sieve and lower it into the boiling water. Untangle the noodles with chopsticks, and boil until tender but firm, about 7 seconds. Remove and drain the noodles, then place them in a large soup bowl. Repeat this step until you have 4 individual servings.

4. Set a few slices of raw beef eye of round on top of the rice noodles (or if you prefer, cook them first using the same strainer and boiling water as in step 3). At this time you can also add some slices of one or more of the special cuts of beef. Pour a generous amount of hot broth with some onions over each serving and garnish with some traditional herbs, mung bean sprouts, chilies, and fried shallots, and

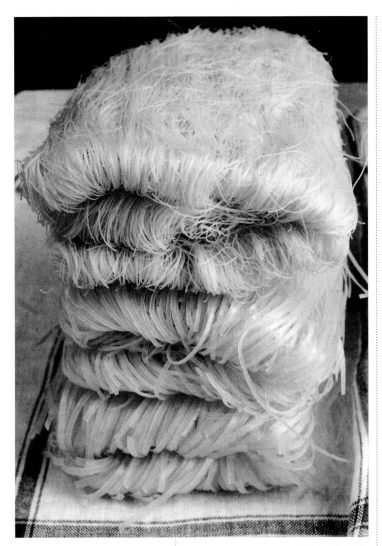

DRIED RICE VERMICELLI AND SMALL AND MEDIUM RICE STICKS

namese tradition, one that my family most definitely observes when we eat Vietnamese food. In order to make sure your guests do not take their food for granted, they must be involved in the ritual of garnishing their own soup. Specifically, they should tear a desired amount of fresh herbs and select fragrant sauces and other condiments to add to the soup. Just as mine do, I think your guests will enjoy being involved in such rituals, ensuring that the soup is exactly to their taste. My family and friends have requested this dish on many occasions. If I may offer some advice, make sure you prepare enough to take care of everybody who wants seconds.

squeeze a wedge of lime over each serving. Sweeten the broth with hoisin sauce and adjust the seasoning with fish sauce as desired.

VARIATION: This *pho* can also be prepared with *bo vien,* beef meatballs (page 215). Substitute 1 recipe *bo vien* for the raw beef and cooked exotic cuts of beef. Add the beef balls to the heated beef broth in step 2. Then proceed with steps 3 and 4.

This is a recipe that requires a great deal of caring preparation on the part of the cook, and the guest as well! It demonstrates a Viet-

Pho Heo
Rice Noodle and Ground Pork Soup

Serves 4

8 ounces small or medium
    dried rice sticks
8 cups pork stock (page 62)
    made with dried shrimp
    and preserved cabbage
1 pound ground pork
1 cup cilantro leaves
1 cup mung bean sprouts,
    root ends trimmed
2 scallions, white parts only,
    thinly sliced on the diagonal
2 to 3 bird's eye or Thai
    chilies, stemmed, seeded,
    and thinly sliced
¼ cup fried garlic oil, variation
    (page 50)
1 lime, quartered
Fish sauce

PHO HEO is a family variation based on the classic Saigon soup *hu tieu do bien* (page 92). Dried shrimp (rather than the traditional dried squid) and preserved *tien sin* cabbage (instead of preserved daikon) make this version distinctive. My aunt Lang, hoping to save a little time and effort, substituted ingredients that were a little easier to prepare and created a simplified but equally delicious version of this hearty soup.

1. Place the rice sticks in a dish with lukewarm water to cover. Let stand until pliable, about 20 minutes.

2. Pour the pork stock into a pot and bring to a gentle boil over medium heat. Reduce the heat to medium-low. Place some ground pork in a ladle and slowly lower it into the stock. Allowing some stock into the ladle, with a pair of chopsticks, stir the ground pork until it separates, then let it go into the stock. Continue this process until you have added all the ground pork to the stock, and gently simmer for 30 minutes.

3. Bring a pot filled with water to a boil over high heat. Drain and divide the rice stick noodles into 4 equal portions. Place them, one portion at a time, in a sieve and lower it into the boiling water. Untangle the noodles with chopsticks and boil until tender but firm, about 7 seconds. Remove and drain the noodles, then place them in a large soup bowl. Repeat this step until you have 4 individual servings.

4. Pour a generous amount of hot broth, along with an equal amount of ground pork, dried shrimp, and preserved *tien sin* cabbage, over each serving and garnish with some cilantro leaves, mung bean sprouts, scallions, chilies, and fried garlic oil. Squeeze a wedge of lime over each serving and adjust the seasoning with fish sauce.

MI VIT
Egg Noodles and Roast Duck Soup

Serves 4

1 pound fresh thin egg
   noodles or 8 ounces dried
   thin egg noodles
8 cups chicken stock (page 61)
12 ounces *laqué* duck
   (page 189), thinly sliced
3 scallions, trimmed and
   thinly sliced on the diagonal
½ cup cilantro leaves

MI VIT, egg noodle soup with roast *laqué* duck, is traditionally Chinese, brought from the North. The egg noodles in this soup are slightly thicker than rice vermicelli and are available either dried or fresh. Although this noodle soup is made with *laqué* duck, there is no reason why you could not use, for example, garlic-roasted baby chickens (page 186). Leftover grilled meats will also give this noodle soup great flavor.

1. If using dried egg noodles, put them in a dish with lukewarm water to cover. Let soak until pliable, about 20 minutes.

2. Pour the chicken stock into a pot and bring to a gentle boil over medium heat. Reduce the heat to medium-low and partially cover until ready to use.

3. Meanwhile, bring a pot filled with water to a boil over high heat. If using dried egg noodles, drain and divide them into 4 equal portions. Place one portion at a time in a sieve and lower it into the boiling water. Untangle the noodles with chopsticks, and boil until tender but firm, 2 to 3 minutes. If using fresh egg noodles, cook them for 3 to 5 minutes. Remove, drain, and place in a large soup bowl. Repeat this step until you have 4 individual servings.

4. Ladle a generous amount of hot broth over each serving of noodles, add the sliced duck meat, and garnish with scallions and cilantro leaves.

HU TIEU DO BIEN
Saigon Seafood and Rice Noodle Soup

Serves 4

1 pound fresh thin flat egg
   noodles or 8 ounces dried
   thin flat egg noodles
   or 8 ounces small or
   medium dried rice sticks
8 cups pork stock made with
   squid (page 62)
8 ounces pork tenderloin
12 medium shrimp, shelled
   and deveined
12 fish *quenelles* (page 150)
Traditional herbs (page 53)
1 cup mung bean sprouts,
   root ends trimmed
2 scallions, white part only,
   thinly sliced on the diagonal
2 or more bird's eye or Thai
   chilies, stemmed, seeded,
   and thinly sliced
¼ cup fried garlic oil, variation
   (page 50)
1 lime, quartered
Fish sauce

HU TIEU DO BIEN, a specialty of Saigon, is traditionally made with rice noodles or Cambodian-style thin flat egg noodles. Much like its northern *pho* counterpart, this soup relies heavily on the intensity of its stock. If the stock is flavorful, then your soup will be good. If the stock is weak, then the soup will be weak as well. Accordingly, the secret to this pork-based stock is the use of dried squid, which ensures an extra layer of smoky flavor. In a more Vietnamese variation, *hu tieu do bien* can be made with rice sticks. My aunt Loan, whose recipe this is, prefers to make this soup with rice sticks, which are lighter than egg noodles.

1. If using, place the dried egg noodles or rice sticks in a dish with lukewarm water to cover. Let stand until pliable, about 20 minutes.

2. Pour the pork stock into a pot and bring to a gentle boil over medium heat. Reduce the heat to medium-low, add the pork tenderloin, and cook through at a simmer, about 20 to 30 minutes. Transfer the pork to a cutting board and continue simmering the broth, partially covered. When cool enough to handle, thinly slice the pork, place it in a bowl, and cover with plastic wrap.

3. Bring a pot filled with water to a boil over high heat. Divide the egg noodles or rice sticks into 4 equal portions. Place one portion at a time in a sieve and lower it into the boiling water. Untangle the rice sticks or egg noodles with chopsticks and boil until tender but firm, about 7 seconds for the rice sticks, and 1 to 2 minutes for egg noodles. If using fresh egg noodles, cook them for 3 to 5 minutes. Remove, drain, and place in a large soup bowl. Repeat this step until you have 4 individual servings.

4. Cook the shrimp in the same pot of boiling water until they turn opaque, about 1 minute. Drain and place atop the 4 servings of rice sticks or egg noodles along with slices of pork tenderloin.

5. Add the fish *quenelles* to the pork stock and cook for 3 minutes.

Pour a generous amount of hot broth, along with an equal amount of fish *quenelles*, over each serving and garnish with some traditional herbs, mung bean sprouts, scallions, chilies, and fried garlic oil. Squeeze a wedge of lime over each serving and adjust seasoning with fish sauce.

One hot summer day my mother decided to prepare soup without the stock—dry soup, literally. She simply placed the pork, shrimp, and fish *quenelles* over her lightly cooked noodles. Then she seasoned the noodles with Chinese thin soy sauce, garnished them with fresh herbs, and added some fried garlic oil for extra flavor and also to untangle the rice noodles, which can easily get stuck together. My father, when asking for his second serving, did the same but kept the broth next to him in a separate bowl to slurp and help him clear his palate. Traditionally, the noodles can be served in the broth or with the broth in a separate bowl on the side.

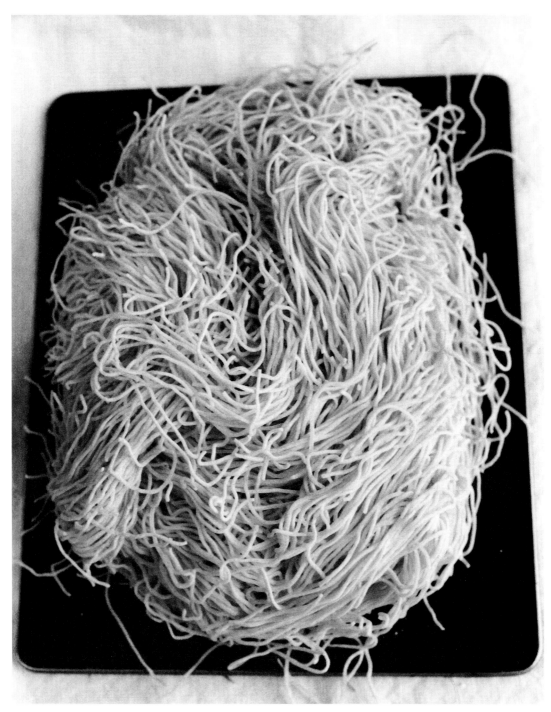

SHANGHAI-STYLE FRESH THIN EGG NOODLES

CHAPTER THREE

RICE, NOODLES, & BREAD

 IN VIETNAM, as in most Asian cultures, rice is a basic staple and a fundamental building block of the cuisine. It is eaten at all times of the day and night, by young and old alike, and is at least as ubiquitous as bread in Western cultures. The Vietnamese prepare rice in several ways. The simplest are steaming, stir-frying, and cooking the grain down to a porridge consistency. It is also ground into flour and combined with salt and water to make fresh rice noodles, thin crêpes, or rice paper. For the past century rice flour has also been used in bread making, which the Vietnamese learned from the French. Less popular than rice-based noodles, egg noodles are made of wheat flour and eggs and are often used in soups or stir-fries. ◆ A day in Vietnam traditionally began with a bowl of *chao*, rice porridge, or *pho bo*, beef and rice noodle soup (page 88), which was eaten only for breakfast. Nowadays, these dishes are eaten all day long. Also eaten are *baguettes*, which are based on the French classic bread of the same name but made with rice flour. These crusty loaves are served either with butter for a simple breakfast, or with *cha lua*, pork pâté (page 197), and fresh herbs such as cilantro and holy basil for lunch. ◆ The fundamental assumption about rice and other starches in Vietnamese culture is that they are the underpinnings of a meal. That is to say, whatever meat, fish, seafood, poultry, or vegetable item is being offered, it is most likely accompanied by a starch. A significant body of folk wisdom and superstition has grown up around this cultural fact. My father, for example, always told my brothers that if they didn't eat every grain of rice, their wives would have pimples. Rice has also been associated with peasant armies in Vietnamese poetry, the idea of sacrifice for a greater good being the common thread. When there is little or no rice, people eat sweet potatoes and cassava as replacements. (Buddhist monks, who are strict vegetarians, will often have combinations of several starches to compensate for the lack of animal protein in their diet.)

Rice, when eaten in its natural state as a grain, is most often steamed alone, traditionally cooked in a clay pot over an open wood fire or a gas flame. It can be flavored with broth and herbs and served with different items to create an impromptu meal. My earliest memories as a child are of my mother cooking rice in our kitchen. Whenever we saw the clay pot on the stove and smelled a minty aroma, we knew she was making her chicken and rice casserole, infused with mint and shallots. And one of my father's favorite midnight snacks is rice porridge, *chao*, with preserved meats and vegetables.

There are several types of noodles in Vietnamese cuisine. They vary in size, shape, thickness, flavor, ingredients, and cooking time and technique, as well as specific use and derivation. Some are borrowed from or inspired by Chinese noodles, others are indigenous, and still others are imported from neighboring countries.

The most popular rice noodles are flat like linguine, *banh pho*, or round like spaghetti, *bun*. They are long, somewhat translucent when dried, and opaque white when fresh. An important difference between fresh Vietnamese and Western noodles is that the Vietnamese versions are already cooked and need only be heated through. The dried ones must first be soaked in warm water until pliable, then blanched for a few seconds. The fresh varieties are not soaked but are cooked directly in stir-fries and soups. Besides these common noodles, there are some interesting variations. A sort of Vietnamese ravioli (page 113), *banh cuon*, is filled with ground pork and cloud ear mushrooms, then drizzled with scallion oil and dipped in *nuoc cham*. *Mi*, Shanghai-style noodles, also called Cambodian-style noodles by the Vietnamese, are used for stir-fries such as *mi xao don do bien*, crispy egg noodles with seafood (page 116), or prepared in soups like *mi vit*, egg noodle and roast duck soup (page 91). *Mien*, glass noodles or bean threads, referred to as Chinese noodles by the Vietnamese, are made of mung beans and are considered vegetables. They are used mostly for their crunchy texture in pâtés or in stuffing to fill *cha gio*, spring rolls (page 198). They are sometimes stir-fried with vegetables, *mien xao rau cai* (page 117) or used in soups such as the classic *mien ga*, glass noodle and chicken soup (page 79).

In order to make the rather cumbersome topic of starches a bit more accessible, I have divided this chapter into three main categories, under the headings of "Rice," "Noodles," and "Bread." Each is described in detail within the context of Vietnamese cuisine.

RICE

R ICE PADDIES form a virtual carpet across the Vietnamese
countryside, their rectangular patterns and terracing creating perhaps the most compelling images of rural life. This distinctive agricultural landscaping knows no regional boundaries and is
found wherever land is cultivated and water is readily available. The
Red River in the North and, to a much larger extent, the Mekong
Delta in the South are Vietnam's rice bowls. Although other crops,
including mangoes, oranges, peppers, coconuts, and pineapples,
as well as sugar cane and shrimp, are grown, rice is the single most
widely cultivated crop. Vietnam, in fact, is the third largest
rice exporter in the world, after the United States and Thailand.

There are dozens of types of rice, and each varies in flavor, col-
or, starch content, texture, and aroma. Many Vietnamese can dif-
ferentiate between rice varieties simply by the aroma given off
during cooking. Throughout the country the preferred grain for
everyday meals is long-grain white rice, which is tender and flaky
after it is cooked. Rice grains that contain an herbal scent, like jasmine rice, are more expensive. When people cannot afford scent-
ed rice, they add a few herbs to plain rice during cooking. Other
white rices include short- and medium-grains. The medium-grain
is cooked in the same way as long-grain rice. Plain short-grain
rice is similar in flavor to these other common rices but is generally preferred for making rice porridge, as it breaks down evenly.

Short-grain sticky rice, also known as sweet rice or glutinous
rice, is chalky white when uncooked and literally sticky, firm, and

translucent when cooked. ("Glutinous" is a misleading term as rice in general does not contain gluten but starch.) It is sometimes mixed with vegetables and meats, wrapped in bamboo, lotus, or banana leaves, then boiled. An example of this is *banh chung*, sticky rice cake with pork and mung beans (page 107), eaten during Tet, the New Year's celebration. Traditionally, everyone made *banh chung* at home, but today in Vietnam, these 4- to 5-inch square bundles are made commercially and sold in the market during that time of the year.

Short-grain sticky rice is often preferred by vegetarians. Combined with legumes and nuts, it is more nutritious and makes up for the absence of meat protein.

COM
Cooked Rice

Serves 2 to 4

1 cup long-grain rice, such as jasmine (yields 3 cups cooked), or medium-grain rice

LONG-GRAIN RICE is the most commonly eaten of all rice grains and part of nearly every meal. I have been cooking rice for as long as I can remember, and I found that the best results come from cooking it in Chinese clay pots. The rice always turns out perfectly, the grains intact, tender on the inside, fluffy, separate, and moist. I find that rice cooked in electric cookers—especially when left on "warm" for hours—tends to be dry. If you prefer using an electric rice cooker, you are better off with the simplest models because they have no extended warming cycles. The women in my family have always measured the water-to-rice ratio with their index finger, placing the tip of the finger above the rice and adding water until it reaches the first knuckle. Of course, that all depends on how long your finger is! A less arbitrary method is simply to use a measuring cup.

1. Put the rice in a medium pot with a few cups of water. Gently swirl your fingers in the pot to allow the starch to separate from the grains. Once the water becomes white, tilt the pot over the sink to drain out the water. Be careful not to let your rice go in the sink. Repeat this process twice more. With each time, the water will get less cloudy. The idea is not to get rid of all the starch, just enough so that the rice will not be too sticky or too dry when cooked. Three times has always given me the best results.

2. After you have drained the rice the third time, add 1¾ cups clean water. Swirl your fingers in the pot once to ensure the rice is leveled and place the lid on the pot. Cook the rice over medium heat until it has absorbed all the water, about 20 minutes. Remove from heat, stir the rice with a wooden spoon a few times, then let rest, covered, for 5 minutes.

VARIATION: Here are two useful rice-to-water ratios. Steps 1 and 2 still apply, but the initial cooking time differs.

2 cups long-grain rice
  2¾ cups water
  25 minutes
  yields 6 cups (serves 4 to 6)

3 cups long-grain rice
  4 cups water
  30 minutes
  yields 9 cups (serves 6 to 8)

VARIATION: For *chao*, or plain rice porridge, substitute 1 cup short-grain rice for the long-grain rice, triple the amount of water, and cook over medium-low heat for 1½ hours.

Plain short-grain rice is used to make this porridge, which is often served for breakfast. At other times of the day, it replaces a bowl of steamed long- or medium-grain rice, and is served with meat, fish, and vegetable dishes on the side. When rice supplies are low, *chao* is also a good way to make a small amount of rice go a long way. The formula: 1 uncooked bowl of rice, when steamed, will feed 4 persons, but when cooked as porridge, it will feed 8 persons.

XOI NEP
Steamed Sticky Rice

Serves 2 to 4

1 cup sticky rice (yields about 2 cups cooked)
Cheesecloth, about 12 inches square

STICKY RICE, or glutinous rice, as it is often called, is not cooked the same way as long-grain or medium-grain rice. Instead, it is soaked for several hours or overnight, then steamed in a bamboo steamer. This rice is used for making *Hue com sen*, a steamed meat and rice cake wrapped in lotus leaf (page 106). Sticky rice approximately doubles in volume when cooked, but because it is more filling than regular rice, not as much is needed to fill the stomach.

1. Soak the sticky rice in 3 cups water, refrigerated, for at least 6 hours. Drain, then rinse and drain two more times.

2. Fill the bottom third of a wok with water (about 6 cups) and place a bamboo steamer with lid over it. Bring the water to a boil over high heat. Then place the damp cheesecloth over the bamboo rack, and spread the rice on it, leaving a 1-inch border all around to let the steam through. Fold over the cheesecloth, cover the steamer with the lid, and steam until the rice is tender but firm, about 25 minutes.

VARIATION: Here are two useful quantities of rice. Steps 1 and 2 still apply, but the cooking time differs.

2 cups sticky rice
    steam 25 minutes
    yields 4 cups (serves 4 to 6)

3 cups sticky rice
    steam 30 minutes
    yields 6 cups (serves 6 to 8)

Growing up, we did not eat a lot of sticky rice, although I often wished for it. Its firm, chewy texture is especially wonderful with salads such as *ga xe phay*, shredded chicken, cabbage, and carrot salad (page 188), or *goi du du*, green papaya salad (page 124). When preparing meals of several courses, you are probably better off using long-grain rice for these salads, as it is less filling. When the salads are served alone, the sticky-rice version will make for a more satisfying meal.

COM GA
Ginger and Garlic Rice with Chicken

Serves 4 to 6

2 cups long-grain rice, such as
   jasmine
2 tablespoons vegetable oil
2 large cloves garlic, peeled
   and chopped
2 tablespoons chopped ginger
2¾ cups chicken stock made
   with a whole chicken
   (page 61)
1 bunch cilantro, tough stems
   removed
Chicken (from making the
   stock)
Nuoc mam gung (page 47)

COM GA is a meal in itself. In order to make this dish properly, it is necessary first to make chicken stock using a whole chicken. The rice is then flavored with fried garlic, ginger, and fresh cilantro, and steamed in the chicken stock. The same chicken used for the stock is cut into medium-size chunks through the bone and placed atop the mounded fragrant rice. An effective way to serve this is on an oval platter that the rice fills completely. Drizzled with *nuoc mam gung*, ginger dipping sauce, it is a welcome dish for any time of the year.

1. Put the rice in a bowl with a few cups of water. Gently swirl your fingers in the bowl to allow the starch to separate from the grains. Once the water becomes white, drain and repeat this process twice more. With each time, the water will get less cloudy. The idea is not to get rid of all the starch, just enough so that the rice will not be too sticky or too dry when cooked. Three times has always given me the best results. Put the rice in a sieve and drain until the rice is fairly dry again.

2. Heat the oil in a medium clay pot or heavy-bottomed pot over medium heat. Add the garlic and ginger and stir-fry until golden and crisp, 5 to 7 minutes. Add the rice and stir with a wooden spoon until lightly golden, 3 to 5 minutes.

Add chicken stock and stir to level the rice. Scatter the cilantro across the top, cover, and cook until the rice has absorbed all the stock, about 25 minutes. Turn the heat off and with a wooden spoon, stir the rice a few times. Allow to rest, covered, for 5 to 10 minutes before serving.

3. With a cleaver, carefully chop the drumsticks and thighs in half crosswise through the bone. Then, chop the breast in half lengthwise and crosswise three times through the bone. Serve with the ginger and garlic rice and *nuoc mam gung* on the side.

RAU THOM COM GA
Mint Rice with Shredded Chicken

Serves 4 to 6

2 cups long-grain rice,
  such as jasmine
2¾ cups chicken stock
  (page 61)
3 shallots or 1 small red onion,
  peeled and minced
1 cup mint leaves, julienned
  or finely chopped
1 pound cooked chicken
  breast meat, skinned and
  shredded (from chicken
  stock)
Nuoc cham (page 42)

RAU THOM COM GA is a refreshing dish made with fresh mint leaves. The rice is cooked in chicken stock. Then, just before serving, finely chopped shallots, julienned mint, and shredded chicken breast are mixed into the rice while it is still hot. This dish is served as a full meal with *nuoc cham* drizzled over it.

1. Put the rice in a bowl with a few cups of water. Gently swirl your fingers in the bowl to allow the starch to separate from the grains. Once the water becomes white, drain and repeat this process twice more. With each time, the water will get less cloudy. The idea is not to get rid of all the starch, just enough so that the rice will not be too sticky or too dry when cooked. Three times has always given me the best results. Put the rice in a sieve and drain until the rice is fairly dry.

2. Put the rice and chicken stock in a medium clay pot or heavy-bottomed pot and stir to level the rice. Cover the pot and cook the rice over medium heat until it has absorbed all the stock, about 25 minutes. Turn off the heat and with a wooden spoon stir in shallots, mint, and chicken until evenly mixed. Allow to rest covered for 5 to 10 minutes. Drizzle *nuoc cham* over each serving.

COM CHIEN
Fried Rice

Serves 6 to 8

1 tablespoon vegetable oil
2 Chinese sweet pork sausages,
  quartered lengthwise and
  diced (or any leftover meat)
1 scallion, root end and tough
  green tops removed, thinly
  sliced into rounds
8 large napa cabbage leaves or
  any Asian greens, thinly
  sliced
4 cups cooked long-grain rice,
  refrigerated overnight
1 large egg
2 tablespoons soy sauce
Freshly ground black pepper

FRIED RICE is an excellent way to prepare leftover cooked rice. It is important, however, that the rice be completely dry prior to stir-frying. For this reason, and for the best results, refrigerate it overnight. Rice that is not completely dry will get sticky when stir-fried, whereas chilled rice will separate beautifully. Fried rice can be made with cut-up leftover meats and vegetables or with fresh ingredients. This is one of those dishes for which you should really have fun experimenting.

1. Heat the oil in a wok or large nonstick skillet over high heat. Add the sausages, scallion, and cabbage and stir-fry until the sausages render their fat, 3 to 5 minutes. Add the rice and continue to stir-fry and mix all the ingredients evenly. Add the egg and stir-fry quickly until the rice dries out completely, about 10 minutes. Add soy sauce and season to taste with black pepper. Stir-fry an additional 5 minutes and serve.

VARIATION: Rather than add the egg to the rice, you can whisk it and make a thin omelette. Once cooked, julienne the omelette and place some over each serving of fried rice.

CHINESE SWEET PORK SAUSAGES

HUE COM SEN
Sticky Rice with Pork and Lotus Seeds

Makes 2 cakes

1 tablespoon vegetable oil
1 large clove garlic
8 ounces pork butt, cut into
    bite-size chunks
Pinch sugar
2 tablespoons fish sauce
2 teaspoons freshly ground
    black pepper
1 cup dried lotus seeds, soaked
    overnight and drained
2 lotus or banana leaves, soaked
    in warm water and cut into
    8-inch-square pieces
4 cups cooked sticky rice
    (page 102)

HUE COM SEN is a specialty of central Vietnam, where the tradition of beautifully presented food started. The tender pork cooked slowly in a peppery fish sauce base is counterbalanced with firm lotus seeds and sweet sticky rice. Just as bamboo is widely used in the North, lotus is as popular in the central region. This rice cake is wrapped in a lotus leaf (traditionally used) or banana leaf (an acceptable substitute) and steamed in a bamboo steamer. When served, it is presented with the lotus flower (water lily) on the side for decoration. If lotus leaves are hard to find, use heavy-duty aluminum foil for wrapping.

1. Heat the oil in a clay pot or heavy-bottomed pot over medium heat. Stir-fry the garlic until fragrant, 3 to 5 minutes. Reduce the heat to medium-low and add the pork, sugar, fish sauce, black pepper, and 1 cup water. Cook until the pork is fork tender, about 2 hours. Remove from the heat and allow to cool.

2. Bring a pot of salted water to a boil over high heat. Lower the heat to medium, add the lotus seeds, and cook until tender, 10 to 15 minutes. Drain and allow to cool.

3. Blot the lotus leaves dry and lay them flat on a work surface. Divide rice into 4 portions (2 slightly larger than the others). Flatten the smallest rice portions in the center of each lotus leaf (about 4 inches square). Roughly shred the pork and scatter half of it on each of the rice squares. Place a layer of cooked lotus seeds on top of the pork and drizzle with some of the cooking juices (from the pork). Spread the remaining rice on top, shaping it so the pork and lotus seeds are completely enclosed. Fold one side of the lotus leaf over the rice once, then fold in the sides and fold over once more. Tie the package with kitchen string as you would a gift box, in a crisscross fashion, and place on a plate.

4. Fill the bottom third of a wok with water and place a bamboo steamer with lid over it. Bring the water to a boil over high heat. Place

STRUNG DRIED LOTUS SEEDS

beans. Legend has it that one year King Hung of the First Dynasty asked each of his children for a gift. His third daughter gave him a cake containing peppery pork and mung beans surrounded by sticky rice, all wrapped in a banana leaf. Pleased with the outcome, he ordered the cake to be eaten in celebration of the New Year, and it has been ever since.

a rice cake (on a plate) on the bamboo rack, set the lid on top, and steam the rice cake for 45 minutes. If you have a double-tier bamboo steamer, place a cake on each tier; if not, repeat the process. To serve, use scissors to cut an opening through each lotus leaf.

VARIATION: For *banh chung,* New Year's cake, substitute 1 cup dried mung beans (soaked for 3 hours and drained) for the lotus seeds. Proceed with step 1. In step 2, bring 2 cups water to a simmer in a pot over medium heat. Add the mung beans and cook, stirring constantly, until the water is completely absorbed, 10 to 15 minutes. Proceed with steps 3 and 4.

Tet is incomplete without *banh chung,* the famous sticky rice cake filled with peppery pork and mung

NOODLES, PAPERS, SHEETS, AND CRÊPES

I N VIETNAM rice is ground into flour to make dried and fresh rice noodles, which are used in great abundance. Dried noodles need to be soaked in lukewarm water and blanched to be reconstituted. Fresh noodles need not go through this process and can be added directly to dishes. Although there is a slight difference in texture (just as there is in dried and fresh pasta), both types of noodles can be stir-fried with vegetables, meat, or seafood or added to fragrant soups.

The three most widely used noodles in Vietnamese cooking are *banh hoai*, thin rice vermicelli, used to wrap meats and seafood and, as such, often part of the table salad, *sa lach dia* (page 52); *banh pho*, thin flat rice noodles, used to prepare Hanoi chicken or beef noodle soup, *pho* (pages 87 and 88); and *bun*, fresh rice vermicelli, tossed with meat or seafood and shredded raw vegetables in *bun thit bo xao* (page 111). Although I've mentioned classic dishes using specific noodles, these same noodles (like most Vietnamese noodles) can be used with great latitude. It is up to the individual cook to decide whether he or she prefers a lighter or heavier noodle with any given dish.

Another common source of starch is egg noodles made of wheat and eggs. Roughly double the size of vermicelli and either round or flat, these egg noodles are stir-fried with seafood, as in *mi xao don do bien* (page 116), or added to soups such as *mi vit*, roast duck and egg noodle soup (page 91).

Cellophane noodles, also known as glass noodles or mung bean thread, are made of mung bean starch. They are often used in fillings because their crunchy texture is perfect for such use. Because they are close to tasteless, they are valued for their ability to absorb flavors. Cellophane noodles are considered vegetables by Asians because they are light and definitely not as filling as wheat- or rice-based noodles. I include a cellophane noodle and vegetable casserole, *mien xao rau cai* (page 117), because it is starch-based and delicious.

Rice flour is also used to make dried rice papers, which are unique to Vietnamese cookery. Rice papers, *banh trang*, are brittle round (6 to 10 inches in diameter) or triangular (about 4 inches on each side) sheets made from rice flour, salt, and water and laid out to air-dry on bamboo mats, the source of their distinctive crosshatch pattern. These shapes, when reconstituted, are used for making fried *cha gio*, spring rolls (page 198), or fresh *goi cuon*, summer rolls (page 156), or are served as part of the table salad, for example, as wrappings for *nem nuong*, pork meatballs (page 200).

Another wrap made with rice flour is the fresh sheets called *banh uot*, which are used to wrap ground meats, *banh cuon* (page 113). (These sheets can also be julienned and stir-fried or added to soups.) Rice flour is also used to create one of my all-time favorites, *banh xeo*, sizzling "sound" crêpes, which are thin and lacy and flavored with coconut milk and turmeric, then filled with stir-fried mung bean sprouts, pork, and shrimp (page 114). These golden colored crêpes are unique to Vietnamese cooking, and I was lucky enough to learn the somewhat tricky technique of making them from my mother. There are a few regional (and personal) variations, which I discuss in the recipe. The first time I made *banh xeo* for my husband, he was shocked, as he could not imagine anything so simple having such subtle and complex flavors.

Bun Thit Bo Xao
Rice Vermicelli with Beef

Serves 4

½ pound dried rice vermicelli
or 1 pound fresh *bun*

8 romaine lettuce leaves, ribs
removed, julienned

2 carrots, peeled and
julienned

½ cucumber, peeled, seeded,
and thinly sliced into
crescents

12 large mint leaves, julienned

Bo xao, stir-fried beef
(page 219)

Cha gio, spring rolls (page 198)
(optional)

Nuoc cham (page 42)

Bun Thit bo xao is a refreshing dish of rice vermicelli, stir-fried beef, shredded lettuce, carrots, and cucumber, topped with ground peanuts and drizzled with *nuoc cham*. Although this recipe uses *bo xao*, stir-fried beef, another grilled meat or seafood, such as *suon nuong xa*, grilled lemongrass marinated pork tenderloin skewers (page 202), and *tom nuong xa*, grilled lemongrass prawns (page 153), would also be good. (If using prawns, remove the shells first.) Sometimes *chao gio*, spring rolls, are cut into bite-size pieces and added to this dish for texture and extra flavor. Because it is served at room temperature, this dish is a good choice for warm-weather days.

1. If using dried rice vermicelli, put it in a bowl with lukewarm water to cover. Let stand until pliable, about 20 minutes. Bring a pot filled with water to a boil over high heat. Drain and divide the rice vermicelli into 4 equal portions. Place one portion at a time in a sieve and lower it into the boiling water. Untangle the noodles with chopsticks and boil until tender but firm, about 3 seconds. Remove, drain, and place in a large bowl. Repeat this step until you have 4 individual servings. If using fresh *bun*, there is no need to boil them.

2. Over each serving of noodles, scatter some lettuce, carrot, cucumber, mint, and beef. Drizzle with *nuoc cham* and toss well.

When we first moved to the United States, it was hard for us to get to New York's Chinatown. When my mother could not find the correct Vietnamese ingredients, she would go to a local Korean-Japanese market and try her luck. She found Japanese *somen* noodles, thin and made of wheat flour, which she used to prepare *bun thit bo xao*. Firm, tender, and delicate in flavor, they were a good substitute. We were pleased to learn that other Vietnamese living in the United States used the same noodles when making *bun thit bo xao*.

BANH PHO XAO SATE
Stir-Fried Rice Noodles with Sate

Serves 4

½ pound medium dried rice
    sticks
1 tablespoon vegetable oil,
    plus extra if necessary
1 tablespoon *sate* (page 49)
10 ounces beef sirloin, sliced
    thinly against the grain
2 scallions, root ends and tough
    green tops removed, cut into
    1½-inch-long pieces and
    halved lengthwise
1 cup mung bean sprouts,
    root ends trimmed
Fish sauce

STIR-FRIED rice noodles with *sate* (peanut, garlic, and chili paste), scallions, and shrimp is a simple and flavorful dish. It reminds me a little of Thailand's national rice noodle dish, *pad thai*, in appearance, texture, and the use of peanuts, but its flavor is distinctly different. Stir-frying rice noodles can be a little tricky, as they tend to stick to one another. Do not be afraid to use enough oil so each strand stays separate. If you do not mind the oil, you'll enjoy this dish. Pickled vegetables make a nice complement.

1. Put the rice sticks in a bowl with lukewarm water to cover. Let stand until pliable, about 20 minutes, and drain.

2. Heat 1 tablespoon oil in a wok over high heat. Stir-fry the beef and scallions until just cooked, about 5 minutes. Transfer to a plate. Heat the *sate* in the wok until fragrant, about 1 minute, add the rice noodles, and stir-fry, making sure each strand is evenly coated (if the noodles start to stick to each other or the bottom of the wok, add a little more vegetable oil), until cooked through, about 7 minutes. Add the beef and scallions to the noodles, then the mung bean sprouts; season to taste with the fish sauce and continue stir-frying until well mixed, 1 to 2 minutes. Transfer to a platter and serve hot.

BANH CUON
Steamed Rice Sheets with Pork

Makes 20

¼ cup dried cloud ear
  mushrooms
1 tablespoon fish sauce
1 teaspoon sugar
12 ounces ground pork
  (70% lean)
1 cup rice flour
⅓ cup tapioca starch
Pinch of salt
⅓ cup vegetable oil
Scallion oil (page 50)
Nuoc cham (page 42)

BANH CUON is a classic dish that is often served as an appetizer and can be great as a party finger food. Ground pork is marinated in sugar and fish sauce. It is then stir-fried with cloud ear mushrooms and garlic, wrapped in *banh uot*—fresh rice sheets—and steamed. Serve with scallion oil and *nuoc cham*.

1. Soak the mushrooms in hot water to cover in a bowl until rehydrated and softened, about 30 minutes. Drain and squeeze the mushrooms to extract any remaining water. With a knife, remove and discard any hard knobs from the mushrooms. Mince and place the mushrooms in a bowl. Add the fish sauce, sugar, and pork and mix well. Allow to marinate at room temperature for 30 minutes or refrigerate for 1 hour.

2. For the *banh uot*, whisk rice flour, tapioca starch, and salt with 2¼ cups water in a bowl. Allow to rest for 1 hour. Stretch a cheesecloth over the edges of the bamboo rack and tighten it with kitchen string around the rim. Fill the bottom third of a wok with water and place the bamboo rack and lid over it. Bring the water to a boil over high heat. When the steamer is filled with steam, brush some of the batter on top of the cheesecloth, spreading with the back of a ladle to about 4 inches in diameter. Close the lid and steam until cooked, about 3 minutes. Loosen the edges with a spatula and transfer the sheet to an oiled plate. Brush some oil on the sheet to keep it from sticking to the next. Repeat process for the remaining batter.

3. Stir-fry the pork until cooked through, about 4 to 6 minutes, and divide into 20 equal portions. Place each portion on one side of a rice sheet. Fold the sheet over once, fold in the sides, and fold all the way to form a bundle. Place *banh cuon* on a plate.

4. Remove the cheesecloth from the bamboo rack, place the plate of *banh cuon* on the rack, and steam, with the lid on, for 5 minutes. Drizzle scallion oil over each *banh cuon* and dip in *nuoc cham*.

NOTE: You can also use Cantonese fresh rice sheets, *sha ho fen*. Longer, wider, and slightly thicker, they are sold in sheets, which need to be cut into 4-inch squares.

BANH XEO
Sizzling "Sound" Crêpes

Makes 20

1½ cups rice flour
Pinch turmeric
½ cup coconut milk
Vegetable oil
⅓ cup thinly sliced scallions
½ pound pork tenderloin,
 thinly sliced
½ pound small shrimp,
 shelled, deveined, and
 halved lengthwise
1½ pounds mung bean
 sprouts, root ends trimmed
Table salad (page 52)
Traditional herbs (page 53)
Nuoc cham (page 42)

THE WORD *banh* means "cake," while *xeo* comes from the actual sizzling sound made when the crêpe is cooking. As prepared in Saigon, *banh xeo* are paper-thin lacy pancakes filled with pork, shrimp, and bean sprouts. They are very delicate in flavor and structure, and here we can feel the French influence of the "crêpe" and the cooking technique of pan-frying. Although this pancake originates in the South, there is a smaller and thicker version called "happy pancake," a specialty of Hue, in the central region. Because these crêpes are crisp only when hot, they should be eaten right away.

1. Whisk together the flour, turmeric, coconut milk, 2 cups water, 2 tablespoons oil, and scallions until well combined. Allow the batter to rest for 30 minutes.

2. Heat 2 teaspoons oil in a wok or skillet over high heat and stir-fry the pork for 3 minutes. Add the shrimp and cook until opaque, 1 to 2 minutes. Add the bean sprouts and cook until just translucent but still firm, about 1 minute. Transfer to a platter and set aside.

3. Heat 1 teaspoon oil in an 8-inch nonstick skillet over medium-high heat. While tilting the pan add ¼ cup of the batter, swirling the pan at the same time to evenly distribute the batter. (Starting from the center of the pan and swirling so the batter moves outward is a good technique, but if you are used to another method, please apply it here.) Once the crêpe starts to bubble gently in the center and loosen itself at the edges, 3 to 5 minutes, add ⅓ cup of the stir-fried pork, shrimp, and bean sprouts, fold over one half of the lacy crêpe, and slide onto a serving dish. Continue making *banh xeo* as you serve them. Serve with table salad and herbs, and *nuoc cham* on the side.

In Saigon I watched a street vendor make *banh xeo*. She was barely twenty years old, but she had the necessary "swirling" technique down to a science, and it was beautiful to watch. First she stir-fried some shrimp, split mung beans, and pork in a cured shallow, thin cast-iron pan. She shook the pan around, distributing all the ingredients evenly across the surface of the pan. Then she added and swirled the batter into the ingredients and poured extra hot oil over everything so that the inside would be just as crisp as the outside. Holding back the crêpe and its filling with a large flat sieve, she poured off the excess oil. She then folded the crêpe over (as you would an omelette) and transferred it to a platter. She served it with the traditional herbs and table salad and *nuoc cham*. Although my family's technique of making *banh xeo* is easier (making the crêpe and adding the cooked filling afterward) and perhaps a little less greasy, I enjoyed seeing it made locally. It certainly was delicious.

MI XAO DON DO BIEN
Crispy Egg Noodles with Seafood

Serves 4

½ pound fresh thin egg
noodles

¼ cup vegetable oil, plus extra
if necessary

Do bien xao, stir-fried seafood
(page 166)

DERIVED FROM the classic Chinese recipe for double-crisp egg noodles, this popular Vietnamese dish is a celebration of the sea's bounty. The best egg noodles for this dish are fresh, thin, and round, and available only in Asian markets. Often referred to as Shanghai-style noodles, they are formed into a thick round pancake, laid flat in the skillet, and crisped on both sides. Shrimp, squid, and scallops are stir-fried and heaped on top. This dish is a meal in itself, delicious with just a touch of chili sauce. Variations include using stir-fried meat or vegetables.

1. Bring a pot of water to a boil over high heat. Add the noodles and cook, untangling them with chopsticks, until tender but firm, about 5 minutes. Drain, spread them into a thick pancake on a plate, loosely cover with plastic wrap, and allow to dry.

2. Heat 2 tablespoons oil in a nonstick skillet over medium-high heat. Add the egg noodles, being careful not to destroy their pancake form, and allow to crisp until golden brown, 5 to 7 minutes. Slide onto a plate. Add the remaining oil to the pan and flip the noodle pancake into the pan so the crisp side faces up. Crisp the underside until golden brown, 5 to 7 minutes. (While the noodles are getting crisp on this second side, you should be stir-frying the seafood.)

Transfer crispy egg noodles to a serving dish and top with the stir-fried seafood. Serve while hot.

MIEN XAO RAU CAI

Glass Noodles with Vegetables

Serves 4

4 ounces dried cellophane
  noodles
¼ cup dried shrimp
4 medium dried shiitake
  mushrooms
1½ tablespoons vegetable oil
2 cloves garlic, peeled and
  lightly crushed
2 ounces fresh ginger, peeled
  and thinly sliced
4 ounces pork tenderloin, thinly
  sliced against the grain
6 ounces baby bok choy
  or similar greens, leaves
  separated and halved
  lengthwise
2 scallions, root ends and
  tough green tops removed,
  cut into 1½-inch-long pieces
  and halved lengthwise
1 cup light pork stock
  (page 62)
2 tablespoons fish sauce
1 tablespoon thick soy sauce
1 teaspoon sesame oil

MIEN XAO RAU CAI is a light dish made with pork, vegetables, and cellophane noodles. It can also be made with shrimp, lump crabmeat, or any other protein. Although I consider this dish to be a meal in itself, my father, like many Asians, considers it a vegetable. "Cellophane noodles are made from mung beans," he says, asking for a bowl of rice on the side.

1. Soak the cellophane noodles in lukewarm water to cover in a bowl until pliable, about 20 minutes. Drain. Soak the dried shrimp in lukewarm water to cover in a separate bowl for 15 minutes and drain. Soak the shiitake mushrooms in hot water to cover in a third bowl until rehydrated and softened, about 30 minutes. Drain and squeeze mushrooms between the palms of your hands to extract any remaining water. With a knife, remove and discard any hard stems. Cut the caps in half.

2. Heat the oil in a large clay pot or heavy-bottomed pot over medium heat. Stir-fry the garlic and ginger until fragrant, about 1 minute. Add the pork, shrimp, and mushrooms and stir-fry until the pork is just cooked, 3 to 5 minutes. Add the bok choy and scallions and stir-fry for 2 minutes. Reduce the heat to medium-low and add the cellophane noodles, stock, fish sauce, soy sauce, and sesame oil. Mix the ingredients well, cover with a lid, and braise for 5 to 7 minutes, until the noodles have absorbed the liquid and turned completely transparent. Serve hot.

BREAD

THE FRENCH *baguette* has made quite an impact on the daily diet of the Vietnamese. They took this quintessential Gallic invention and made it their own by substituting rice flour for half of the wheat flour. The result is a lighter bread with a uniquely subtle flavor. Consumed on a daily basis, it is eaten toasted with butter for breakfast. For a quick lunch it is filled with slices of meat pâté or grilled meat, freshly torn herbs, and shredded lettuce, carrots, cucumber, and a bit of chili sauce. In the South it is often served with curries, an intriguing substitute for the more traditional rice. I learned something of this wonderful variation when I was a child, because whenever we made curries in France, my mother would ask my older brother to run to the *boulangerie* and get a *baguette* so we could scoop up the sauce. Years later, while visiting Saigon, I had the opportunity to taste an authentic Vietnamese bread with a curry. It was then that I learned the rice flour secret, and that I came to love the Vietnamese variation. If you're curious, as I was, about the Saigon *baguette*, try the recipe given here.

Banh Mi
Saigon Baguette

Makes 2 loaves

2¼ teaspoons active dry yeast
1 tablespoon sugar
1 cup all-purpose flour
1 cup rice flour
1 teaspoon salt
2 tablespoons butter, melted

T HE KEY to the special flavor of these loaves is in combining rice flour with wheat flour for the dough. As is traditional, these *baguettes* should be slit across the top three times on the diagonal or once lengthwise with a clean, sharp razor blade. (This is what makes the "open eye" design on each loaf.) Although similar in color and texture, Saigon *baguette* is shorter and wider than its French counterpart.

1. Place the yeast, 1 cup lukewarm water, and sugar in the bowl of a mixer with a dough hook. Sift together the all-purpose flour, rice flour, and salt in a separate bowl.

2. Starting the mixer at the lowest speed, add the butter to the yeast, then gradually add the dry ingredients and beat until well combined, about 3 minutes. Increase the speed to medium and continue beating the dough until it is smooth and comes away from the sides of the mixing bowl easily. Put the dough on a lightly floured surface, cover with plastic wrap, and allow to rise (double in volume), 45 minutes to 1 hour.

3. Punch down the dough and knead it for about 2 minutes. Separate into 2 portions and shape each into an 8-inch-long *baguette*. (The dough may be sticky and hard to handle at this point. Do not overwork it, just gently shape it.) Cover loosely with plastic wrap and allow to rise a second time, about 45 minutes. Meanwhile, place a baking stone on a rack set in the middle of the oven and preheat the oven to 400°F.

4. With a sharp knife blade or a clean razor blade, make 1 slit lengthwise or three diagonal slits along the top of each *baguette*. With the help of a wooden pastry paddle, carefully slide 2 *baguettes* onto the baking stone and bake until golden, 20 to 25 minutes. To test for doneness, tap the underside of a loaf. If it sounds hollow and the exterior is crisp, then it is done. Remove from the oven and allow to cool before handling.

N O T E : A perfect substitute, if you do not feel like baking, is a traditional French *baguette*.

SPRING BAMBOO SHOOTS AND DRIED SHIITAKE MUSHROOMS

CHAPTER FOUR

VEGETABLES

 THE VIETNAMESE have taken an enormous variety of both indigenous and imported vegetables and developed recipes for each of them reflecting traditional Asian-based cooking techniques and, to a certain extent, their regional climates. Paralleling the development of soups, meats, and fish, cooking vegetables in the cool northern region is influenced both by centuries of Chinese cultural influence and by the need to preserve perishables. Northern ingredients include salt-preserved leafy greens such as cabbage and canned bamboo shoots. Dishes include *rau muong xao*, stir-fried water spinach (page 125), and *mang xao nam dong co*, stir-fried bamboo shoots and shiitake mushrooms (page 130), both of which were traditionally cooked in China and have been transplanted to Vietnam. A slight, yet important, modification is the use of fish sauce rather than soy sauce in these dishes. ◆ The people of the warm South, enjoying a long growing season, abundant indigenous edible plants, and the influence of south Asian trade routes, have developed vegetable dishes that emphasize fresh or raw vegetables and include the spicy curries of India. Many of their menus are so dominated by vegetable dishes that they are akin to vegetarian cuisines.

The Buddhist monks of Vietnam are, in fact, strict vegetarians. They believe that all living things have souls and so refuse to eat meat or fish and their by-products. Instead, they eat fruits, vegetables, soy-based proteins such as tofu, and rice or other starches. Some Vietnamese Buddhists, depending on how strictly they observe their religion, either will or will not use pork fat and fish sauce in their cooking, relying on vegetable oil and soy sauce as acceptable substitutes. During religious celebrations, however, even the less strict adhere to vegetarian principles, preparing pure vegetarian dishes.

The central region, with the principal port of Vietnam at DaNang and the former imperial capital at Hue, has long been a sophisticated portal onto the sea and a link to the West. Since at least the late 1500s, DaNang has been involved in overseas trade. This was where the French first stepped on Vietnamese soil and, about a century later, where American soldiers first made camp. It was also here that the South Vietnamese admitted defeat in 1975. The people of DaNang have been gathering such fruits and vegetables as strawberries, pineapple, asparagus, potatoes, corn, and tomatoes from the West and offering them up to the sophisticated culinary culture of Vietnam for centuries. These items have, in turn, been widely dispersed throughout the country, defying regional differences and climatic variations. You see them in such dishes as *ca chien sot ca chua*, pan-fried fish with tomato sauce (page 145), and *sup cua mang tay*, crab and asparagus soup (page 80). Because fruits, with a few exceptions, such as *canh ca nau dua*, fish and pineapple soup (page 75), are often considered sweets, they are treated in Chapter 7, "Sweets & Drinks."

Curiously, while the Vietnamese have enthusiastically adopted Western fruits and vegetables, they have not embraced Western techniques of vegetable preparation. Not even the French, with their massive inroads in the fused cuisine of Vietnam, have ever made much headway in this regard. I have included *mang tay xao*, stir-fried asparagus (page 127), as an example of Western ingredients enjoyed through Asian preparation techniques.

In general, vegetable dishes are so delicate that they tend to be very simple, and so not much explanation is needed. There are two basic preparation methods, the most important being stir-frying and the second braising. The recipes included here are pure vegetable dishes that I would serve during an elaborate meal to complement meat and seafood dishes. I have also included dishes that combine vegetables and protein, such as pan-fried bitter melon (page 133) stuffed with a combination of ground pork and shrimp. These I would serve with a clear soup and rice for a simple lunch meal.

Whenever possible, the Vietnamese eat a lot of fresh raw herbs at almost every meal. For them, herbs are vegetables that provide contrasting textures with the cooked food. They are listed in the condiments chapter as *rau*, traditional herbs (page 53), as well as *sa lach dia*, table salad (page 52). Other types of vegetables listed in that chapter are pickled carrots, daikon, and cucumber, often served with grilled meat and seafood because of the crunchy and refreshing counterbalance they provide.

Among all this diversity is one plant that may be considered the national vegetable of Vietnam: *rau muong*, or water spinach. It grows quickly and profusely and can be found in nearly every part of the country. Southerners enjoy it almost daily. Northerners, who also eat copious amounts of it, consider it a sort of bodily appendage. When cooked, water spinach's hollow stems stay firm and crunchy, while its leaves wilt and become tender, a sort of embodiment of the coincidence of opposites that the Vietnamese enjoy in all their cuisine. Sometimes water spinach is added to soups, but most often it is stir-fried with garlic, vegetable oil, and either fish sauce or preserved bean curd.

One note: My family has always avoided stir-frying cauliflower, snowpeas, carrots, bamboo shoots, and bell peppers together, a dish popularly known in restaurants around the world as Buddha's Delight. We find the combination to be a bit too much. All those flavors can be rather bland when mixed together, and the mix makes it difficult to enjoy any of the flavors separately. For those of you who do enjoy this vegetarian dish, I hope you will try some of the recipes here and begin to enjoy the subtle flavor of each and every ingredient as you move from one dish to another.

GOI DU DU
Green Papaya Salad

Serves 4

1 to 1½ pounds green papaya or
    green mango, peeled, halved
    lengthwise, and seeded
Juice of 2 limes or lemons
3 tablespoons fish sauce
3 tablespoons sugar
2 red bird's eye or Thai chilies,
    seeded and julienned
1 tablespoon finely chopped
    unsalted roasted peanuts
4 sprigs cilantro, root ends
    and tough stems removed

GOI DU DU is a refreshing salad with tangy, sweet, and spicy characteristics perfect with any barbecued meat. It is also a great appetizer. Its principal ingredient, green papaya, sometimes called pawpaw, varies in shape from round to elongated. It has dark green skin and light green flesh. Green papaya is used as a vegetable because, unlike the rich, orange-colored papaya, it is mild, not sweet, and crunchy. When green papaya is not available, use green mango. Both can be purchased in Asian or Latin markets. One hint: For a heartier variation of *goi du du*, add steamed shrimp and sliced cooked pork tenderloin.

1. Cut the papaya or mango into matchstick strips. Whisk together the lime juice, fish sauce, and sugar in a bowl until the sugar is completely dissolved. Add the papaya and chilies and toss until well combined. Let stand for 20 minutes. Transfer to a serving plate, sprinkle with peanuts, and garnish with cilantro.

VARIATION: Bring water to a boil in 2 separate saucepans over medium heat. Add 6 small to medium shrimp in one saucepan and cook until opaque, about 1 minute. Add a 4-ounce piece of pork tenderloin to the other saucepan and simmer until cooked through, about 8 minutes. Remove the shrimp and run under cold water, then shell, cut in half lengthwise, and devein. When cool enough to handle, thinly slice the pork tenderloin against the grain. Proceed with step 1, tossing in the shrimp and pork tenderloin.

When we get together for a family gathering, it is a big deal because there are so many of us. One way to feed everyone successfully is with a barbecue, and my uncle Niep Seng and aunt Kim often share the cooking. While he marinates chicken, pork, and beef, she prepares all sorts of pickled vegetables (page 48) and this wonderful green papaya salad, *goi du du*, as refreshing accompaniments.

Rau Muong Xao
Stir-Fried Water Spinach

Serves 4 to 6

1½ tablespoons vegetable oil

1 large clove garlic, peeled
and minced

1 pound water spinach, stems
trimmed, washed, drained,
and halved crosswise

Freshly ground black pepper

1 tablespoon preserved bean
curd or fish sauce

WATER SPINACH grows in both wet and dry soils. Available in every season, it is the most widely eaten vegetable in Vietnam. In this recipe, water spinach, *rau muong*, is stir-fried with garlic and preserved bean curd or fish sauce for seasoning. There are two types of water spinach. One has large leaves, thick stems, and a light green color. It is often preferred because it is the sweeter and more tender of the two. The second type has narrower leaves, slim stems, and is dark green. While slightly compromised in character, it is also widely eaten. Water spinach is a favorite among the Vietnamese because, when cooked, it retains two different, complementary textures: tender leaves and crunchy stems. Be sure to soak and rinse water spinach a few times, as its hollow stems tend to retain sand and soil. NOTE: Although the difference in texture between the stems and the leaves will not be nearly as apparent, regular spinach is a delicious substitute.

1. Heat the oil in a wok over high heat and stir-fry the garlic until fragrant and lightly golden, about 1 minute. Add the water spinach, season with pepper, and stir-fry until wilted, about 3 minutes. Add the bean curd, stir-fry until it is evenly distributed, then cover and cook until done, 2 to 3 minutes more.

DAU XAO
Stir-Fried Yard-Long Beans

Serves 4 to 6

1½ tablespoons vegetable oil
2 medium cloves garlic, peeled
  and thinly sliced or minced
1 pound yard-long beans,
  stem ends trimmed and cut
  into 2-inch-long pieces
1 tablespoon fish sauce
Freshly ground black pepper

YARD-LONG BEANS, also known as Asian beans and long beans, get their name from the simple fact that they grow up to about 3 feet long. There are two types of yard-long beans. One is light green, thick, and smooth; the other is thin, dark green, and less smooth. The latter is preferred over the former because it is crunchier and sweeter. The texture of the yard-long bean is very different from the Western green or string bean, including the very thin French *haricot vert*. It has a tight pod wall that stays crunchy when cooked and can be extremely tough if undercooked. And sometimes these beans "squeak" when eaten! If you have a hard time finding yard-long beans, use French *haricot vert* or regular green beans. Although the texture and flavor will differ slightly, they will still make a wonderful dish.

1. Heat the oil in a wok over high heat and stir-fry the garlic until lightly golden, about 1 minute. Add the beans and stir-fry about 3 minutes. Add the fish sauce, season with pepper, and continue to stir-fry until cooked through, about 10 minutes more.

YARD-LONG BEANS

Mang Tay Xao
Stir-Fried Asparagus

Serves 4 to 6

1½ tablespoons vegetable oil
1 large clove garlic, peeled
   and minced
1 bunch white asparagus,
   stems peeled, thinly sliced
   diagonally
1 tablespoon fish sauce
Freshly ground black pepper

THIS RECIPE is an interpretation of the ubiquitous Vietnamese stir-fried vegetable, created in the spirit of dishes transposed from France to Asia. While asparagus comes in white, purple, and green varieties and can be thick or thin, here I use thick and tender white asparagus, best during the spring season. This "Western bamboo," as the Vietnamese like to call it, is thinly sliced on the diagonal and stir-fried with minced garlic and a good dash or two of fish sauce. It is a perfect complement to any meat or seafood dish and an excellent way to use asparagus whenever it is available.

1. Heat the oil in a wok over high heat and stir-fry the garlic until fragrant, about 1 minute. Add the asparagus, season with fish sauce and pepper, and stir-fry until tender, about 7 minutes.

GIA XAO
Stir-Fried Mung Bean Sprouts

Serves 4 to 6

1½ tablespoons vegetable oil
2 scallions, root ends
  trimmed, cut into 1½-inch-
  long pieces and halved
  lengthwise
1½ pound mung bean
  sprouts, root ends trimmed
1 tablespoon fish sauce
Freshly ground black pepper

THE MUNG BEAN sprout is used raw as a garnish in soups, preserved in salt brine and served as a table condiment, and stir-fried with scallions as a main vegetable dish like this one. A mung bean sprout has a small yellow head and a short, thin white stem. (It should not be confused with the soybean sprout, which has a large yellow head.) *Gia xao* is a simple stir-fry I often make at home. For presentation's sake and texture, I like to snap off the thin, often discolored root end from the sprout. It is tedious work, and many cooks, especially in restaurants, do not bother. This step is entirely up to you, as the flavor is unaffected.

1. Heat the oil in a wok over high heat and stir-fry the scallions until fragrant, about 1 minute. Add the mung bean sprouts, season with fish sauce and pepper, and stir-fry until just wilted, 2 to 3 minutes.

Mung bean sprouts are used in several different ways in Vietnamese cooking. The bean itself is used to make the classic sweet mung bean soup *che dau xanh* (page 227), while the sprout is used as a raw garnish for the Hanoi noodle soups *pho ga* (page 87) and *pho bo* (page 88), or is stir-fried as a vegetable dish, as here (sometimes with thinly sliced beef added). Other times it is stir-fried with fresh rice noodles and shredded omelette. Although the flavor of mung bean sprouts is delicate, it is very distinctive. Accordingly, there is no substitute.

TRIMMING THE ROOT ENDS OF MUNG BEAN SPROUTS

MANG XAO NAM DONG CO
Stir-Fried Bamboo Shoots and Shiitakes

Serves 4 to 6

**8 large dried shiitake
    mushrooms**
2 tablespoons vegetable oil
**2 ounces fresh ginger, peeled,
    sliced, and lightly crushed**
**6 ounces canned bamboo
    shoots, blanched, drained,
    and julienned**
⅓ cup chicken stock (page 61)
2 tablespoons fish sauce
Pinch sugar
Freshly ground black pepper

BAMBOO is a popular vegetable in the North. It is eaten fresh or preserved, stir-fried, braised, or added to soups. Bamboo shoots have contrasting textures, ranging from firm and crunchy at the bottom to tender at the very tip. Young winter tips are preferred, as they are tender and sweet. Spring shoots are also available but are generally not as tender. Bamboo shoots are occasionally available fresh-frozen. They require fairly elaborate preparation, because they contain natural toxins that must be blanched out. *Mang xao nam dong co* is a simple dish that incorporates canned bamboo shoots very well. It can be served with meat and seafood dishes any time of the year.

1. Soak the mushrooms in hot water to cover in a bowl until rehydrated and softened, about 30 minutes. Drain and rinse. Squeeze the mushrooms between the palms of your hands to extract any remaining water. With a knife, remove and discard any hard stems, then cut the mushroom caps into julienne strips.

2. In a wok or skillet, heat the oil and stir-fry the ginger over high heat until fragrant, about 1 minute. Add the mushrooms and the bamboo shoots and stir-fry for about 5 minutes. Reduce the heat to medium, add the chicken stock, fish sauce, and sugar and season to taste with black pepper. Mix well, cover with a lid, and cook until heated through, about 20 minutes more. Serve hot.

Dau Hu Kho Gung
Braised Tofu with Ginger

Serves 4 to 6

1 tablespoon vegetable oil

1 large clove garlic, peeled and minced

2 ounces fresh ginger, peeled and minced

6 ounces ground pork (70% lean)

1 teaspoon or more Vietnamese chili and garlic sauce

2 scallions, root ends trimmed, cut into 1½-inch-long pieces and halved lengthwise

1 pound firm tofu, cut into ½-inch cubes

1 tablespoon fish sauce

Coarse sea salt

Freshly ground black pepper

D AU HU KHO GUNG is what I call comfort food: warming with its ginger, garlic, and chili, yet soothing with its rich tofu and silky sauce. Perhaps one of my favorite vegetable dishes ever, when served over rice, it is a full meal. There is a small amount of pork, primarily to add flavor. You will also need Vietnamese chili and garlic sauce, which can be found in most Asian markets. It comes in two versions, smooth sauce in a squirt bottle or slightly chunky in a jar, which is preferred here.

1. Heat the oil in a clay pot or heavy-bottomed pot over medium heat. Stir-fry the garlic and ginger until fragrant and lightly golden, about 5 minutes. Add the pork and stir-fry so it separates into pieces and just cooks through, about 3 minutes. Reduce the heat to low, add the chili and garlic sauce, scallions, tofu, and fish sauce, and carefully mix (so as not to break up the tofu too much) until well combined. Cover and cook for 5 minutes. Season to taste with salt and pepper and continue cooking, covered, until all the flavors have blended together, another 10 minutes. Serve with rice.

In this dish the tofu cooks for a good 15 minutes, and so it is a good idea to use firm tofu because it will not break down as easily as soft tofu. It is also important not to overstir the dish while cooking, as this will break up the tofu. Let it simmer quietly. Just before serving, mix it carefully to coat each tofu piece with the juices.

VIETNAMESE CHILI AND GARLIC SAUCE, TOFU, AND FRESH GINGER

CARI RAU CAI
Vegetable Curry

Serves 4 to 6

1 large shallot

3 large cloves garlic

3 tablespoons vegetable oil

2 stalks lemongrass, outer
leaves and tough green tops
removed, root ends
trimmed, and stalks sliced
paper-thin in rounds

3 tablespoons good-quality
Indian curry powder

2 teaspoons Thai shrimp paste
(optional)

3 or more dried red chilies

1 cup canned unsweetened
coconut milk

1 cup chicken stock (page 61)
or vegetable stock (page 66)

1 tablespoon fish sauce

3 lime leaves or lime peels

4 ounces green beans, stem
ends trimmed, and cut
diagonally into 1½-inch-
long pieces

4 ounces carrots, peeled
and sliced diagonally into
¼-inch-thick pieces

8 ounces small yellow new
potatoes, peeled

8 ounces Japanese eggplant,
quartered lengthwise, then
cut into 1½-inch-long pieces

I N THIS SIMPLE CURRY the texture of the different vegetables—waxy potatoes, crunchy green beans, and tender
eggplant—makes this one of the most interesting dishes of its
type. Although I like chicken stock for a more pronounced flavor, if you are a vegetarian purist, you can certainly use vegetable
stock, which is also delicious. To add extra flavor to the curry, I
like to char the shallot and garlic. As with all stews, I generally
make this curry a day ahead of time to let the flavors come
together overnight.

1. Char the shallot and garlic in a dry skillet over high heat, until all sides have darkened, about 3 to 5 minutes. Remove from the heat. When cool enough to handle, peel and crush the garlic and peel and thinly slice the shallot. Heat the oil in a clay pot or heavy-bottomed pot over low heat. Increase the heat to medium and stir-fry the garlic and shallot until lightly golden, about 10 minutes. Add lemongrass, curry powder, shrimp paste, and chilies and cook until the flavors come together, about 5 minutes.

2. Add the coconut milk, chicken or vegetable stock, fish sauce, and lime leaves. Cover and bring just to a boil. Reduce the heat to medi-um-low and add the green beans, carrots, potatoes, and eggplant.

Cook, partially covered, until all the vegetables are tender, 45 to 50 minutes. Serve with Saigon *baguette* or rice on the side.

MUOP DANG XAO
Pan-Fried Stuffed Bitter Melon

Serves 4 to 6

8 ounces ground pork (70% lean)
8 ounces shrimp, shelled and
   minced
1 scallion, root end removed,
   minced
1 teaspoon sesame oil
Coarse sea salt
Freshly ground black pepper
1 pound whole bitter melon,
   cut into ½-inch-thick
   rounds, spongy core and
   seeds removed
2 tablespoons vegetable oil

BITTER MELON is a lumpy, light green, elongated gourd that contains naturally occurring quinine, which makes it bitter and gives it medicinal qualities. It is used in many Asian cuisines and is usually steamed, braised, or stir-fried, often with other ingredients to tame the bitterness. For many people it is an acquired taste, and you may need a few tries before you actually enjoy it. When selecting a bitter melon, be sure it is firm and small so it will be less bitter and have a crisp texture. You need not peel it, but you should remove the soft core, which is spongy and contains seeds. In this recipe the sweet pork and shrimp mediate the strong flavor of this quirky vegetable.

1. Put the pork, shrimp, scallion, and sesame oil in a bowl. Season with salt and pepper and mix until well combined. Stuff each bitter melon slice with the mixture.

2. Heat 1 tablespoon vegetable oil in a nonstick skillet over medium-high heat and cook half the stuffed bitter melon slices until tender and golden, about 2 to 3 minutes per side. Heat the remaining oil and cook the remaining bitter melon slices. Serve with rice and chili sauce on the side.

STUFFED BITTER MELON

CA PHAO KHO
Braised Eggplant

Serves 4 to 6

2 pounds Japanese eggplant,
   halved lengthwise
1 tablespoon vegetable oil
2 large cloves garlic, peeled
   and minced
6 ounces ground beef
1 tablespoon fish sauce
Coarse sea salt
Freshly ground black pepper

THIS BRAISED EGGPLANT recipe is reminiscent of a Mediterranean-style eggplant caviar in texture because it is cooked until the eggplant breaks down into a chunky purée. A small amount of ground beef or pork is often added for flavor, and the fish sauce gives it a distinctly Vietnamese taste. When selecting an eggplant, make sure it is young, firm, unbruised, and smooth. (When young, an eggplant has fewer seeds.) I prefer to use slender Japanese eggplant because it tends to have fewer seeds even when mature and to be firmer than Western eggplant. In a pinch, however, any eggplant will do for this dish.

1. Char the eggplants on all sides over an open flame on medium-high heat or in a dry skillet on an electric stove. When the skin has blackened on all sides, allow to cool. Peel the eggplant and cut into large chunks.

2. Heat the oil in a clay pot or heavy-bottomed pot over medium heat. Add the garlic and stir-fry until golden, about 10 minutes. Add the ground beef and stir so the beef separates, about 5 minutes. Reduce the heat to low, add the eggplant and fish sauce, and season with salt and pepper. Braise, partially covered, until the eggplant has cooked down but is still slightly chunky, about 30 minutes.

VARIATION: If you do not like the smoky flavor of the charred eggplants, simply skip step 1. Instead, cut the eggplants, skin on, into large chunks and proceed with step 2.

In my family we love to eat eggplant. We grill, stir-fry, and braise it. *Ca phao kho* is a dish my mother has been preparing ever since my brothers and I were infants. We were never fed commercial baby food. Instead, my mother would make all sorts of dishes including *ca phao kho*, mixing in some rice. Today she continues to make it for her grandchildren.

BONG CAI XAO THIT BO
Stir-Fried Cauliflower and Beef

Serves 4 to 6

1 tablespoon vegetable oil

1 large clove garlic, peeled and minced

1 scallion, root ends trimmed, cut into 1½-inch-long pieces and halved lengthwise

½ small to medium head cauliflower, leaves removed, head separated into small florets

8 ounces beef sirloin, sliced thinly against the grain

Dash sesame oil

1 tablespoon fish sauce

1 teaspoon thick soy sauce

Freshly ground black pepper

THE VIETNAMESE often include cauliflower in their stir-fries because they enjoy its crunchy texture and bright white color. In this simple stir-fry, *bong cai xao thit bo*, the crisp cauliflower florets complement the tender reddish brown slices of beef. Choosing a cauliflower is easy. Just look for bright green leaves and a white to creamy white head. If the head has brown spots and the leaves are yellow, it is too old. This simple recipe can be served with rice as a full meal.

1. Heat the vegetable oil in a wok over high heat. Stir-fry the garlic until fragrant, about 3 minutes. Add the scallion and cauliflower and stir-fry for 10 to 15 minutes. Add the beef, sesame oil, fish sauce, and soy sauce, season to taste with pepper, and stir-fry for 5 to 10 minutes more. Transfer to a serving dish and serve with rice.

VARIATION: Substitute chicken breast meat for the beef.

STUFFED CRAB SHELLS

CHAPTER FIVE

FISH & SEAFOOD

THE COASTLINE of Vietnam runs like a pearl necklace along its eastern shores, from the Gulf of Tonkin in the North to the Gulf of Thailand in the South. The South China Sea, which links the two, sits like a jewel in the center. Inland, Vietnam has hundreds of rivers that flow toward the sea. The three most important are the Red River in the North, the Perfume River in the Center, and the most bountiful of all, the Mekong River in the South. With all this water and its riches, it is no wonder that the Vietnamese enjoy seafood as their second most important staple, after rice. ◆ In Vietnam, the sea coast and rivers are open markets, and anyone can fish and sell or eat their daily catch. For children it is a game; for adults it is a way to make ends meet; and for all it is a way of life. Long ago the Chinese introduced nets, bamboo fishing poles, and the skills to use them to the Vietnamese. Today it is with those skills that the Vietnamese have prospered as fishermen. They fish everywhere, at sea and in rivers. But, as if all the waters in the world weren't enough, they also fish in rice paddies and dig ponds for raising carp, catfish, shrimp, crabs, and other seafoods. ◆ Every day throughout the year, the fishermen go out to the shallow waters in barks, special round "bucket" boats called *thuyen thung*, made of woven bamboo. *Thuyen thung* resemble oversized coconut shells as they float around in the Gulf of Thailand where the island of Phu Quoc lies. As you approach the island, its beautiful white-sand beaches and palm trees appear, but soon your eyes start to tear from the intense odor of the fermenting fish called *ca com*, a small, silvery, translucent type of anchovy. This is the essence of *nuoc mam*, the famous fish sauce used as the basis for many Vietnamese dishes, whether northern, central, or southern in origin.

In Vietnam, as in many developing nations, fish and seafood are eaten fresh. This is as much due to circumstance as anything else, as refrigeration is a luxury most Vietnamese cannot afford, and seafood is simply sold and consumed the same day it is caught. As a result, many recipes rely on the sweet and delicate flesh of fresh fish as a primary component of flavor. Steamed dishes, especially, often combine fresh whole white fish with the most minimal fresh herb infusions, resulting in marvelously delicate and balanced *poisson du jour*, such as *ca hap bia* (page 144), fish steamed in beer infused with ginger and served with a spicy lemongrass soy dipping sauce (page 45).

Abundance has proved to be the mother of invention, as more is often caught than can be eaten at once, and different types of preservation have evolved. Drying and salting are the most common, although pickling is also employed. Squid and shrimp, for example, are so abundant that they are often salted and dried, then used as seasoning and texture in cooking or eaten as a snack. A brief soaking in water is sufficient to remove most of the salt, as is, alternatively, a quick pan toasting. Dried squid and shrimp, for example, can be used as flavor enhancers in stir-fries or pork stock (page 62). One of my mother's favorite dishes is cellophane noodles with pork and vegetables (page 117), which uses dried shrimp. My father, on the other hand, enjoys dried squid when it is pan-toasted, torn into thin strips, and eaten while sipping hot jasmine tea or ice-cold beer. It is a treat that can become addictive, especially when watching TV.

Fish and seafood are abundant in most of Vietnam's waters, but regional preferences make for slight differences in the way they affect the cuisines. In the warm South and Center, for example, there is a slightly stronger emphasis on light seafood dishes. In the North, where the weather is cooler, heavier meat dishes are often preferred, so fish is eaten somewhat less frequently. Throughout Vietnam the fish and seafood in markets are reasonably priced and abundant, leading to simple home-cooked dishes like *ca chien*, fried butterfish (page 147), and *tom nuong xa*, grilled lemongrass prawns (page 153). Dishes such as *ca nhoi*, steamed fish stuffed with pork and herbs (page 142), and *do bien xao*, stir-fried seafood (page 166), however, are considered a bit more involved and are often reserved for family gatherings and other special occasions, or eaten in restaurants, where they can be a bit expensive.

My favorite seafood restaurants in New York's Chinatown are clustered on the Bowery and Elizabeth Street. There huge water tanks are set against street windows, displaying all sorts of live fish and seafood to entice potential diners. Going to these restaurants with my father is a real treat, as fish and seafood are subjects on which he is quite expert. While our family is shown to a table, he personally selects fish, crustaceans, and mollusks for our meal, discussing each with the restaurant manager. They'll go back and forth, pointing to specific items, evaluating each for freshness and flavor, and proposing different menus. Moments later the selections will arrive, one at a time, each prepared in a different way. Whether the dishes are steamed, fried, stir-fried, or braised, the unspoken goal is to make each one more delicious than the previous, until the evening ends in a kind of culinary intoxication and *bonhomie*.

FISH

FRESHWATER FISH, such as carp and catfish, and fish from the sea, such as sea bass and mackerel, are part of the daily diet of the Vietnamese people and are usually prepared in similar ways. Fish can be cut up into bite-size morsels, lightly fried, and served with fresh herbs, *cha ca thang long* (page 148); sliced into thick steaks and braised in a caramel sauce, *ca kho* (page 146); or steamed whole in beer, *ca hap bia* (page 144). Another approach to fish is the preparation of fish cakes and *quenelles* — small rolled fish balls with a soft, textured, meatball-like consistency. In France, *quenelles* are technically any finely ground fish or meat that is bound with fat and eggs. In Vietnam, they are similar but are bound with fat and potato starch. *Quenelles* are often served in seafood and noodle soups such as *hu tieu do bien* (page 92). Fish cakes are sometimes thinly sliced, stir-fried with other seafoods, and served with crispy egg noodles, *mi xao don do bien* (page 116).

Even with all the different ways of preparing fish, the Vietnamese are partial to one method. They prefer the fish whole and steamed. Whole fish is a sign of prosperity, so when it is ordered by your host, you are honored. The head of the fish is a delicacy and is believed to bring good luck to the one who eats it. The numerous bones and bits of cartilage in the head make its flesh the most flavorful. To an Asian the Western habit of discarding fish heads is anathema!

Steamed fish, whether whole, cubed, or filleted, is usually not complicated to make. The preparation time can be long, but these dishes are often reserved for evening meals. For a quick lunch, if fish is the desired protein, it is usually small fried fish such as butterfish or pompano. These little delights, which are particular favorites of my brothers William and Philippe, are served with rice, pickled vegetables, and some *nuoc cham* (page 42) for dipping.

CA NHOI
Stuffed Fish

Serves 4

2 medium dried shiitake
    mushrooms
8 ounces pork (70% lean),
    thinly sliced
1 tablespoon fish sauce
1 teaspoon sesame oil
1 tablespoon potato starch
One 3-pound whole carp or
    sea bass, scaled, cleaned,
    and central bone removed
2 scallions, root ends trimmed,
    thinly sliced in rounds
12 sprigs cilantro, root ends
    trimmed, chopped
2 ounces fresh ginger, peeled
    and minced
Coarse sea salt
Freshly ground black pepper
2 teaspoons vegetable oil
Spicy lemongrass soy dipping
    sauce (page 45)

CA NHOI is a northern specialty usually served during seasonal celebrations because of its involved preparation. The key to executing this beautiful stuffed fish is to properly remove the central bone without tearing the flesh, because it is this technique that will keep the stuffing in place. I use kitchen shears to snap the bone right where it connects to the head and at the tail end on the inside of the fish, then I run a small knife along both sides of the bone to lift it out. Although *ca nhoi* is traditionally steamed, my mother also likes to roast it, which produces a crispy skin. If you cannot find a carp small enough to fit in your steamer or roasting pan, sea bass, although different in texture and flavor, is equally delicious.

1. Put the mushrooms in a bowl with hot water to cover, then set a plate over the bowl to prevent steam from escaping. Let stand until the mushrooms rehydrate and soften, about 30 minutes. Squeeze the mushrooms between the palms of your hands to get rid of the excess water. Using a paring knife, remove any hard stems, then mince the caps.

2. Combine the pork, fish sauce, and sesame oil in a bowl and mix well. Transfer to a plastic bag, squeeze out the air, and seal the bag. Place in the freezer for 30 minutes.

3. Meanwhile, to remove the central bone from the fish, use kitchen shears to snap the bone where it connects to the head and tail on the inside. Then run a knife blade (being careful not to tear the flesh) along both sides of the bone and remove it.

4. Place the slightly frozen pork in a food processor and, adding the potato starch gradually, pulse to make a fine paste. Transfer the paste to a bowl. Add the mushrooms, scallions, cilantro, ginger, season with salt and pepper, and mix until well combined. Season the fish with salt and pepper in-

side and out, then stuff it with the pork paste.

5. Fill the bottom third of a wok with water, fit a bamboo steamer with lid over it, and place the wok over high heat. Place the stuffed fish on a plate. When the steamer is filled with steam, place the plate on the bamboo rack and cover the steamer with the lid. Steam until the fish is cooked through, 20 to 25 minutes. Drizzle spicy lemongrass soy sauce over the fish. Serve with rice.

VARIATION: At the end of step 2, preheat the oven to 375°F. At the end of step 4, rub vegetable oil over both sides of the stuffed fish. Place it in a baking dish and bake until golden crisp, 15 to 20 minutes per side. Drizzle spicy lemongrass soy sauce over the fish and serve with rice.

When we lived in France among my mother's family, my uncles would often go fishing on the Loire River on weekends. Most of the time there would be at least one carp among their catch. My grandmother would always make roasted carp *farci*, a popular French dish with a pork stuffing and aromatics such as curly parsley, onions, and garlic. Although the seasonings and aromatics differ, *ca nhoi* is likely derived from or strongly influenced by this classic French recipe.

CA HAP BIA
Carp Steamed in Beer

Serves 4

5 large dried shiitake
    mushrooms
4 cups beer
1 stalk lemongrass, outer
    leaves removed and tough
    green tops removed, root
    end trimmed, and stalk
    lightly crushed
One 2½- to 3-pound whole
    carp or flounder, scaled and
    cleaned
2 scallions, trimmed, cut into
    2-inch-long pieces and
    julienned
3 ounces fresh ginger, peeled
    and julienned
Coarse sea salt
Freshly ground black pepper
Spicy lemongrass soy dipping
    sauce (page 45)

CARP, A NATIVE Asian freshwater fish, is a favorite among the Vietnamese. Found all year round, its sweet flesh is best in the fall and spring (during the summer, when the water level is low, carp tend to feed on the bottom of the pond, picking up impurities and a muddy flavor). Beer-steamed carp is a modern classic, born of the 1960s, when beer was brought to Vietnam by Westerners, and local breweries were developed. Carp's fatty flesh absorbs a subtle, yeasty flavor from the beer. Enhanced with ginger and scallions, it is delicate in texture and flavor.

1. Put the mushrooms in a bowl with hot water to cover, then set a plate over the bowl to prevent steam from escaping. Let stand until the mushrooms rehydrate and soften, about 30 minutes. Squeeze the mushrooms between the palms of your hands to get rid of the excess water. Using a paring knife, remove any hard stems, then julienne the caps.

2. Pour the beer into a wok and add enough water to fill the bottom third of the wok. Add the lemongrass. Fit a bamboo steamer with lid over it, and place the wok over high heat. Place the carp on a plate, scatter mushrooms, scallion, and ginger over the fish, and season with salt and pepper. When the steamer is filled with steam, place the plate on the bamboo rack and close the steamer with the lid. Steam until the fish is cooked through, about 20 minutes. Remove from the steamer and drizzle the spicy lemongrass soy sauce over the fish. Serve with rice.

While in Hanoi, I was invited to eat whole fish at a private home. Honored, I nonetheless noticed that the fish was quite plump. Unusually plump. When I asked my host why this was so, she explained to me, pointing to the stomach of the fish, that the intestines and internal organs were left intact—that is, the fish had not been gutted. This was done, she explained, so the fish would sit fuller on the serving plate, creating a nicer presentation. "Just eat around the guts," she suggested. I most certainly did just that.

CA CHIEN SOT CA CHUA
Pan-Fried Fish with Tomato Sauce

Serves 4

4 small to medium
   vine-ripened tomatoes
One 2½-pound whole striped
   bass, scaled and cleaned
Coarse sea salt
Freshly ground black pepper
2 tablespoons plus 1 teaspoon
   vegetable oil
1 large clove garlic, peeled
   and thinly sliced
1 tablespoon fish sauce
12 sprigs dill, trimmed
12 sprigs cilantro, root ends
   trimmed
12 large holy basil leaves

A CLASSIC DISH, *ca chien sot ca chua* uses dill and tomatoes (no seeding, blanching, or peeling required), ingredients of Western origin. Vine-ripened tomatoes from Holland or Israel are best for this recipe, as they do not become mealy when cooked down. The finished dish—pan-fried fish with what is essentially a chunky red sauce—may at first seem Mediterranean, but the refreshing garnish of lemony herbs, cilantro and holy basil, and fish sauce makes it distinctly Vietnamese.

1. Halve tomatoes, then quarter each half and set aside.

2. Rinse, drain, and blot dry the fish inside and out. Season with salt and pepper. Heat 2 tablespoons oil in a nonstick skillet over high heat. Pan-fry the fish until golden and crisp on the outside and cooked through, 5 to 7 minutes per side. Transfer to a platter. Add the garlic to the same skillet and stir-fry until golden, about 5 minutes. Add the tomatoes, fish sauce, season to taste with pepper, and stir-fry until softened, 10 to 15 minutes. Carefully pour the chunky tomato sauce around the fish. Wipe the skillet with a paper towel and heat the remaining oil. Add the dill, cilantro, and holy basil and stir-fry until just wilted, 1 to 2 minutes. Place the herbs over the fish. Serve with rice.

VARIATION: Substitute four 6-ounce striped bass fillets for the whole fish. Pan-fry the fillets skin-side down until golden and crisp, 3 to 4 minutes. Flip fish skin-side up and continue cooking for an additional 1 to 2 minutes. Proceed with the recipe.

CA KHO
Braised Fish in Caramel

Serves 4

1½ pounds mackerel or eel,
  bone-in, about 1-inch-thick
  steaks
Coarse sea salt
Freshly ground black pepper
3 tablespoons sugar
1 tablespoon thick soy sauce
3 tablespoons fish sauce
6 ounces daikon, peeled and
  sliced into thin rounds
2 large cloves garlic, peeled
  and lightly crushed
2 scallions, trimmed, cut into
  1½-inch-long pieces and
  quartered lengthwise
3 dried red chilies or 2 or more
  bird's eye or Thai chilies
2 tablespoons vegetable oil
3 ounces fresh ginger, peeled
  and julienned

BRAISED FISH in caramel originated in the North but is now eaten all over Vietnam. Because it is slow-cooked, using fatty fish such as mackerel or eel makes sense. These fish tend to have a distinct flavor, slightly more pronounced than other, leaner fish, and braising either one in caramel sauce sweetens it. The fat rendered from the fish gradually melts into the sauce, making it velvety. Chilies and scallions counterbalance the rich caramel, while the rice served alongside gives texture and unifies all these great flavors.

1. Season the fish steaks with salt and pepper on both sides.

2. Make a caramel by combining the sugar and 2 tablespoons water in a large sand pot or heavy-bottomed pot over medium-low heat. When the sugar melts and turns golden, about 10 minutes, remove the pot from the heat and stir in ⅓ cup water, thick soy sauce, and fish sauce. Reduce the heat to low and add the daikon, garlic, scallions, chilies, and fish steaks. Cover and simmer until the fish is cooked through, about 20 minutes.

3. Meanwhile, heat the oil in a saucepan over high heat and stir-fry the ginger until golden crisp, about 2 minutes. Transfer the braised fish to a serving platter and scatter the ginger over it. Serve with jasmine rice on the side.

CA CHIEN
Fried Butterfish

Serves 4

**Eight 4-ounce whole butterfish
or similar small fish, cleaned
Vegetable oil for deep-frying
Pickled vegetables (page 48)**
Nuoc cham **(page 42)**

SMALL FISH such as butterfish, pompano, or trevally jack, about 4 inches long, are often prepared deep-fried. Unlike Westerners, my family does not dredge their fish in flour. Instead, we dry the fish thoroughly prior to deep-frying. Sometimes the fins and bones are so crisp that the entire fish is edible, head to tail, and this is a real treat. *Ca chien* is perfect for lunch, uncomplicated to make and delicious. At home we like to serve it over fragrant jasmine rice with pickled vegetables on the side and *nuoc cham* for dipping. *Nuoc cham* is especially complementary because its acidity cuts the fat.

1. Rinse, drain, and blot dry the fish, inside and out. Heat the vegetable oil in a wok over medium-high heat. When the oil has reached a temperature of about 375°F, deep-fry the fish two at a time until deep golden and very crisp, 4 to 5 minutes per side. Drain on paper towels. Serve with rice, pickled vegetables, and *nuoc cham* on the side.

CHA CA THANG LONG
Hanoi Fried Fish with Dill

Serves 4 to 6

½ pound dried rice vermicelli
Vegetable oil for deep-frying, plus one tablespoon for stir-frying
½ cup rice flour or all-purpose flour
½ teaspoon turmeric
1 to 1½ pounds white fish fillets, such as flounder or striped bass, skinned and cut into 1-inch squares
4 scallions, trimmed, cut into 1-inch-long pieces and halved lengthwise
¼ cup roasted unsalted peanuts, split
½ cup small holy basil leaves
½ bunch cilantro, root ends trimmed
½ bunch dill, trimmed
Nuoc cham (page 42)

THIS DISH OF FRIED fish nuggets with fresh herbs is northern. Ever since I picked up the recipe on my last trip to Hanoi, it has become one of my family's favorites. Unlike small whole fish, morsels are dredged in rice flour so they do not fall apart when fried. The fried fish is surprisingly light, and the licorice-like dill—a popular herb used in Vietnamese cooking—uplifts the palate when eaten with the fish. In this dish one can get a sense of how herbs are used in Vietnamese cooking. They are not just garnishes sparingly sprinkled, but are used in great quantities with every bite of fish.

1. Soak the rice vermicelli in lukewarm water to cover in a bowl until pliable, about 15 minutes. Bring a pot filled with water to a boil over high heat. Drain and divide the vermicelli into 4 equal portions. Place them, one portion at a time, in a sieve and lower it into the boiling water. Untangle the noodles with chopsticks and boil until tender but firm, about 5 seconds. Remove, drain, and place in a bowl. Repeat this step until you have 4 individual servings. For 6 servings simply divide vermicelli into six smaller portions.

2. Heat the oil in a wok over medium heat to about 350° to 375°F. Meanwhile, mix the rice flour and turmeric in a plastic bag. Add the fish to the flour mixture, seal the bag, and shake it to coat each piece evenly. Put the fish pieces, a few at a time, in the palms of your hands and shake off the excess flour. Working in batches, deep-fry the fish until golden crisp, about 2 minutes per side. Drain on paper towels and arrange in the center of a serving platter.

3. Heat 1 tablespoon oil in a wok or nonstick skillet over high heat. Add and stir-fry the scallions for 1 minute. Add the peanuts, holy basil, cilantro, and dill and continue stir-frying for 30 seconds more. Arrange the stir-fried herbs around the fried fish. To eat, place some herbs and fish pieces on top of the vermicelli and drizzle some *nuoc cham* over the ingredients.

One day, during the week prior to Tet, the Vietnamese New Year celebration, I was walking through Hanoi's old French Quarter, also known as 36 Streets. I noticed that each street was named after the business it catered to. On Paper Street, vendors sold paper products, including gift wrapping and ceremonial make-believe money. Leather was sold on Leather Street, flowers on Flower Street, and so forth. Then I stumbled upon Cha Ca Street, where several restaurants offered *cha ca*. I walked into Cha Ca La Vong, which I later found out was the original restaurant offering this specialty. A small hibachi made of sand—much like a sand pot—was filled with red-hot coals and placed on my table. The waiter then set a cured cast-iron pan with sizzling golden pieces of fish over the coals and proceeded to add scallions, peanuts, holy basil, cilantro, and dill. The fragrance of the herbs sizzling with the fish was amazing. Added to a bowl of *bun*, rice vermicelli, and drizzled with the indispensable *nuoc cham*, the dish was refreshing and more delicious with every bite.

NEM CA
Fish Quenelles

Makes 24

2 tablespoons fish sauce

2 teaspoons sugar

2 tablespoons vegetable oil

Freshly ground white pepper

1 pound cod, skin and bones
removed, cut into chunks

2 tablespoons potato starch

1 teaspoon baking powder

Spicy lemongrass soy dipping
sauce (page 45)

NEM CA, fish *quenelles* about the size of cherries, are made with white fish, such as cod, mackerel, or whiting, or sometimes with a combination of all three. I like using cod because its flavor is more delicate than that of mackerel and because it has far fewer bones than whiting, making the task of deboning much easier. Making fish *quenelles*, or fine-textured balls, is quite simple. If you are not up to the task, however, you can find them frozen in most Asian markets. Look for the smaller ones, as the larger ones tend to be filled with meat.

1. Whisk together fish sauce and sugar in a bowl until the sugar is completely dissolved. Stir in 1 tablespoon vegetable oil and white pepper to taste.

2. Place the fish in a food processor and pulse to make a fine paste, about 1 minute. Add the fish sauce mixture, potato starch, and baking powder and continue pulsing until the mixture has a firm, paste-like consistency, about 1 minute more.

3. Bring a pot filled with water to a boil over high heat. Pinch off about 1 teaspoon of the fish paste and form it into a ball. Repeat the process, dropping each ball into the boiling water to cook. Once the balls float to the surface, cook for 1 minute more and remove with a slotted spoon. Drain and cool completely. At this point you can use fish balls in *hu tieu do bien*, seafood noodle soup (page 92), or freeze them.

4. Heat the remaining vegetable oil in a nonstick pan over medium-high heat. Pan-fry the fish balls, shaking the pan occasionally, until golden on all sides, 3 to 5 minutes. Serve with spicy lemongrass soy sauce for dipping.

Fish *quenelles* are one of the true delights of Vietnamese cuisine. In the soup *hu tieu do bien*, they provide texture and subtle flavor, and unlike fish chunks, they never fall apart when cooked. Their springy consistency is also excellent stir-fried with garlic and a dash or two of sesame oil.

CRUSTACEANS AND MOLLUSKS

LIKE THE CHINESE, the Vietnamese steam, braise, stir-fry, deep-fry, and grill seafood. Seasoning crustaceans—shrimp, lobsters, and crabs—and mollusks—squid, scallops, clams, and snails—with fish sauce or soy sauce and fresh herbs is common. Except in deep-frying and grilling, the liquids given up by these shellfish during cooking, together with their seasonings, make for marvelously rich sauces.

Shrimp and squid are among the most commonly eaten shellfish in Vietnam, with the emphasis in preparation being on simplicity. *Tom nuong xa*, grilled lemongrass prawns (page 153), are marinated with lemongrass, sugar, and fish sauce, then quickly grilled over red-hot coals. *Goi muc* (page 160), grilled squid tossed with fresh holy basil and chilies and dressed with a tamarind, sugar, and fish-sauce mixture, is another uncomplicated dish to prepare. Both have long been favorites of my family, often enjoyed in the warm summer months, when grilling is a simple pleasure. Perhaps the most classic Vietnamese shrimp dish is *chao tom* (page 154), minced shrimp meat mixed with toasted rice flour and wrapped around a sugar cane stick, then grilled. This elegant dish, which originated in the former imperial city of Hue, in central Vietnam, is now found in Vietnamese restaurants around the world. You can easily recognize *chao tom* enthusiasts: After they have enjoyed the cane-sweetened shrimp paste, they chew the sugar cane itself, savoring every last bit of flavor.

Clams and scallops are traditionally stir-fried with ginger, scallions, and chilies and seasoned to taste with fish sauce. These stir-fries develop a velvety sauce created from the seafood's juices during cooking that clings to every morsel. Sometimes they are shelled and stir-fried with vegetable oil and sugar. The result is caramelized clams, or candied clams, a recipe I discovered in a private home in the beautiful colonial section of Hanoi. The caramelized clams can also be eaten alone as a snack, with tea or beer, or used to garnish stir-fried vegetables.

Specialties such as *goi cuon,* summer rolls (page 156), and *cua farci,* stuffed crab shells (page 158) are prepared in ways specific to Vietnam. These dishes have the same complex balance of texture and flavor as meat, poultry, and other dishes, and they are noticeably absent from other Asian cuisines. Similarly, they deny any allegiance to Western cooking. Although crab cakes are a delicacy commonly eaten in France, the Vietnamese recipe has almost nothing in common with its European counterpart. Having evolved in Vietnam, it now bears no resemblance to the original. Somewhat curiously, expatriate Vietnamese in France and the United States have adopted the habit of eating raw clams and oysters, but in Vietnam this has never caught on. Despite the numerous incidences of fusion in the cuisine, some things simply never change.

Tom Nuong Xa
Grilled Lemongrass Prawns

Serves 4 to 6

16 king prawns (8 to 9 inches
   long) or 24 medium prawns
   (4 to 5 inches long), heads
   and shells intact
¼ cup sugar
⅓ cup fish sauce
1 tablespoon vegetable oil
2 stalks lemongrass, outer
   leaves and tough green tops
   removed, root ends
   trimmed, and finely ground

THE BEST PRAWNS for this recipe are king prawns, which measure about 8 to 9 inches long. Plump and tender but firm, their heads are often filled with sweet tomalley, full of flavor. If these are not available, use medium prawns, usually about 4 to 5 inches long. Marinated in a combination of lemongrass, fish sauce, and sugar, both are excellent grilled over a barbecue or on an indoor grill any time of the year. Sometimes in my family, we make this recipe using squid or frog's legs. If you cannot find fresh lemongrass, substitute garlic or ginger; although much different in flavor, they are equally tasty.

1. With a paring knife, make an incision through the shell along the back of the prawns. Devein, leaving the shell intact; rinse the prawns and pat dry.

2. Whisk together the sugar and fish sauce in a bowl until the sugar is completely dissolved. Stir in the oil and lemongrass, then the prawns, and toss, running your fingertips between the flesh and shells. Place the prawns in a plastic bag and seal the bag. Marinate the prawns, refrigerated for 2 to 3 hours, turning the bag over every 30 minutes or so.

3. Grill over a barbecue (make sure the flames have subsided and coals are red with white ashes), or on a well-oiled grill pan over medium-high heat, until prawns are cooked through and turn pink, about 3 minutes per side for king prawns, 2 minutes for medium prawns.

VARIATION: *Muc nuong xa,* the squid version, is equally delicious. Substitute 1 pound whole squid, skinned and cleaned, for the prawns. In step 2, marinate for 1 hour, and in step 3, grill for 1 to 2 minutes per side.

CHAO TOM
Grilled Shrimp Quenelles on Sugar Cane

Serves 4 to 6

1 pound shrimp, shelled and
    deveined
2 ounces pork fatback or
    2 tablespoons vegetable oil
1 teaspoon sugar
⅓ cup toasted rice flour
    (page 24) or rice flour
1 teaspoon baking powder
2 scallions, trimmed and
    minced
Coarse sea salt
Freshly ground black pepper
8 sugar cane sticks, ¼ inch thick
    by 3 inches long (optional)
Nuoc cham (page 42)
Table salad (page 52)

THIS DELICATE DISH originated in Hue, the culinary capital of central Vietnam. The shrimp paste is traditionally wrapped around a sugar cane stick, then grilled. Fresh and sweet sugar cane is hard to find, however, and rather than use canned sugar cane in syrup, I prefer to omit it altogether and shape the paste into small patties. Toasted rice flour, which binds the shrimp meat, is not sold in markets but is made at home. To make this flour, I toast medium-grain semi-sticky rice in a dry pan and grind it to a fine powder. Baking powder is used to give the shrimp paste extra volume when grilling or pan-frying. The pork fat not only adds flavor but also keeps the paste moist.

1. Mince the shrimp with the pork fatback (if using). Transfer the paste to a bowl and add the sugar, 2 tablespoons toasted rice flour, baking powder, scallions, and salt and pepper to taste. (If not using pork fatback, add the oil at this time.) Mix until well combined.

2. Divide the shrimp mixture into 12 equal portions and wrap a portion around each sugar cane stick, leaving about ½ inch of cane visible at each end. If not using sugar cane, form portions into round patties about 1 inch in diameter. Put the remaining toasted rice flour on a plate and dredge each shrimp *quenelle* in it. Grill over a barbecue (make sure the flames have sub-sided and the coals are red with white ashes) or on a well-oiled grill pan over medium-high heat until the shrimp mixture is cooked through (pink) and slightly golden, about 2 minutes per side. Serve with *nuoc cham* and table salad on the side.

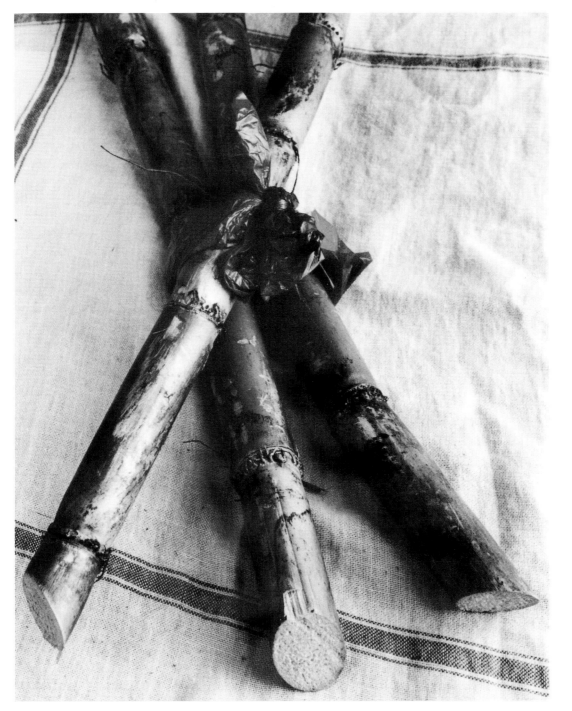

FRESH SUGAR CANES

GOI CUON
Summer Rolls

Serves 4 to 6

4 ounces dried rice vermicelli

4 ounces pork tenderloin

18 small-medium shrimp, shelled

12 round rice papers (about 8 inches in diameter)

1 head Boston lettuce, leaves separated and ribs removed

24 large mint leaves

1 cup julienned carrot

Nuoc leo (page 44)

SHRIMP, PORK, and rice vermicelli are mixed with mint, tender lettuce, and crunchy carrot and wrapped in softened rice paper to create this Vietnamese classic. Friends often tell me, however, that they are reluctant to order *goi cuon* in restaurants because the rice paper tends to be dried up and chewy. There is a simple fix: Cover the prepared rolls with a damp cotton towel or plastic wrap until just before serving, and the rice paper will stay soft and tender. Also, try to find the thinnest rice paper you can. Although not as thin as the rice papers in Vietnam, the Erawan (Three Elephant) brand is available in most Asian markets in the United States and is consistently good.

1. Soak the rice vermicelli in lukewarm water to cover in a bowl, until rehydrated and softened, about 15 minutes. Drain and squeeze the noodles to get rid of the excess water.

2. Bring a pot filled with water to a boil over high heat. Place the rice vermicelli in a sieve and lower it into the boiling water for 5 seconds. Remove the vermicelli and transfer to a bowl. When cool enough to handle, divide the vermicelli into 12 equal portions. In the same boiling water, cook the pork tenderloin until cooked through, about 10 minutes. When cool enough to handle, thinly slice the pork. In the same water, cook the shrimp until they turn opaque, about 1 minute. When cool enough to handle, cut in half lengthwise and devein.

3. Pour lukewarm water about 1 inch deep into a square or rectangular dish. Separate and soak 4 wrappers at a time until pliable, about 5 minutes. Place a clean kitchen towel on your work surface, then place each rice paper on the towel. With another kitchen towel, gently blot each wrapper until it is no longer wet but remains sticky. Leaving 1 inch uncovered on the side closest to you and the adjacent sides, place a lettuce leaf, vermicelli portion on top, 3 shrimp halves (overlapped), 2

DRIED RICE PAPERS

pork slices (overlapped), 2 mint leaves, and some carrot on each rice paper. Fold wrapper once over the filling, then fold in the sides, and continue rolling tightly to the end. Repeat this process with the remaining ingredients to make 12 rolls. Wrap in a damp towel or with plastic wrap until ready to eat. Serve with *nuoc leo*.

People have asked me why pork and shrimp or another seafood are often cooked together in Viet- namese cuisine. I found the ques- tion curious because I grew up eat- ing these combinations, whether in soups, stir-fries, or refreshing sum- mer rolls, and never questioned the idea. While I have never found a definitive answer, one explanation is that such mixings are consistent with the idea of complementing op- posites, or *yin* and *yang*. In the case of *goi cuon*, the textures do com- plement each other: tender pork combined with firm shrimp.

CUA FARCI
Stuffed Crab Shells

Serves 4

½ ounce dried cellophane
noodles

6 dried cloud ear mushrooms

1 pound fresh lump crabmeat

2 ounces pork fatback,
ground, or 1 tablespoon
vegetable oil

1 large egg

1 small shallot, peeled and
minced

1 small clove garlic, peeled
and minced

Coarse sea salt

Freshly ground black pepper

4 Atlantic blue crab shells,
about 5 inches across (point
to point), cleaned

Vegetable oil or 4 thin slivers
unsalted butter

Scallion oil (page 50)

Nuoc cham (page 42)

THIS IS AN INCREDIBLY tasty dish of French derivation, as the word *farci* ("stuffed") suggests, and its shredded crab combined with cellophane noodles, cloud ear mushrooms, shallot, and garlic, stuffed and baked in a shell, makes a beautiful presentation. Because the prep time for these is fairly long, they are often eaten in restaurants. There are a few tricks, however, to simplify things. You will need blue crab shells, which are perfect for a single serving and can be saved from the preparation of *tom hum cua hap*, steamed lobsters and crabs (page 159). (If this is impossible, just form individual crab cakes.) You can also buy lump crabmeat from a fishmonger to avoid having to pick the meat out of each crab. Of course, if you feel up to it, steam Dungeness crabs and pick the meat out yourself!

1. Preheat the oven to 350°F. Soak the cellophane noodles and cloud ear mushrooms in lukewarm water to cover until rehydrated and softened, about 15 minutes. Drain and squeeze the noodles and cloud ears to get rid of the excess water. Finely chop noodles and cloud ears and put them in a mixing bowl.

2. Add the crabmeat, pork fatback or oil, egg, shallot, and garlic, season with salt and pepper, and mix until well combined. Divide the stuffing into 4 equal portions. Stuff a portion into each shell, pushing it in if necessary. Place the stuffed crab shells, stuffing side up, on a baking sheet. Brush with oil or place a thin shaving of butter on top and bake until the stuffing is cooked through, browned, and crispy, about 20 minutes. Drizzle with some scallion oil and serve with *nuoc cham* on the side.

Some cooks like to deep-fry stuffed crab shells. I find that baking them gives lighter results, and I do not have to worry about the stuffing falling out of the shells, as they are usually deep-fried stuffing side down.

TOM HUM CUA HAP
Steamed Lobsters and Crabs

Serves 4

Four 1- to 1¼-pound lobsters
8 blue crabs
4 ounce fresh ginger, peeled, cut into 4 slices, and lightly crushed
4 scallions, trimmed, halved, and lightly crushed
2 stalks lemongrass, outer leaves removed, tops trimmed, and stalks lightly crushed
Coarse sea salt
Freshly ground black pepper
Nuoc chanh ot **(page 43)**

THIS IS PERHAPS the easiest recipe in the entire book, as you simply scatter fresh lemony herbs over the seafood prior to steaming. I usually buy 1- to 1¼-pound lobsters rather than larger ones because their meat is sweet, tender, and firm. In Asian cookery, steaming fish and seafood is generally preferred over boiling. Steaming allows the lobsters and crabs to retain their delicious juices instead of filling up with water. This dish provides an opportunity to save crab shells for making *cua farci*, stuffed crab shells (page 158). Wash the shells thoroughly in hot water, removing any leftover bits. Then air-dry and store them in a plastic bag for later use. Steamed crustaceans are best eaten with *nuoc chanh ot*, a spicy and sweet lemon relish, and rice.

1. Being very careful, scrub the lobsters and crabs under cold water. Fill the bottom of a large pot (or two large pots) with about 2 inches of water, position a rack so that it fits just above the water level, cover the pot, and place over high heat. When the water starts to boil and the pot is filled with steam, add the lobsters and the crabs. Scatter the ginger, scallions, and lemongrass on top. Season with salt and pepper, cover the pot, and steam the crustaceans until they turn red, 8 to 10 minutes. Serve with *nuoc chanh ot* for dipping.

While my lobsters and crabs are steaming, I have just enough time to set the table. I cover it with double or triple layers of kraft paper or newspaper and spread out spoons, seafood picks, nut crackers, and wooden mallets. When they are ready, I present the fragrant, heaping platter of crustaceans. I suggest you seriously consider doubling the quantity of lobsters and crabs you think you might need. Once people get going on these, it's hard to get them to stop. While you're at it, make extra *nuoc chanh ot*. Oh, and ice-cold beer—forget the glasses if you like—is perfect here.

GOI MUC
Spicy Squid Salad

Serves 4 to 6

1 tablespoon tamarind pulp
1 tablespoon sugar
2 tablespoons fish sauce
1 tablespoon lime juice
1 large clove garlic, peeled
   and minced
1 small yellow onion, peeled
   and sliced into thin wedges
1 or more bird's eye or Thai
   chilies, seeded and julienned
3 tablespoons vegetable oil
1 pound baby or medium-size
   squid (tentacles optional),
   skinned and cleaned
1 medium ripe tomato, halved
   crosswise and seeded
½ cup holy basil leaves, torn
½ cup cilantro leaves

GOI MUC is made with steamed or grilled squid tossed in a refreshing tamarind-based sauce. In my family we prefer grilled squid because, when lightly charred, it gets a wonderful flavor. Baby or medium-size squid (2 to 4 inches long) are best because they are tender and sweet in flavor. (Avoid larger squid when possible, as they tend to be chewy.)

1. In a bowl, mix the tamarind pulp with ¼ cup lukewarm water and crush the pulp with the back of a spoon. Strain the mixture through a fine sieve set over a bowl, pressing the pulp against the sieve with the back of the spoon. Discard the solids. Add the sugar, fish sauce, and lime juice to the tamarind and whisk until the sugar is completely dissolved. Add the garlic, onions, and chili and allow to stand for 20 minutes.

2. Separate the squid bodies from the tentacles, rinse under cold water, drain, and pat dry thoroughly. Heat the vegetable oil in grill pan over medium-high heat. Grill the squid, pressing them down with a heatproof spatula, 2 to 3 minutes per side. If using medium squid, with a sharp knife, make a light crisscross pattern on the outside of the body; grill for 3 to 4 minutes per side, halve lengthwise, then cut into 1-inch pieces.

3. Meanwhile, in a separate oiled pan over medium-high heat, grill the tomato halves until lightly charred, 3 to 5 minutes per side. Cut the tomato halves into bite-size chunks, toss with the squid, holy basil, cilantro, and tamarind dressing, and transfer to a platter.

FRESH TAMARIND PODS
AND PULP

MUC CHIEN GION
Salt-and-Pepper-Fried Squid

Serves 4 to 6

1 pound baby or medium
   squid (tentacles optional),
   skinned and cleaned
Vegetable oil for deep-frying
2 tablespoons coarse sea salt
1 tablespoon freshly ground
   black pepper
½ cup cornstarch
1 or 2 limes, each cut
   crosswise into 8 wedges

THIS DISH is as much Chinese as it is Vietnamese and is commonly seen on both kinds of restaurant menus. It is also a favorite among Westerners. The fried squid is lightly dusted with a cornstarch, salt, and pepper mix, and you can substitute a chili-salt mix for the coarse sea salt and freshly ground black pepper if you like. Either way, it is wonderful served with lime wedges on the side, and light enough to be a finger food or appetizer.

1. Rinse squid bodies and tentacles under cold water, drain and pat dry thoroughly. Slice into ⅛-inch rings. If using medium-size squid, cut open the squid and make a light crisscross pattern on the outside with a paring knife, then cut into approximately 1-inch square pieces.

2. Heat the vegetable oil in a wok over medium heat to about 375°F. Meanwhile, mix the salt, pepper, and cornstarch in a plastic bag. Add the squid, seal the bag, and shake it to coat each piece evenly. Put a few squid pieces at a time in the palms of your hands and shake off the excess cornstarch mix. Working in batches, deep-fry the squid until the rings turn golden and crisp, about 1 minute, or if using 1-inch square pieces, until they curl up and crisp, about 1 minute. Drain on paper towels and serve with lime wedges on the side.

VARIATION: *Tom chien gion* is the shrimp version of this recipe. I often use small shrimp because they are just right when served as a finger food. Remove all the shell except the very tail end, which will serve as a "handle." Butterfly and devein the shrimp. Proceed with step 2, frying the shrimp for about 1 minute.

NOTE: A chili-salt mix is easy to make. Substitute ¼ teaspoon finely ground dried red chili pepper for the black pepper.

MUC NHOI
Stuffed Squid

Serves 4

12 baby squid with tentacles,
   skinned and cleaned
6 ounces ground pork
   (70% lean)
1 small shallot, peeled and
   chopped
1 small clove garlic, peeled
   and chopped
1 tablespoon fish sauce
1 teaspoon sugar
Freshly ground black pepper
1 tablespoon potato starch
2 tablespoons vegetable oil
Nuoc cham (page 42)

STUFFED SQUID is a classic from the central region. This recipe does take some preparation, but the end result is beautiful and well worth it, especially when using baby squid. This can also be made with larger squid, then sliced in rings and served as a main course. The advantage of using baby squid, however, is that they are bite-size and perfect to serve as an appetizer.

1. Rinse the squid bodies and tentacles under cold water, drain, and pat dry thoroughly. With a paring knife, separate the tentacles from the bodies. Refrigerate the bodies. Chop the tentacles and mix with pork, shallot, garlic, fish sauce, sugar, and a pinch of pepper until well combined. Transfer to a plastic bag. Seal the bag and place it in the freezer for 45 minutes.

2. Transfer the frozen mixture to a food processor and pulse until it is ground. Add potato starch and continue pulsing to make a fine paste. Stuff each squid body with the paste and close the bodies with a toothpick.

3. Heat 1 tablespoon oil in a nonstick pan over medium-high heat. Add half of the stuffed squid and brown on all sides, about 2 minutes per side. Make sure you roll the squid to ensure even browning, 6 to 8 minutes total. Repeat with the remaining oil and squid. Serve with *nuoc cham* on the side.

Nghieu Xao Ot
Spicy Stir-Fried Clams

Serves 4

24 to 36 cockles, or Venus or
  razor clams
1 tablespoon vegetable oil
2 cloves garlic, peeled and
  minced
3 ounces fresh ginger, peeled
  and julienned
1 teaspoon Vietnamese chili-
  garlic sauce
2 teaspoons fish sauce
2 scallions, root ends trimmed,
  cut into 2-inch-long pieces
1 bunch cilantro, stems
  removed

MY FAVORITE MOLLUSKS for this stir-fried dish are cockles, or Venus or razor clams, because they are especially tasty and tender when cooked. I prefer smaller shellfish for cooking because they tend to be the least chewy. The one thing to remember when preparing clams is to soak and rinse them several times in cold water to get rid of any sand prior to cooking.

1. Put the cockles, or Venus or razor clams, in a bowl and fill with water to cover. Place in the refrigerator and allow to soak for 30 minutes. Drain and repeat twice more.

2. Heat the oil in a wok over high heat. Add the garlic and ginger and then stir-fry until fragrant, about 3 minutes. Add the mollusks, chili-garlic sauce, and fish sauce and stir-fry until well mixed. Scatter the scallions and cilantro on top, cover, and cook until the mollusks open, 5 to 7 minutes. Serve hot.

SO XAO XA
Stir-Fried Scallops with Lemongrass

Serves 4

12 to 24 large scallops or
queenies, with or without
shell or coral
1 tablespoon vegetable oil
2 cloves garlic, peeled and
minced
2 stalks lemongrass, outer
leaves and tough green tops
removed, root ends
trimmed, and stalks finely
ground
2 teaspoons fish sauce
2 or more bird's eye or
Thai chilies, seeded and
julienned
2 scallions, root ends
trimmed, cut into 2-inch-
long pieces and julienned
1 bunch cilantro, tough stems
removed

F OUND ALL YEAR round in Atlantic, Mediterranean, and Pacific waters, scallops can grow to 7 inches across their fan-like shells. The smaller variety, known as queen scallops or queenies, grows to 3 inches. If you have a really good fishmonger, ask for scallops on the shell with their coral, or roe, intact, as it is the tastiest part of the scallop. If you find only shelled scallops, that's fine, too. Clams or periwinkles, tiny black sea snails (use 2 pounds), are delicious substitutes.

1. Put the scallops in a bowl and fill with water to cover. Place in the refrigerator and allow to soak for 30 minutes. Drain and repeat twice more. (This step is not necessary if using shelled scallops.)

2. Heat the oil in a wok over high heat. Add the garlic and lemongrass and stir-fry until fragrant, about 1 minute. Add the scallops, fish sauce, and chilies and stir-fry until well mixed. Scatter the scallions and cilantro on top. Cover, and cook until the scallops open, 5 to 7 minutes. Serve hot.

CARI DO BIEN
Seafood Curry

Serves 4

3 tablespoons vegetable oil

3 large cloves garlic, peeled and crushed

1 large shallot, peeled, halved, and thinly sliced

2 stalks lemongrass, outer leaves and tough green tops removed, root ends trimmed, and stalks sliced paper thin

2 tablespoons good-quality Indian curry powder

2 teaspoons Thai shrimp paste (optional)

3 or more dried red chilies

1 cup canned unsweetened coconut milk

1 cup chicken stock (page 61) or water

1 tablespoon fish sauce

3 lime leaves or lime peels

12 ounces cod fillet, cut into 8 equal pieces

8 medium shrimp, shelled, butterflied, and deveined

12 baby squid, cleaned

8 large sea scallops, shelled

12 holy basil leaves, julienned

THIS COCONUT-BASED curry—made with cod, shrimp, squid, and scallops—is one of my favorite dishes from the South. The balance between savory, sweet, and spicy is perfect with the four seafoods, whether they are used in combination, as in this dish, or alone. The addition of the lemony-sweet herb holy basil both complements and lifts the flavor of the seafood beautifully.

1. Heat the oil in a clay pot or heavy-bottomed pot over low heat. Increase the heat to medium and stir-fry the garlic and shallot until lightly golden, about 5 minutes. Add the lemongrass, curry powder, shrimp paste, and chilies and cook until the flavors come together, about 5 minutes.

2. Add the coconut milk, chicken stock or water, fish sauce, lime leaves, fish, shrimp, squid, and scallops. Cover and bring just to a boil. Reduce the heat to medium-low and cook until the seafood turns opaque, 5 to 10 minutes. Remove from the heat, add the holy basil leaves, and serve with jasmine rice or Saigon *baguette* on the side.

Do Bien Xao
Stir-Fried Seafood

Serves 4

2 tablespoons vegetable oil

3 ounces fresh ginger, peeled and julienned

3 scallions, root ends and tough green tops removed, cut into 1½-inch pieces and halved lengthwise

1 carrot, peeled and thinly sliced diagonally

4 ounces snowpeas

8 medium shrimp, shelled, butterflied, and deveined

8 large sea scallops, shelled

12 baby squid, halved lengthwise, then carefully scored in a crisscross pattern

½ cup chicken stock (page 61) or light pork stock (page 62)

1 tablespoon fish sauce

Coarse sea salt

Freshly ground black pepper

4 sprigs cilantro, tough stems removed

STIR-FRIED SEAFOOD is generally made with shrimp, squid, and scallops, species that are firm and tender and will not fall apart when stir-fried (fish doesn't fare as well). It usually includes aromatics such as ginger and scallions and little else, relying on the freshness and natural flavor of the seafood for its character. Snowpeas and thinly sliced carrots are added for color and texture. This stir-fry is often served over thin and crispy egg noodles, *mi xao don do bien* (page 116), or over rice as one-course meals.

1. Heat the oil in a wok over high heat. Stir-fry the ginger and scallions until fragrant, about 3 minutes. Add the carrots and stir-fry for 3 minutes. Add the snowpeas, shrimp, scallops, squid, chicken stock, and fish sauce, and season with salt and pepper. Stir-fry until the seafood turns opaque and is cooked through, about 6 minutes total. Transfer to a serving platter, garnish with cilantro, and serve with rice or thin and crispy egg noodles.

FROGS AND SNAILS

ALTHOUGH SNAILS AND FROGS are considered delicacies, for many people the idea of eating either of them is daunting. In Europe and Southeast Asia they are popular, appearing on the menus of fancier restaurants. In France, for example, they are usually sautéed or baked with a *beurre persillé*, parsley-and-garlic-butter combination. In Vietnam, lemongrass, fish sauce, and curry are the common aromatics.

Frog's legs are delicious, especially when they are plump, about the size of the wing drummettes of a 2- to 3-pound chicken. I buy them live in Chinatown because they are consistently big and tender and I can select the ones I want. Although the legs are the only part of the frog that are prepared and offered in restaurants, the whole frog (with the exception of the head and innards) is edible. The sight can be offputting for some, as I found out when I served headless frogs for dinner one night. My guests were mildly shocked (and it's hard to shock the French) when whole, headless frogs were presented on a platter. Since then I have served only the legs when friends come to my home to dine. The rest I freeze for later use, usually in a curry.

It is believed that snails were among the first animals to be eaten by man. The ancient Romans were reportedly the first to cook them, and according to the *Larousse Gastronomique*, the Gauls liked them as dessert!

On a recent trip to Vietnam, I saw snails prepared. The live snails were simply minced and mixed with ground pork and lemongrass, then stuffed back into the shell and steamed. This was a curious approach to preparing snails, I thought. Prior to that experience, I had only eaten *escargots* with the French side of my family. Prepared in the most classic style, *escargots à la bourguignonne* (snails baked with a cognac-spiked parsley-and-garlic butter) are a specialty of France's Burgundy region. The Vietnamese cook apparently thought it unnecessary to purge the snails for 3 hours, and she also eliminated the 2-hour blanching normally associated with French-style preparation. (I had always assumed that these steps were necessary to get rid of the slime and other impurities.) Instead, she simply rinsed the snails several times and, discarding the tail ends, minced and combined them with ground pork, lemongrass, and minced chilies. Then she would fill the shells with the stuffing and steam them. The finished dish was delicate and quite tasty served with a fragrant lemongrass-infused soy sauce. Overall, I was pleasantly surprised. When I returned to New York, I invited my family for dinner and told them I was making snails. They came with a bottle of wine, ready for the beautiful *escargots* to come out of the oven. Instead, they were confused as I opened a bamboo steamer to reveal steamed stuffed snails. It was much different from what they were used to, but they enjoyed the snails nonetheless.

Ech Xao Cari
Curried Frog's Legs

Serves 4 to 6

4 to 6 pairs frog's legs, depending on the size (about 1½ pounds)
1 tablespoon vegetable oil
1 small yellow onion, peeled and sliced into thin wedges
4 ounces fresh ginger, peeled and julienned
1 tablespoon curry powder
2 tablespoons fish sauce
Coarse sea salt
Freshly ground black pepper
6 sprigs cilantro, root ends and most stems removed

P EOPLE SAY that frog's legs taste like chicken, and while they are light and succulent like well-prepared poultry, they have their own distinctly subtle flavor. Try to find large frog's legs about the size of the chicken wing drummettes of a 2- to 3-pound bird. If you have an Asian market near you, chances are they stock live frogs. If you buy frozen ones, make sure they're not too small. The texture may not be as tender because of the freezing, but they certainly will be more than adequate.

1. Rinse, drain, and blot dry the frog's legs thoroughly with paper towels. Then split them in half through the pelvic bone so you have single legs.

2. Heat the oil in a wok or non-stick pan over high heat. Add the onion and ginger and stir-fry until the onion is just translucent and the ginger is crisp and fragrant, 3 to 5 minutes. Add the frog's legs, curry powder (sprinkled evenly), and fish sauce. Season with salt and pepper and stir-fry until the frog's legs are cooked through and crisp on the outside, about 7 minutes. Transfer to a serving plate and garnish with cilantro.

VARIATION: Substitute 1 pound baby squid, cleaned and halved lengthwise, for the frog's legs. In step 2, stir-fry the squid until cooked, 2 to 3 minutes.

FRESH FROGS FROM THE FISHMONGER IN CHINATOWN

ECH XAO XA
Stir-Fried Lemongrass Frog's Legs

Serves 4 to 6

4 to 6 pairs frog's legs, depending on the size (about 1
  pound)
¼ cup sugar
⅓ cup fish sauce
3 tablespoons vegetable oil
2 stalks lemongrass, outer
  leaves and tough green
  tops removed, root ends
  trimmed, and stalks
  finely ground
2 unripe star fruit, thinly
  sliced into stars
Scallion oil (page 50)

STAR FRUIT, OR carambola, a fruit that can be used as a vegetable when unripe, is very popular in Vietnam. In this dish, it complements the sweetness of the lemongrass-marinated frog's legs and makes for a beautiful presentation. Overlap thin star fruit slices in a circle and place two to three single frog's legs in the center. The legs have plenty of flavor, but you can optionally drizzle scallion oil over them while they are still hot.

1. Rinse, drain, and blot dry the frog's legs thoroughly with paper towels. Then split them in half through the pelvic bone so you have single legs.

2. Whisk together the sugar and fish sauce in a bowl until the sugar is completely dissolved. Stir in 1 tablespoon oil and the lemongrass. Transfer the frog's legs and marinade to a plastic bag, seal it, and refrigerate 2 to 3 hours, turning the bag over every 30 minutes.

3. On each plate, overlap 8 to 10 star fruit slices in a circle. Working in batches if necessary, heat the remaining 2 tablespoons oil in a nonstick pan over high heat. Add the frog's legs and sear until golden and crisp, about 3 minutes per side. Cover and continue cooking for 1 to 2 minutes. Transfer 3 single frog's legs to each plate, carefully placing them in the center of the star fruit garnish. Drizzle with scallion oil and serve hot.

STAR FRUIT

FRESH SQUAB FROM A BUTCHER IN CHINATOWN

CHAPTER SIX

POULTRY & MEATS

CHICKEN, DUCK, SQUAB, quail, pork, and beef are a large part of the Vietnamese diet. They are collectively thought of as animal protein and are often cooked in similar ways. (Accordingly, all are included in this chapter but separated under the headings "Domesticated and Game Birds," "Pork and Beef," and "Exotics.") From a breakfast bowl of chicken or beef *pho*, to a lunch of grilled squab or skewered pork, to a dinner with all sorts of dishes, including roast duck or braised beef short ribs, poultry and meat are ever present. It is important to understand, however, that the quantities of poultry or meat, methods of preparation, and overarching philosophy of balance in the cuisine combine to render it lighter than many Western cuisines and certainly lighter than you might expect. ◆ Although there are several different techniques for preparing poultry or meat, marinating and grilling are favored. The coals lend a smoky flavor to the flesh of the animal, and much of the fat is melted away in the cooking process. In my family we especially look forward to late spring, summer, and early fall because the weather permits outdoor barbecuing. We use only natural wood coals and moistened wood chips for grilling. Our marinades have evolved from generation to generation, each in its own way, accentuating the flavor of poultry and meat. When in contact with the grill, the herbs and spices blend with the smoke of the burning wood. The air is filled with such strong fragrances that we would gladly spend the entire day cooking and nibbling on the food. When the weather gets too cold, we grill indoors over the stove, or broil or roast in the oven.

In winter, however, we find braised stew meats—pork shank, beef tendon, neck meat, or even an old hen—more satisfying. The slow and gentle braising method traditionally employed allows the flesh of the animal to increase gradually in temperature during cooking. The fat melts over a period of hours, moistening the flesh throughout the simmering process, making the meat so tender that it falls off the bone. Any sauce created during braising is enriched as a result of the spices, having steeped in it for hours.

Tender, lean cuts of poultry and meat can be served in any season and are best cooked quickly by stir-frying or grilling (such cuts include chicken breast, beef sirloin, and pork tenderloin). Sliced thinly against the grain or cubed, they are commonly combined with vegetables and served over stir-fried noodles or plain rice, or sometimes for a fun snack, in a sandwich made with a rice flour *baguette* (page 119).

A note: In many instances, one marinade will complement several types of poultry, meat, or seafood. If you feel like eating chicken but the marinade included in this chapter is combined with pork, do not be concerned about it; experiment with confidence. Just be sure to adjust the seasoning and cooking time according to the meat you will be using.

DOMESTICATED AND GAME BIRDS

D OMESTICATED BIRDS such as chickens and ducks are raised throughout Vietnam, including densely urbanized Hanoi and Saigon. They are plentiful, easy to care for, and considered valuable investments because they provide not only meat but eggs. You will not see dressed birds at local markets in Vietnam. They are selected live by the customer, then are killed on the spot, as the Vietnamese prefer their poultry fresh (and you cannot get fresher than that). A typical morning street scene has bicycle riders with woven baskets full of live chickens, ducks, or squabs dodging traffic on busy city streets. In the markets poultry farmers set up huge vats of boiling water for plunging and dressing (removing the feathers) birds as quickly as customers buy them.

Vietnamese chickens—indeed, chickens throughout Asia generally—are smaller and tougher than their Western counterparts. I find them slightly rubbery in texture, but many Vietnamese would argue that they are juicier and more flavorful. In my opinion, U.S. organic free-range chickens compare favorably to both Asian and other U.S. chickens, and I recommend them for any chicken recipe.

Poultry in Vietnam, especially chicken, is considered properly cooked when the bones are pink—what Westerners might think of as undercooked. This is consistent with Chinese cooking preferences, which recommend "pink bones and red marrow," and most likely derived from traditional braising, wok frying, and steaming techniques. (Whole steamed fish is also considered properly cooked when prepared this way.) Whether the bird is spit-roasted, as is traditional, or oven-roasted, which is a recent adopted Western technology, the "pink bones and red marrow" preference persists.

When appropriate, the recipes in this book presume the "pink bones and red marrow" cooking method. Once you try it, I think you will understand its popularity in Asia and use it in all your cooking. In this method the dark meat is cooked all the way through, and the breast meat stays tender and juicy, all without the use of additional fat or oil. I have experimented with different roasting techniques and found that the best results come with a high temperature and careful timing—a kind of sophisticated balancing act. The intense heat (generally 450°F) seals in the juices, keeping the bird moist, and crisps the skin. Roasted baby chickens (page 186) are a perfect example. You will need to check the bird carefully as you get closer to the recommended cooking time. If the tendons on the drumsticks detach from the bone, for example, the bird is already overcooked.

Chicken recipes vary from the relatively complex, such as chicken curry, *cari ga* (page 184), to the exceedingly simple, such as boiled chicken served cut up over ginger- and garlic-flavored rice, *com ga* (page 103). Even this basic dish, however, can have its subtleties. Rice is cooked in the stock created by boiling the bird, a cooking method in which delicate flavors are introduced and all the ingredients are used to maximum advantage. Exploring this dish and learning from the traditional method of toasting rice prior to cooking, I have developed variations using a medley of toasted rice, fried garlic, and ginger with the stock, that yields very pronounced flavors.

Ducks are prized for their gamy meat and their eggs. They have a rich flavor, abundant fat, and consistently dark meat but take more time and effort to raise than chickens. Whole ducks are usually reserved for special or formal occasions, but cut-up duck served over egg noodles, as in *mi vit* (page 91), can be found in restaurants throughout the country.

The Vietnamese often prefer (larger) duck eggs over (smaller) chicken eggs in many of their dishes that call for eggs. Cooked and served as omelettes, duck eggs can also be julienned and served over fried rice (page 105). Used whole and shelled, they are sometimes included in special braised meat dishes such as *thit heo kho nuoc dua*, braised pork shank in coconut juice (page 206), in which they absorb the braising liquid and become a caramel brown color on the outside. Tender and moist, velvety in contrast to the texture of the braised meat, the flavors of the dish are a marvelous combination of sweet and piquant.

Duck eggs containing partial embryos, *trung vit long*, are a delicacy in Vietnam, derived from Chinese custom. (Chicken embryos are eaten in China, but Southeast Asians prefer the larger duck eggs.) The prospect of eating an embryo is offputting to many Westerners, including my mother, who is quite a gourmet and still shies away from it. I assure you, however, that hard-boiled and seasoned with a sprinkle of salt and pepper, these eggs are excellent. They are found in Chinese and Vietnamese shops; just ask for duck egg with embryo or small duck inside.

When cooked, the whites of these eggs are so hard they are often discarded. The yolks, which contain the embryo, are tender and have a slightly more pronounced flavor than regular chicken egg yolks. You may encounter the occasional crunchy (but edible) underdeveloped bone, but this is normal. If you find a feather, however, the egg was taken beyond the recommended one-week incubation time and is past its prime. My father used to tell me that the more you eat these special eggs—which are regarded as fortifiers—the smarter you get. (Whatever the specifics, I really enjoy them.)

Quail are small birds. They are harvested full grown, weighing 4 to 5 ounces. Usually spit-roasted or fried everywhere in Vietnam, when served grilled, as street vendors do, they are crispy enough to eat bones and all. Asian quail are generally meatier in proportion to their bone mass than Western quail. The quail sold in the United States, however, still yield a good amount of meat. I usually serve two per person unless I am giving a banquet at which I offer all sorts of different dishes and one will do. Because quail eggs are small, seasonal, and delicate, they are valued as a delicacy. When available, we eat them for fun, soft-boiled and braised in soy sauce (page 192).

Squab are nestling pigeons, usually harvested at 25 to 30 days old and weighing about 10 ounces. Larger than quail, and considered game meat, they are smaller than chickens. (The Vietnamese rarely prepare them at home, as one bird is too costly to prepare for one person and too small to feed a whole family.) Spit-roasted or fried, these "in-between" size birds are a bit of a treat, enjoyed most often in restaurants and at banquets. At such occasions, when enjoyed with many dishes, squab are served one-quarter bird per person. The Vietnamese dish *bo cau quay, laqué* squab (page 190), is loosely related to Chinese dishes like Peking duck. The crispy skin (the French word *laqué* derives from *lacquer*, as in furniture lacquer) and juicy, tender meat complement each other perfectly, a balance of texture and flavor, often pulled together with a sprinkle of lime-based chili and salt dip.

In Vietnamese cooking, as in Vietnamese culture in general, waste is considered anathema. Accordingly, poultry offal such as hearts and gizzards, and even specialty items like duck tongues, are eaten. Often stir-fried with vegetables throughout Vietnam, and in the South with *sate*, a chili and peanut dry paste, they are delicious. Chicken and duck feet are also braised in the style of braised pork shank in coconut juice (page 206) and may be used as a variation.

GA XAO XA
Stir-Fried Chicken with Lemongrass

Serves 4

2 tablespoons fish sauce
2 teaspoons sugar
2 tablespoons vegetable oil
2 stalks lemongrass, outer leaves
  and tough green tops
  removed, root ends trimmed,
  and stalks finely ground
2 large cloves garlic, peeled
  and minced
4 boneless chicken thighs
1 or more bird's eye or Thai
  chilies, seeded and thinly
  sliced diagonally
Scallion oil (page 50)
Nuoc cham (page 42)

T HE SOUTH, unlike the North, of Vietnam, is known for its spicy chili-based cuisine. Hot chilies are often combined with sweet, sour, and salty seasonings and herbs in order to create balance and harmony in the cooking. Rooted in a *yin* and *yang* philosophy adopted from the Chinese, Vietnamese ingredient selection strives for complementary and interdependent flavors, ultimately resulting in a uniquely balanced approach to food preparation. Unlike Thai dishes, in which "heat" really counts, or Indonesian dishes, in which chili fried rice must bring tears to your eyes or be regarded as inferior, the use of hot chilies in southern Vietnamese cooking is an integral part of a complex dualistic structure. In *ga xao xa*, one of the most popular items on any Vietnamese menu, bird's eye chilies, or more common Thai chilies, are selected to complement the sugar, lemongrass, and fish sauce.

1. Whisk the fish sauce and sugar until the sugar is completely dissolved. Stir in 1 tablespoon oil, the lemongrass, and garlic, then add the chicken and mix to coat the pieces evenly. Allow to marinate, refrigerated, for 2 hours.

2. Heat the remaining oil in a wok or nonstick pan over high heat. Cook the chicken with the chili until the chicken is cooked through and crisp at the edges, 5 to 7 minutes per side. Serve over rice, with scallion oil and *nuoc cham* on the side.

VARIATION: *Ga xao xa* can also be made with chicken breast. Thinly slice 1 pound breast meat against the grain. Then marinate it as in step 1, reducing the time to 30 minutes. In step 2, stir-fry until chicken is cooked through, about 5 minutes total.

As a time-saver, my aunt Loan often makes lemongrass and garlic paste in large amounts. Kept moist with just enough vegetable oil to cover, this paste lasts up to a week in the refrigerator. During the week, Loan often prepares either this grilled chicken or the pork chop version (page 203). Following her efficient footsteps, my mother would often make *ga xao xa* using this paste and sliced chicken breast for our meal when we came home from school. It was quick to prepare and uncomplicated for my brothers, William and Philippe, and me to eat. The flavorful chicken was simply placed over rice in a bowl, and with a pair of chopsticks we would use the "shovel method" (literally pushing rice into the mouth with the chopsticks), as most Asians do when they eat rice. My mother had it planned out so that we could eat quickly and still have plenty of time to do our homework before we went to bed. No excuses allowed!

GA KHO GUNG
Braised Chicken with Ginger

Serves 4 to 6

1 ounce dried tiger lilies
8 medium-large dried shiitake
  mushrooms
¼ cup fish sauce
2 tablespoons sugar
1 tablespoon thick soy sauce
2 pounds whole chicken legs,
  skinned (optional)
1 tablespoon vegetable oil
2 large cloves garlic, peeled
  and crushed
2 scallions, trimmed, cut into
  1-inch-long pieces and
  halved lengthwise
3 ounces fresh ginger, peeled
  and julienned
3 or more dried red chilies
2 cups chicken stock (page 61)
6 ounces bamboo shoots, thinly
  sliced into 2-inch-long by
  ½-inch-wide pieces

A SAND POT over low heat is used to braise the chicken in this dish. The pungent aroma comes from the abundant use of ginger, as well as dried shiitake mushrooms and tiger lilies, two Chinese ingredients adopted by the Vietnamese. I like to use only the best-quality dried shiitake mushrooms, which are light in color and meaty. Because they tend to sponge up the braising liquid, when you bite into them they create an explosion of sweet and spicy juices on the palate. Tiger lilies, golden-colored flower buds also known as golden needles, are prized for their texture, sweetness, and floral fragrance. They are often added to braised dishes, such as this one, or to clear soups.

1. Soak the tiger lilies and mushrooms in hot water in a bowl until rehydrated and softened, about 30 minutes. Drain and rinse. Squeeze the excess water out of the lilies and mushrooms. With a knife, remove and discard the hard stem ends of the lilies and stems of the mushrooms. Tie each lily into a knot and cut mushroom caps in half.

2. Whisk together the fish sauce, sugar, and thick soy sauce until the sugar is completely dissolved. With a cleaver, split the chicken legs at the joints so you have 2 sets of drumsticks and thighs. Then carefully chop each piece in half crosswise through the bone. Add the chicken to the sauce and allow to marinate, refrigerated, for 2 hours.

3. Put the oil, garlic, scallions, ginger, and chilies in a clay pot or heavy-bottomed pot over low heat. Increase the heat to medium and stir-fry the ingredients until fragrant, about 5 minutes. Add the chicken, marinade, stock, and mushrooms, cover, and bring to a boil. Reduce heat to low, add the tiger lilies and bamboo shoots, and simmer, partially covered, until the chicken is cooked, about 45 minutes. Serve with rice.

My father, Nhu Minh, thinks that I am a bit "over the top" for using the best-quality dried shiitake

TIGER LILIES SOAKING IN WATER

mushrooms, which are quite expensive, when making this braised chicken dish. He says, "These are for eating alone or with abalone." He has a point. Usually a braised dish containing meat and vegetables (such as this one) and served with a bowl of rice is a meal in itself. "A humble meal," he expresses, "and the best-quality mushrooms are hardly humble, but an indulgence." I cannot quite give them up, however, as these mushrooms lend their own flavor to the braising liquids as much as they soak up the combined flavors of the tiger lilies, ginger, chilies, and other ingredients. It is an indulgence, but a delicious one!

CARI GA
Chicken Curry

1¾ to 2 pounds chicken legs and wings, with or without skin

¼ cup vegetable oil

3 large cloves garlic, peeled and crushed

1 large shallot, peeled, halved, and thinly sliced

2 stalks lemongrass, outer leaves and tough green tops removed, root ends trimmed, and stalks sliced paper thin

2 tablespoons good-quality Indian curry powder

2 teaspoons Thai shrimp paste (optional)

3 or more dried red chilies

1 cup canned unsweetened coconut milk

1 cup chicken stock (page 61) or water

1 tablespoon fish sauce

3 lime leaves or lime peels

6 ounces green beans, ends trimmed, cut diagonally into 1½-inch-long pieces

12 ounces small yellow new potatoes, unpeeled or peeled

12 ounces Japanese eggplant, quartered lengthwise, then cut into 1½-inch-long pieces

CURRY POWDER, lime leaves, lemongrass, and coconut milk are essential to southern Vietnamese *cari*, or curry. Although spared from Chinese colonization, the South was introduced to Indian spices and spicing by the Khmers from neighboring Cambodia. Curry refers not only to the dish but also to the spice base—a combination of ginger, curry leaves, chilies, and seeds such as coriander, cumin, fennel, fenugreek, and mustard, as well as turmeric, which imparts a deep yellow color. To round out the flavor of the curry paste, I use preserved shrimp paste; although it is not necessary, I recommend it. I love to make curry for friends who know and enjoy Asian dishes, because even the most knowledgeable are stunned if I serve it with a Saigon *baguette* (page 119). Bread now rivals rice as an accompaniment as more Vietnamese enjoy this French-derived "sauce scoop" when they eat their *cari*.

1. With a cleaver, separate the chicken legs at the joint, so you have 2 drumsticks and thighs, then cut each piece in half crosswise through the bone. Discard the wing tips and separate the wings at the joints.

2. Heat the oil in a clay pot or large heavy-bottomed pot over low heat. Increase the heat to medium and stir-fry the garlic and shallot until lightly golden, about 3 minutes. Add the lemongrass, curry powder, shrimp paste, and chilies and cook until the flavors come together, about 3 minutes.

3. Add the chicken pieces and brown on all sides, 8 to 10 minutes total. Add coconut milk, chicken stock or water, fish sauce, and lime leaves, cover, and bring just to a boil. Reduce heat to medium-low, add the green beans, potatoes, and eggplant, mix well, and cook, partially covered, until the chicken starts to fall off the bone and potatoes are fork tender, 45 to 50 minutes, turning once or twice during cooking. At this point skim off as much fat as you desire. Serve with Saigon *baguettes* or rice on the side.

VARIATION: Duck can be substituted for the chicken. Unlike chicken, the entire duck is dark meat, so I usually use any parts I have. Cut duck into medium-size chunks through the bones.

Cari ga is a great use of the less expensive cuts of chicken, such as legs and wings. Dark meat tends to stay moist and is preferable in a dish that cooks for an hour or more. Curiously, in many Vietnamese restaurants, you may find curry to be quite oily. Vietnamese chefs do not bother degreasing it because they prize the fat. In my family, the fat content is determined by the taste of the person who sits at the head of the table. When I make this dish for my husband, I take the skin off the chicken, but when I make curry for my father, I leave the skin on.

GA NUONG TOI
Garlic-Roasted Baby Chickens

Serves 4 to 8

½ cup mushroom soy sauce

2 tablespoons sugar

1 tablespoon honey

2 tablespoons vegetable oil

6 large cloves garlic, peeled, crushed, and minced

2 tablespoons freshly cracked black pepper

Four 10- to 12-ounce baby chickens or 2½ pounds of chicken parts

GARLIC-ROASTED baby chicken is popular not only in Vietnam but in Cambodia, too. The spiciness of the garlic and freshly cracked black pepper combined with the honey and mushroom soy sauce creates a balance of flavors that is memorable. The tender meat and crispy texture of the skin are "finger-lickin'" good. This dish is most often prepared with whole chicken, chicken parts, or quail. I prefer using whole baby chickens, often sold as *poussin* at the butcher's. They are more tender and juicier than quail because of their higher fat content. You can also use cornish hens; although not as juicy and tender as baby chickens, they have a great flavor. The plump birds make a generous single serving.

1. Whisk together the mushroom soy sauce, sugar, and honey in a bowl until the sugar is completely dissolved. Stir in 1 tablespoon oil, the garlic, and pepper. Carefully loosen the skin of the chickens by gently running your fingers between the skin and the meat (breast and legs). Try not to tear the skin in the process. Put the birds in a plastic bag, add the marinade, seal the bag, and shake it a few times. Marinate the chickens, refrigerated, for 2 hours, shaking the bag every 30 minutes.

2. Place the rack in the middle of the oven and preheat oven to 450°F. With a cleaver, cut through the center bone of the breast lengthwise and flatten the birds. Place skin side up on a rack set over a roasting pan and roast until the juices run clear, about 40 minutes.

3. To roast the chickens whole, tie the drumsticks together with kitchen string and roast the chickens breast side down for 15 minutes, then breast side up for 30 minutes. Serve with *com ga*, ginger and garlic rice (page 103), substituting the garlic roasted baby chickens for the boiled chicken.

VARIATION: *Chim nuong toi* is a variation on the recipe using

QUAIL AND BABY CHICKEN

quail. You will need eight 4- to 5-ounce quail. Follow the recipe, roasting the birds for 20 minutes in step 2. If you prefer to serve the quails whole, then follow step 3, roasting them breast side down for 10 minutes, then breast side up for 15 minutes more.

Walking through Hanoi one afternoon, I was pleased by the sight of spit-roasted quail, *chim nuong* *toi*, sharing space with incense, imitation paper money edged with gold or silver, candies, pastries, desserts, fruit, and other prepared foods. All items were available either for offerings at the Buddhist temple or for tourists who were enticed by the aromas.

GA XE PHAY
Chicken Salad

Serves 4 to 6

2 tablespoons fish sauce
2 tablespoons lime juice
1 tablespoon white rice
   vinegar or white vinegar
2 tablespoons sugar
3 cups julienned green cabbage
1 tablespoon coarse sea salt
1½ cups julienned carrot
1 large shallot, peeled and
   thinly sliced lengthwise
1 large clove garlic, peeled
   and minced
1 or more red bird's eye or Thai
   chilies, seeded and julienned
1 pound cooked chicken
   breast meat, shredded or
   thinly sliced
⅓ cup julienned mint leaves
2 tablespoons chopped unsalted roasted peanuts

THIS COLD SHREDDED chicken, cabbage, and carrot salad is sort of the Vietnamese equivalent of coleslaw. Served as an appetizer in many Vietnamese restaurants, it is tossed with a rice vinegar or plain white vinegar dressing. (Western wine vinegars should not be used, as their distinct flavors would be overpowering.) While the salad is best made with either freshly boiled or steamed chicken, leftover roast chicken is also acceptable. Although the vegetables are normally served raw, I prefer to cure them in salt, which tenderizes them a bit and at the same time gets rid of their excess water content. They become more pleasant to the palate but still retain their necessary "crunch."

1. Whisk together the fish sauce, lime juice, vinegar, and sugar in a large bowl until the sugar is completely dissolved.

2. Toss the cabbage with 2 teaspoons salt and the carrot with 1 teaspoon salt in separate bowls. Allow to stand for 30 minutes. Drain and rinse both vegetables. Place the cabbage and carrot in a clean kitchen towel, then twist to squeeze out any remaining water. Add the cabbage, carrot, shallot, garlic, and chili to the dressing. Mix well and allow to marinate for 20 minutes. Toss the chicken and all but 1 tablespoon of mint with the salad. Serve the salad garnished with the peanuts and remaining mint.

VIT QUAY
Laqué Duck

Serves 4 to 8

⅓ cup fish sauce

1 tablespoon thick soy sauce

2 tablespoons honey

2 teaspoons five-spice powder

One 5½-pound Long Island
duck

2 ounces fresh ginger, peeled,
cut into 4 slices, and lightly
crushed

4 scallions, trimmed, halved
crosswise, and lightly
crushed

U NLIKE PEKING DUCK, which is generally served in three courses—crispy skin, stir-fried meat, and bone soup—Vietnamese roast duck is enjoyed skin and meat in the same bite and accompanied by pickled vegetables. Although much less time-consuming to prepare than its Chinese counterpart, it is just as tasty. A beautiful crisp skin is achieved by keeping the duck uncovered in the refrigerator overnight, allowing it to dry out, then poking holes in the skin with a skewer to let fat drip out and baste the bird as it roasts. The addition of dried shiitake mushrooms placed under the skin makes an elegant variation on the recipe.

1. Whisk together the fish sauce, thick soy sauce, honey, and five-spice powder in a large dish. Carefully loosen the skin of the duck by gently running your fingers between the skin and the meat (breast and legs). Try not to tear the skin in the process. Place the duck in the marinade and rub the marinade over it, inside and out and between the flesh and the skin. Drain and refrigerate the duck, uncovered and turning occasionally, for 24 hours.

2. Preheat the oven to 425°F. Place the ginger and scallions in the cavity of the duck, then truss it with kitchen string. With a metal skewer, poke the skin of the duck a few times on the breast and legs. Place the duck breast side down on a rack, and roast for 45 minutes, basting it every 15 minutes with the drippings. Turn the duck breast side up, and continue roasting (basting every 15 minutes) until juices run clear, about 45 minutes.

VARIATION: To roast the duck with dried shiitake mushrooms, soak 20 to 24 medium-large mushrooms in hot water to cover in a bowl until rehydrated and softened, about 30 minutes. Drain and squeeze the mushrooms to get rid of the excess water. With a knife, remove the stems. Toss the caps in the marinade until evenly coated. Place the mushrooms between the flesh and skin of the duck's breast and legs. Marinate and roast the duck as directed.

BO CAU QUAY
Laqué Squab

Serves 4 to 8

⅓ cup fish sauce
1 tablespoon thick soy sauce
2 tablespoons honey
1 tablespoon vegetable oil
2 teaspoons five-spice powder
Four 10- to 12-ounce squabs
2 ounces fresh ginger,
    peeled and cut into 4 slices,
    and lightly crushed
4 scallions, trimmed, halved
    crosswise, and lightly
    crushed

L A Q U É ,   A   W O R D taken from the French, meaning "lacquered," refers to a shiny finish, as in lacquered furniture. I like to roast squab at a very high heat in the oven. This allows the meat to sear while keeping the juices in and allowing the skin to crisp. *Bo cau quay* is a special item often ordered at elaborate formal banquets in Asian restaurants. Sometimes, for a birthday, New Year's, or other celebration, I will prepare squabs at home. I especially like to serve them with traditional pickled vegetables and a mix of lime juice, crushed chili, and salt on the side for last-minute seasoning—which complement the sweet honey-glazed, crisp skin and moist flesh of the birds.

1. Whisk together the fish sauce, thick soy sauce, honey, oil, and five-spice powder in a large dish. Carefully loosen the skin of the squab by running your fingers between the skin and the meat (breast and legs) without tearing the skin. Place the squab in the marinade and coat evenly, inside and out and between the flesh and the skin. Drain and refrigerate the birds, uncovered and turning occasionally, for 24 hours.

2. Preheat the oven to 425°F. Place an equal amount of ginger and scallion in the cavity of each bird, then truss each with kitchen string. Place the squab breast side down on a rack and roast 15 minutes. Turn them breast side up and continue roasting for 20 to 25 minutes more. Serve with pickled vegetables and rice.

Friends call me all the time to ask which restaurants to go to in Chinatown and what to order. I always tell them to go as a group so they can order a tasting menu and experience a cultural as well as a culinary event. A traditional banquet is balanced with fish, seafood, vegetables, starch, meat, and poultry. I like to order squab as the poultry course because it is unusual. Squab have a delicious gamy flavor, and their beautiful crisp golden skin makes them the center of conversation.

TRUNG CHUNG
Steamed Egg Pâté

Serves 4 to 6

½ ounce dried cellophane noodles

4 dried cloud ear mushrooms

6 large chicken eggs or regular duck eggs

4 ounces ground pork (70% lean)

3 boneless anchovy fillets, crushed into a coarse paste

2 scallions, trimmed and minced

Vegetable oil

Spicy lemongrass soy dipping sauce (page 45)

THIS STEAMED EGG PÂTÉ—similar in texture to French pâté—is lightly flavored and easy to make. A small amount of ground pork and some preserved salted fish are added to the egg mixture to enhance what might otherwise be a simple steamed omelette. Because preserved fish can be hard to find, I have substituted good-quality anchovies here. The taste is a little less pungent but still good. *Trung chung* is traditionally eaten with rice and served with soy sauce. Serving it with a spicy lemongrass soy sauce is also delicious.

1. Soak the cellophane noodles and cloud ear mushrooms in lukewarm water to cover in a bowl until rehydrated and softened, about 15 minutes. Drain and squeeze the noodles and cloud ears to get rid of the excess water. Coarsely chop the noodles and cloud ears.

2. Mix eggs with 1 tablespoon water in a mixing bowl and whisk until pale yellow. Add the noodles, cloud ears, ground pork, anchovies, and scallions and mix until well combined.

3. Fill the bottom third of a wok with water, fit a bamboo steamer with lid over it, and place the wok over high heat. Pour the egg mixture into a well-oiled small heat-proof bowl (about 2 cups in volume); ideally the mixture should come to about ¼ inch below the rim of the bowl. When the steamer is filled with steam, place the bowl on the bamboo rack and cover the steamer with the lid. Steam the eggs until cooked through, 20 to 30 minutes. Serve with rice and spicy lemongrass soy sauce for dipping on the side.

Trung chung can be served for breakfast, lunch, or dinner. Often part of a simple meal, it is served over cooked jasmine rice with grilled meats, or as a side dish to plain rice porridge accompanied by other side dishes—pan-fried thinly sliced Chinese sweet pork sausages, preserved *tien sin* cabbage, sardines in oil with thinly sliced fresh chilies and soy sauce.

CHIM TRUNG KHO
Braised Quail Eggs

Serves 4

12 quail eggs
1 tablespoon vegetable oil
2 scallions, trimmed, cut into
    1-inch-long pieces, and
    julienned
2 large cloves garlic, peeled
    and lightly crushed
2 ounces fresh ginger, peeled
    and julienned
½ cup chicken stock (page 61)
1 tablespoon thin soy sauce
½ tablespoon thick soy sauce
1 teaspoon sugar

QUAIL EGGS have been a delicacy for thousands of years. Seasonal, hard to find, difficult to harvest, they were expensive. Today, because of quail farming, these eggs—about the size of acorns with black-spotted shells—are more common and have come down in price. In this recipe they are soft-boiled (egg whites are cooked through, but the yolks remain slightly soft) prior to shelling and braising. Although braised quail eggs make a wonderful dish, I also encourage you to try them as a substitute in *thit heo kho nuoc dua*, braised pork shank in coconut juice (page 206), which will give the dish a more delicate presentation.

1. Gently place the eggs in a pot and just cover with water. Bring the water to a gentle simmer over medium-low heat and cook the eggs for about 2 minutes. Remove eggs and rinse under cold water to cool completely. Carefully shell the eggs, being careful to keep the eggs intact.

2. In a small sand pot or heavy-bottomed pot, heat the oil over low heat. Increase heat to medium-low, add the scallions, garlic, and ginger, and stir-fry until fragrant, 3 to 5 minutes. Add the chicken stock, thin and thick soy sauces, sugar, and eggs and simmer until the eggs are a rich golden color, about 15 minutes.

QUAIL EGGS

PORK AND BEEF

PORK IN VIETNAM is an integral part of the cuisine and by far the most commonly eaten meat. This goes beyond simple preference for the meat or its flavor. It is tied to the animal's place in the economy and culture of the country. Pigs are prized farm animals for several reasons. Nearly all of the animal is considered useful, from its meat to its internal organs to even its skin, feet, and head. The animal is simple to raise, living on scraps. It is large enough to feed a family and can easily be slaughtered in times of scarcity. Its meat and fat can be cured and preserved; what is not eaten immediately can be stored or sold. Additionally, the price of pork—especially the fattier cuts such as pork belly—is lower than that of other meats, even lower than the price of poultry.

It is generally believed that the pigs from Hue, former seat of Vietnam's imperial court and its complex culinary culture, are the best. They are traditionally fed on rice and banana tree parts, rendering the meat sweet and tender. This meat complements perfectly the refined and delicate cuisine of Hue, located in Vietnam's central region. One of their more interesting recipes is *Hue com sen*, or sticky rice with pork and lotus seeds, wrapped and steamed in lotus leaf (page 106). Throughout Vietnam, especially at formal holiday dinners or wedding feasts, a roasted whole suckling pig—a great indulgence—is prepared. Seasoned according to the region and its tradition, the basic cooking method is the same: slow spit-roasting over an open wood fire. Derived from its use in Chinese culture, roast whole suckling pig is served as the center of attention and often the crowning achievement at such feasts. It is uniquely delicious: Roast suckling pig is perhaps the most succulent pork you will ever eat. Extraordinarily tender as a result of exclusive milk feeding and slow roasting, the meat falls off the bones as you carve it and melts in your mouth. The skin is crispy and sweet like candy. The internal organs—tongue, heart, kidneys—are edible and exquisite.

In Vietnam, vegetable oil was historically scarce and expensive, so the Vietnamese traditionally prepared many of their dishes using pork fat. *Cha gio*, the ubiquitous Vietnamese spring rolls (page 198), for example, were cooked in lard, or rendered pork fat, as were omelettes and sautéed vegetables. Today, while some Vietnamese continue to prefer pork fat over the lighter vegetable oil, many others have switched. As new ingredients have become available, or simply less expensive, the cuisine has evolved. When I visited Hanoi, I was invited to share in a traditional Tet holiday feast for which the spring rolls were pan-fried in pork fat. This interested me, because at home my mother deep-fried them in vegetable oil. She knew that lard gives the food an extra layer of flavor but preferred to limit the amount of pork fat she used because of its high cholesterol content. Accordingly, we use vegetable oil for day-to-day meals. Like my host in Hanoi, however, we occasionally indulge in the more flavorful pork fat as a holiday treat.

Pork and beef are often cooked in similar ways: ground, sliced, steamed, grilled, stir-fried, and simmered in soups. As with pork, all the parts of beef, including the fat and the white and red offal, are eaten. The availability, price, and popularity of beef in Vietnam vary by region, however. Cattle are most commonly raised in the North because of its plentiful grazing land. Reasonably priced, beef is enjoyed there almost daily, starting in the morning with Hanoi's famous beef and noodle soup, *pho*. Other popular northern dishes include *cha dum*, or beef pâté (page 213), *bo vien*, beef meatballs (page 215), and *bo kho ca rot*, spicy beef and carrot stew (page 216). In the South, where the meat is expensive, the Vietnamese generally reserve it for special occasions. (*Pho*, which uses extremely thin slices of beef, is a notable exception; it is consumed everywhere in Vietnam.) Some Saigon restaurants now import beef from New Zealand and Australia as a specialty item, believing it to be superior meat, much in the way Americans think of Japanese *Kobe* beef. They also offer the extraordinary Hanoi-derived meal, *bo bay mon*, beef seven ways.

When I was in Hanoi, I visited restaurants specializing in *bo bay mon*. Beef is served literally seven different ways, with seven distinctly different beef dishes brought to the table in sequence. This is the tour-de-force of the North, its unique specialty, tied to both its indigenous cattle-raising industry and periods of dominance by beef-loving Mongol invaders. Normally, ritualistic observance of traditional preparation and presentation methods is expected, with only minor variations from one restaurant to another. The meal starts with beef fondue, *bo nhung dam* (page 208), and ends with rice porridge with beef, *chao bo* (page 85). In between come beef in pepper leaves, *bo la lot* (page 209); lime-cured beef salad, *goi bo* (page 210); grilled lemongrass beef, *bo nuong xa* (page 212); beef pâté, *cha dum* (page 213); and grilled beef patties, *cha bo* (page 214). Despite the predominance of beef, the intent here, as in all Vietnamese cuisine, is to balance the meal. Vinegar cuts the fat in one dish, as do lime curing, grilling, fish sauce, and lemongrass in others. The final porridge settles the stomach. If you are a meat eater or you want to offer a special tasting menu, you might consider trying this memorable combination of dishes. Between the traditional recipes and the variations in this book, you will be able to re-create the ritual, or come up with your own interpretation. NOTE: Each beef dish here can and often does stand alone. Rice porridge with beef, *chao bo*, for example, is commonly eaten for breakfast in the North.

CHA LUA
Pork Pâté

Makes 1

3 tablespoons fish sauce
2 tablespoons vegetable oil
1 tablespoon sugar
1 small shallot, peeled and
    minced
1 small clove garlic, peeled
    and minced
Freshly ground black pepper
2 pounds pork butt, thinly
    sliced, or ground pork
    (70% lean)
¼ cup potato starch
2 teaspoons baking powder
1 sheet heavy duty aluminum
    foil, 9 inches by 12 inches
1 sheet plastic wrap, 9 inches
    by 12 inches
1 banana leaf, trimmed to
    roughly 9 inches by 12 inches
    (there is no substitute for
    this leaf; if you cannot find it,
    triple the amount of the
    plastic wrap)

S IMPLE TO MAKE, *cha lua* is the quintessential Vietnamese *charcuterie*. Although it is similar to the French idea of pâté, beginning with pork, it contains no cognac or herbs and is more delicate in flavor and texture. In fact, considering its look and texture, it could be mistaken for Italian bologna! (The taste, I assure you, is very different.) Unlike French pâté, *cha lua* is wrapped in banana leaves rather than fatback and steamed rather than baked. It is excellent served sliced with a rice flour *baguette* (page 119) or with Vietnamese table salad (page 52) and *nuoc cham* (page 42) on the side . Sliced and served in soups such as *hu tieu do bien* (page 92), it is the perfect complement to the aromatic herbs.

1. Whisk together the fish sauce, oil, and sugar until the sugar is completely dissolved. Stir in the shallot and garlic and season to taste with pepper. Add the pork and pound the meat into the marinade until evenly coated. Allow to marinate, refrigerated, for 1 hour.

2. Place the pork in a container and put it in the freezer for 1 hour. Transfer the partially frozen pork to a food processor and pulse to loosen the meat, about 5 minutes. Add the potato starch and baking powder and continue pulsing until the mixture has a firm, smooth, and pale paste-like consistency, about 5 minutes more.

3. Bring a pot filled with water to a boil over high heat. Meanwhile, lay flat the aluminum foil on a clean work surface. Lay a sheet of plastic wrap of the same size on top, then lay the banana leaf on the plastic wrap and lightly oil it. Form the pork mixture into a thick sausage about 3 inches in diameter by 7 inches long and place it on top of the banana leaf. Fold the 3-layer wrap over the pork, fold in the sides, and roll it into a bundle. The foil should be on the outside. Tie the bundle with kitchen string as you would a pork roast. Boil, uncovered, until cooked through, about 50 minutes.

CHA GIO
Spring Rolls

Makes 40

2 ounces dried cellophane
    noodles
1 ounce dried cloud ear
    mushrooms
1 pound ground pork (70% lean)
1 medium yellow onion,
    peeled and minced
1 large clove garlic, peeled
    and minced
1 carrot, peeled and grated
1 large egg
Coarse sea salt
Freshly ground black pepper
40 triangular rice papers
Vegetable oil for deep frying
1 bunch mint, leaves only
Table salad (page 52)
Nuoc cham (page 42)

SPRING ROLLS are made all over Vietnam. In the South they are called *cha gio* and traditionally made with lean pork and carrot; in the North they are called *nem ran* and traditionally made with fatty pork and kohlrabi. At home we use lean pork or a combination of pork with crab or shrimp. All are tasty, and all are "correct," in the sense that variations on the recipe are common. Cellophane noodles and cloud ear mushrooms are used primarily as fillers and for texture, as their flavors are close to none. As delicious as the spring rolls are on their own, they are even better with "the trimmin's." From the table salad, pick a lettuce leaf and place a couple of cucumber slices, some julienned carrot, and a leaf or two of fresh mint on it. Place a spring roll on top, roll up the lettuce leaf to enclose it, and dip it in the *nuoc cham*. The resulting combined textures and tastes—the crispy roll and crunchy vegetables; the sour, sweet, and spicy flavors of the dipping sauce—make it worth spending the time to do it right. In Vietnam, *cha gio* take some time to make, and so are usually reserved for special celebrations or eaten in restaurants.

1. Soak the cellophane noodles and cloud ear mushrooms in lukewarm water to cover until rehydrated, about 15 minutes. Drain and squeeze the noodles and cloud ears to get rid of the excess water. Finely chop the noodles and cloud ears and put them in a mixing bowl.

2. Add the ground pork, onion, garlic, carrot, and egg and season with salt and pepper. Mix the ingredients with your hands until evenly combined.

3. Pour lukewarm water about 1 inch deep into a square or rectangular dish. Separate and soak 4 rice

papers at a time until pliable, about 5 minutes. Place a clean kitchen towel on your work surface, then place each triangle, rounded side near you, on the towel. With another kitchen towel, blot each wrapper until it is no longer wet but remains sticky. Place about 1 teaspoon filling 1 inch from the rounded edge. Fold the wrapper once over the filling, then fold in the sides and continue rolling tightly to the pointed end. Repeat this process with the remaining rice papers and filling.

4. Heat the oil in a wok to 360° to 375°F over medium-high heat. Test the heat of the oil with one roll; the oil should sizzle around the roll but not so vigorously as to destroy the spring roll. Fry a few rolls at a time, turning them once immediately to prevent them from sticking together, then turning them occasionally until golden on all sides, 3 to 5 minutes. Drain on paper towels and serve with mint, table salad, and *nuoc cham.*

VARIATION: Substitute 8 ounces fresh shredded crabmeat or minced shrimp for half of the ground pork amount and follow directions.

HINT: As you make *cha gio,* stack them, covering each layer with plastic wrap to keep them from drying out, and refrigerate. Serve them freshly fried the next day. Freeze leftover rolls for up to a month; reheat them in a 375°F oven for 15 minutes, turning once.

Nem Nuong
Pork Meatballs

Makes 20

2 tablespoons fish sauce

1 tablespoon vegetable oil

2 teaspoons sugar

1 small shallot, peeled and
minced

1 small clove garlic, peeled
and minced

Freshly ground black pepper

1 pound pork butt, thinly sliced,
or coarsely ground pork

2 tablespoons potato starch

Bamboo skewers, soaked for
20 minutes and drained

Table salad (page 52)

Nuoc leo (page 44)

N EM NUONG is a Vietnamese pork meatball and a specialty of the central region of Nha Trang. Potato starch
gives the meatballs their *quenelle*-like smooth and somewhat springy
texture, in contrast to, for example, the grainy texture of Italian
meatballs. The uncooked paste has raw shallot and garlic in it, and
for some it can be hard to digest. If you prefer, do as the French
would: Sauté the shallot and garlic until the shallot is translucent
and slightly golden prior to mixing them into the meat paste. That
step breaks down the acid, releasing the sugars of both shallot and
garlic and making them easier to digest. A perfect and traditional compliment to these sweet meatballs is *nuoc leo*, peanut sauce.

1. Whisk together the fish sauce,
oil, and sugar until the sugar is
completely dissolved. Stir in the
shallot and garlic, and season with
pepper. Add the pork and pound
the meat into the marinade until
evenly coated. Allow to marinate,
refrigerated, for 1 hour.

2. Place the pork between the palms
of your hands and squeeze tightly
to get rid of the excess liquid. Put
the drained meat in a container and
place in the freezer for 1 hour. Put
the partially frozen pork in a food
processor and pulse to loosen the
meat, about 2 minutes. Add the
potato starch and continue pulsing
until mixture has a firm, paste-like
consistency, about 5 minutes.

3. Pinch off about 1 tablespoon of
the pork paste and form it into a
ball. Repeat the process until you
have used up the paste.

POTATO STARCH

4. Depending on how long the skewers are, slide 3 to 5 meatballs onto each skewer. Grill over a barbecue (make sure the flames have subsided and coals are red with white ashes) or on a well-oiled grill pan over medium-high heat until the meatballs are cooked through, rolling them around in the pan, about 6 minutes total.

Traditionally, when making this dish or similar foods such as *bo vien*, beef meatballs (page 215), or *cha lua*, pork pâté (page 197), you begin with a chunk of meat. Then you slice it, marinate it, freeze it for 1 hour or so, and process it into a paste. One time I had leftover ground meat and decided to make this recipe using it so as not to waste the meat. I marinated it, froze it, then processed it. Because it was already ground, it took much less time to process, and the end result was just as delicious. It works well when you are in a hurry.

SUON NUONG XA
Grilled Lemongrass Pork Tenderloin Skewers

Serves 4

¼ cup fish sauce

1 tablespoon thick soy sauce

3 tablespoons sugar

2 tablespoons vegetable oil

2 stalks lemongrass, outer leaves
   and tough green tops
   removed, root ends trimmed,
   and stalks finely ground

1 large shallot, peeled and
   finely chopped

2 large cloves garlic, crushed,
   peeled, and finely chopped

1 pound pork tenderloin, thinly
   sliced against the grain

16 bamboo skewers, soaked
   for 20 minutes and drained

½ cup chopped unsalted
   roasted peanuts

Table salad (page 52)

Nuoc cham (page 42)

THESE THIN STRIPS of pork tenderloin marinated in lemongrass are best grilled outdoors over a barbecue because they absorb the smoky flavor and the edges of the meat become crisp. They are also delicious when prepared indoors, either on a grill or in a skillet over high heat. *Suon nuong xa* can be enjoyed in many different ways: tossed with thin rice vermicelli, shredded lettuce, carrot, cucumber, chopped roasted peanuts, and drizzled with *nuoc cham*; sandwiched in a rice flour *baguette* (page 119) with fresh cilantro, some chili sauce, and a few tomato slices; over rice with a side of pickled vegetables (page 48); or wrapped in a softened rice paper, with some mint, star fruit, and drizzled with scallion oil, then dipped in *nuoc cham*. Full of flavor no matter which way you eat them, these pork tenderloin skewers quickly become a favorite.

1. Stir together the fish sauce, soy sauce, sugar, and oil until the sugar is completely dissolved. Add the lemongrass, shallot, garlic, and pork and mix to coat the meat evenly. Allow to marinate for 1 hour, refrigerated.

2. Depending on how long the skewers are, slide 2 to 4 slices of pork onto each skewer so the meat is flat with the skewer going through the slices several times. Grill over a barbecue (make sure that the flames have subsided and the coals are red with white ashes). Alternatively, heat a well-oiled grill pan or nonstick skillet over high heat and cook half of the skewered pork tenderloin until the edges crisp, about 1 minute per side. Heat remaining oil and cook the rest of the skewered pork. Remove the skewers from the grilled pork.

3. To serve with the table salad: Shred the lettuce and divide among 4 large bowls. Add in layers equal portions of carrot, cucumber, rice

consists of the bare essentials: a sidewalk corner and four bricks set around coals with a grill set on top. The surrounding streets are fragrant with lemongrass. Passersby are enticed by the perfume of spicy meat grilling, then fed subtle, delicious morsels. During the summer, my husband craves grilled meats, especially the lemongrass pork chops. He will offer to grill them over the hibachi, even if it means squatting on our fire escape in the city.

LEMONGRASS: SLICED, CRUSHED, WHOLE, AND GROUND

vermicelli, and grilled pork. Sprinkle peanuts and drizzle *nuoc cham* over each serving.

VARIATION: Substitute eight 4-ounce pork chops cut about ¼ inch thick (bone in or boneless) for the thinly sliced pork tenderloin. In step 1 marinate the chops for 4 hours, refrigerated. In step 2 cook chops 3 minutes per side. Serve over rice with pickled vegetables on the side. Sprinkle peanuts and drizzle *nuoc cham* over each serving.

After *pho*, the fragrant rice noodle soups sold by street vendors, the second most popular streetcart foods are grilled meats. Almost everywhere you go in Vietnam, street vendors set up shop from early morning until late in the evening. A typical shop, no bigger than a couple of square feet,

THIT HEO NUONG
Stir-Fried Pork Ribs

Serves 4 to 6

2 pounds lean pork ribs, cut
    crosswise through the bone
    into 1½-inch pieces
2 tablespoons vegetable oil
2 large cloves garlic, peeled
    and minced
2 tablespoons hoisin sauce
2 tablespoons fish sauce

T HIS STIR-FRIED pork rib recipe uses a sauce developed by a family friend who is of Chinese-Vietnamese heritage. Madame Nguy, a wonderful cook who prepared traditional Vietnamese dishes for her family in Saigon for years and now lives in Paris, loves to experiment with the culinary traditions of both cultures. Her sauce for this recipe is a perfectly balanced combination of sweet Chinese hoisin sauce and salty Vietnamese fish sauce. These ribs are not only delicious stir-fried but also grilled on the barbecue.

1. Bring a pot filled with water to a boil over high heat. Blanch the ribs for 10 minutes and drain.

2. Heat the oil in a wok over high heat. Add the ribs and garlic and stir-fry until the ribs are slightly golden at the edges, about 15 minutes. Add the hoisin sauce and toss until each rib is well coated. Add the fish sauce and continue stir-frying until the liquid cooks out and the hoisin caramelizes on the ribs, about 20 minutes.

VARIATION: Keeping the ribs whole, you can mix all the ingredients and marinate the ribs (without blanching) for about 4 hours, refrigerated. Then grill them.

HOISIN SAUCE

Thit Heo Kho Mang

Braised Pork with Bamboo Shoots

Serves 4 to 6

¼ cup fish sauce
1 tablespoon thick soy sauce
2 tablespoons granulated sugar
4 large cloves garlic, peeled
  and crushed
2 ounces ginger, peeled and
  julienned
1 pound pork shoulder cut
  into 1-inch cubes
2 cups simple pork stock
  variation (page 62) or water
1 pound bamboo shoots,
  thinly sliced lengthwise
Freshly ground white or black
  pepper

Bamboo shoots are a very popular vegetable in the North, and this dish is one of the classic ways of preparing them. Traditionally it is made with bamboo preserved in salt. Rich golden in color, preserved bamboo tends to have a stronger flavor and is firm in texture. It is widely available in Chinatown either sliced or in large chunks. If you feel like experimenting with preserved bamboo, be sure to soak it in water for about 3 hours prior to using to get rid of the excess salt. I like this dish to be a little more subtle, and so I use either fresh or canned bamboo. I recommend small, tender, whole winter shoots (labeled as such). Blanch canned bamboo for a few minutes in boiling water prior to using it in the recipe.

1. Whisk together fish sauce, soy sauce, and sugar in a bowl until the sugar is dissolved completely. Add garlic, ginger, and pork and mix to coat meat evenly. Allow to marinate, refrigerated, turning the meat every hour, for 3 to 4 hours.

2. Put pork with marinade and pork stock in a clay pot, or heavy-bottomed pot, and bring to a gentle simmer over medium-low heat. Cook, covered, for 1½ hours. Add bamboo shoots and continue to cook until meat is fork tender, about 1 hour more. Serve with rice.

THIT HEO KHO NUOC DUA
Braised Pork Shank in Coconut Juice

Serves 4 to 6

4 to 6 chicken or duck eggs or
   12 quail eggs

⅓ cup sugar

3 cups young coconut juice
   (if using fish sauce)

½ cup fish sauce or thin soy
   sauce

Two 2-pound pork shanks,
   bone in and with rind

5 scallions, trimmed, halved,
   and white bulbs lightly
   crushed

2 ounces fresh ginger, sliced
   and lightly crushed

3 large cloves garlic, peeled
   and lightly crushed

3 or more dried red chilies

5 star anise

½ teaspoon five-spice powder

EVERY FAMILY has its own interpretation of this braised pork dish. The traditional Vietnamese approach uses fish sauce in combination with young (or "green") coconut juice, available fresh or canned. The clear coconut juice—as opposed to milk—tames the very pungent fish sauce. Young coconut juice is not always available, however, so we often prepare this dish using the more subtle soy sauce—a product of Chinese origin—to dilute the caramel (see Variation). This is not an unusual substitution, as this dish is derived from the classic Chinese braised caramelized pork. Fatty and gelatinous cuts of pork, such as shank and feet on the bone—with the skin left intact to keep the meat moist during the hours-long braising—are best. Skim off the fat, leaving just a few drops for a glistening effect when serving.

1. Gently place the eggs in a pot and just cover with water. Bring to a gentle simmer over medium-low heat and cook until soft-boiled, about 5 minutes (about 2 minutes for quail eggs). Rinse under cold water and allow to cool completely. Carefully shell the eggs, being careful to keep the eggs intact.

2. Make a caramel by combining the sugar and ¼ cup water in a heavy-bottomed pot over medium heat. When the sugar is melted and turns a rich gold, about 8 minutes, remove the pot from the heat and stir in the coconut juice and fish sauce (or 3 cups water and the soy sauce). Reduce the heat to low and stir until the sauce is completely smooth. Add the pork shanks, turning them to coat evenly on all sides. Add the scallions, ginger, garlic, chilies, star anise, and five-spice powder and simmer, covered, turning the shanks occasionally, until the meat is fork tender, about 4 hours.

3. With a ladle, skim off the fat and add the eggs. Continue simmering, ladling sauce over the eggs occasionally, until the eggs

turn golden and cook through, about 5 minutes.

VARIATION: This sweet braised dish is equally delicious made with whole pig's feet or beef tripe cut in bite-size chunks. Fill a pot with water and bring it to a boil over high heat. Blanch 4 pig's feet or 1½ pounds beef tripe for 15 minutes, then drain thoroughly. Proceed with the recipe, cooking over low heat until fork tender, 6 to 8 hours.

Like most stews, no matter which country of origin, this northern braised pork dish is even better re-heated. When I plan on having friends over for dinner, I braise the pork a day ahead to let the flavors blend overnight. Typically, after feasting on the stew, the meat is gone, but some of the best remains: the sauce. For a second meal, I sometimes add more soft-boiled eggs to the leftover sauce and simmer them over low heat. Served over a bowl of steaming rice, the egg and sauce combination makes a sweet and satisfying lunch, dinner, or snack.

Bo Nhung Dam
Beef Fondue

Serves 4 to 6

1 teaspoon vegetable oil
1 large clove garlic, peeled
  and lightly crushed
1 large shallot, peeled and
  thinly sliced
1 stalk lemongrass, outer leaves
  and tough green tops
  removed, root end trimmed,
  and stalk quartered crosswise
  and lightly crushed
Dash sesame oil (optional)
1 cup beef stock (page 64)
1 cup white rice vinegar
2 tablespoons sugar
1 pound beef eye of round,
  thinly sliced against the grain
  (2-inch by 1-inch strips)
Table salad (page 52)
Traditional herbs (page 53)
Mam nem (page 46)

CLASSIC VIETNAMESE beef fondue is served as the first course of *bo bay mon*, beef seven ways. It is a direct influence of the Mongolian hot pot called *da bin low*. Thin slices of raw beef are served alongside a steaming broth. The broth, which has a strong white rice vinegar base, is usually combined with water and sometimes with beef stock. It is used as a cooking medium, and minor, personal variations are sometimes employed. My aunt Loan's family, who settled in Saigon, uses a light beef stock instead of plain water and also adds a hint of sesame oil. At the table it is up to the individual to cook a serving of beef to his or her desired taste. Once cooked, the meat is wrapped in a softened rice paper, then dipped in a pungent anchovy and pineapple sauce.

1. Heat the oil in a fondue pot set over an open flame. Stir-fry the garlic, shallots, and lemongrass until fragrant and lightly golden, about 7 minutes. Add the sesame oil, beef stock, 1 cup water, vinegar, and sugar and cook until the sugar is completely dissolved.

2. Have each guest pick a slice of raw beef with his or her fondue fork and cook it directly in the pot. From the table salad, grab a rice paper, and on it place some sliced cucumber, julienned carrot, fresh herbs, and a slice or two of cooked beef. Roll it into a bundle and dip it in *mam nem*.

Bo La Lot
Beef Grilled in La Lot Leaves

Serves 4 to 6

12 ounces ground beef
1 shallot, peeled and minced
1 large clove garlic, peeled
and minced
2 tablespoons finely ground
lemongrass from the white
bulb
2 teaspoons sugar
1 tablespoon fish sauce
24 *la lot* leaves or small
grape leaves
Bamboo skewers, soaked for
20 minutes and drained
Nuoc cham (page 42)

L A   L O T   L E A V E S are green and heart-shaped. They are relatively hard to find outside Asia, and when available, they are much smaller in size than the ones found in Vietnam. To make this classic northern recipe, I often use grape leaves to wrap the meat, just as most Vietnamese restaurants do in the West. (Grape leaves are widely available and can be found in the international food aisles of supermarkets as well as Middle Eastern specialty shops.) This dish is often part of the *bo bay mon* ritual, or beef seven ways, in which beef is prepared in seven distinct ways.

1. Mix together the beef, shallot, garlic, lemongrass, sugar, and fish sauce in a bowl.

2. If using *la lot* leaves, put about 2 teaspoons of the beef mixture in the center of each leaf, fold the pointy end over once, then roll carefully, making sure the filling is completely and tightly enclosed. If using grape leaves, rinse, drain, and pat them dry. Put about 2 teaspoons filling in the center, slightly closer to the wider end. Fold the wide end over the filling, fold in the sides, then roll up carefully, making sure the filling is completely and tightly enclosed. Repeat the process with the remaining leaves and beef mixture.

3. Depending on how long the skewers are, slide 3 to 5 beef rolls crosswise onto each skewer. Grill over a barbecue (make sure that the flames have subsided, and the coals are red with white ashes), or on a well-oiled grill pan over medium-high heat, about 2 minutes per side. Serve with *nuoc cham* for dipping.

GOI BO
Lime-Cured Beef Salad

Serves 4 to 6

⅓ cup lime juice
¼ cup fish sauce
2 tablespoons sugar
1 large garlic clove, peeled,
  crushed, and minced
2 stalks lemongrass, outer
  leaves and tough green
  tops removed, root ends
  trimmed, and stalks sliced
  paper thin
1 to 2 bird's eye or Thai
  chilies, seeded, and sliced
  on the diagonal
1 pound beef filet mignon or
  top round, 1 inch thick
¾ cup mung bean sprouts,
  root ends trimmed
20 large holy basil leaves,
  julienned
20 large mint leaves, julienned
Fried shallots (page 51)

THIS LIME-CURED beef salad is traditional in Laos, Thailand, Cambodia, and Vietnam. You can make it in one of two ways. Sear the beef first, crisping the edges but keeping the center rare, and then slice it and cure it in a lime juice–based dressing. Or omit the searing step and simply cure (a cooking process in itself) the raw beef in lime juice. The most common cut of beef used is top round because it is slightly chewy and retains its shape when sliced paper-thin. Other cuts are used as variations. I like top round very much, but sometimes when I want a more buttery texture, especially when the beef is seared, I use filet mignon. This is also one of the dishes served in the traditional *bo bay mon*, beef-seven-ways meal.

1. Whisk together the lime juice, fish sauce, and sugar in a bowl until the sugar is completely dissolved. Add the garlic, lemongrass, and chili and let marinade stand for 20 minutes.

2. Meanwhile, cut the filet mignon into blocks 2 inches wide by any length. Heat a well-oiled nonstick pan over high heat and sear each block of meat 1 to 2 minutes per side. Transfer the meat to a cutting board and, when cool enough to handle, cut into thin slices.

3. Add the beef to the marinade and allow to stand for 30 minutes. Next, drain the meat as much as you can but do not pick out the garlic, lemongrass, and chili.

4. Toss the meat with mung bean sprouts and two-thirds of the holy basil and mint. Arrange the meat in a mound in the center of a serving plate, then scatter the remaining holy basil, mint, and fried shallots on top.

VARIATION: For the top round variation, cut the beef into 2-inch-wide blocks, then wrap each block in plastic wrap and put in the freezer for 1 hour (this facilitates the slicing). Slice paper thin and proceed with steps 3 and 4.

It's hard to know who will be willing to eat raw meat and who won't. When I plan a dinner and I want to make this dish, I remind myself that the concept is not all that strange, as many people eat steak tartare—a French lean ground beef delicacy served with a raw egg and delicately sliced shallot, cornichon, and capers—or the Japanese raw fish specialties known as sushi and sashimi. Curing with salt, sugar, lime or lemon juice, or a spirit is a technique that cooks meat and seafood without the use of heat. Examples of dishes cooked this way are Italian meat *carpaccio*, Swedish salmon *gravlax*, and conch *ceviche*, which I once enjoyed in the Bahamas. All are delicacies that are well worth a try.

BO NUONG XA
Grilled Lemongrass Beef Cubes

Serves 4 to 6

¼ cup fish sauce

1 tablespoon thick soy sauce

2 tablespoons vegetable oil

3 tablespoons sugar

2 stalks lemongrass, outer leaves
  and tough green tops
  removed, root ends trimmed,
  and stalks finely ground

2 large cloves garlic, crushed,
  peeled, and finely chopped

1½ pounds beef sirloin, cut
  into 1-inch cubes

Bamboo skewers, soaked for
  20 minutes and drained

Table salad (page 52)

Traditional herbs (page 53)

½ cup unsalted roasted
  peanuts, finely chopped
  (optional)

Scallion oil (page 50)

Nuoc cham (page 42)

THIS IS AN EXCELLENT way to prepare beef. Marinated in lemongrass, fish sauce, and sugar, it is robust in flavor, yet relatively light on the palate. It is best grilled, which not only crisps the meat but gives it a smoky flavor. *Bo nuong xa* is one of the dishes served in the ritualistic *bo bay mon*, beef seven ways. Served as a one-course meal, it is tossed with rice vermicelli, shredded lettuce, cucumbers, carrots, and fresh herbs; sprinkled with peanuts; and drizzled with scallion oil and *nuoc cham*.

1. Stir together the fish sauce, soy sauce, oil, and sugar until the sugar is completely dissolved. Add the lemongrass, garlic, and beef and mix to coat the meat evenly. Allow to marinate, refrigerated, for 2 hours.

2. Depending on how long the skewers are, slide 2 to 4 cubes of beef onto each. Grill over a barbecue (make sure that the flames have subsided and the coals are red with white ashes) until the edges crisp, about 1 minute per side. Or in a well-oiled grill pan or nonstick skillet over high heat and cook half of the skewered beef at a time.

3. Combine the grilled beef with some rice vermicelli drizzled with scallion oil, fresh herbs (1 to 2 leaves), 1 slice of star fruit, drizzle with scallion oil, then wrap to form a bundle in a lettuce leaf and dip in *nuoc cham*. Another approach to serving this dish is to toss the beef cubes with a little from each of the table salad and traditional herb ingredients. Served on individual plates or in large soup bowls (as is traditional), sprinkle with peanuts, drizzle scallion oil and *nuoc cham*, and toss to combine well.

VARIATION: Serve with jasmine rice and a stir-fried green such as water spinach (page 125) or yard-long beans (page 126) or with pickled vegetables (page 48).

CHA DUM
Steamed Beef Pâté

Makes 2

1 ounce dried cellophane
   noodles
6 dried cloud ear mushrooms
1 pound ground beef (70% lean)
2 large eggs
2 large shallots, peeled and
   minced
2 large cloves garlic, peeled
   and minced
1 teaspoon sugar
Coarse sea salt
Freshly ground black pepper
Vegetable oil for deep-frying
Shrimp chips or table salad
   (page 52)
Scallion oil (page 50)
¼ cup unsalted roasted
   peanuts, finely chopped
¼ cup cilantro leaves
Nuoc cham (page 42)

OFTEN PART OF *bo bay mon*, or beef seven ways, this pâté is usually served with shrimp chips but can also be eaten wrapped in lettuce leaves. When cooked correctly, the dish has a distinctive crunchy texture, which is achieved through the use of cellophane noodles and cloud ears. *Cha dum* can also be served in a *baguette* sandwich with some cilantro or other refreshing herbs, chili and garlic sauce, and scallion oil. Make sure the ground beef you use is 30 percent fat for the best flavor.

1. Soak the cellophane noodles and cloud ear mushrooms with lukewarm water to cover in a bowl until rehydrated and softened, about 15 minutes. Drain and squeeze the noodles and cloud ears to rid them of the excess water. Finely chop the noodles and cloud ears and put them in a mixing bowl.

2. Add the beef, eggs, shallots, garlic, sugar, season with salt and pepper, and mix until well combined. Lightly oil 2 small heatproof bowls (about 2 cups each). Divide and press the meat mixture in each bowl. (Ideally, the mixture should come up to the rim of the bowl.)

3. Fill the bottom third of a wok with water, fit a bamboo steamer with lid over it, and place the wok over high heat. When the steamer is filled with steam, place the bowls on the bamboo rack (if you have a double-tier steamer, place one bowl on each rack) and cover with the lid. Steam until the juices run clear, about 20 minutes. Remove the bowls from the heat and allow to cool for 10 minutes. Pour off the excess liquid, then run a knife blade around the edges to loosen the pâtés slightly and invert onto a serving dish.

4. While the pâtés are steaming, pour the oil into a pot and heat to 375° over medium-high heat. Add a few shrimp chips at a time. Flipping them once, they will expand on both sides in a matter of seconds. Drizzle the pâtés with scallion oil, garnish with peanuts and cilantro, serve with the shrimp chips or table salad, and dip in *nuoc cham.*

CHA BO
Grilled Beef Patties

Makes 2 dozen

1 pound ground beef (70% lean)
2 small cloves garlic, peeled
  and minced
1 large shallot, peeled and
  minced
¼ cup finely ground peanuts
  (not butter)
¼ cup canned unsweetened
  coconut milk
¼ cup vegetable oil
1 tablespoon fish sauce
2 teaspoons sugar
Freshly ground black pepper
Table salad (page 52)
Nuoc cham (page 42)

ONE OF THE SEVEN beef courses served during a *bo bay mon* meal, these patties are far more interesting than a plain burger, being a wonderful combination of ground peanuts, beef, and coconut milk. After they are grilled medium-rare, *cha bo* are eaten wrapped in lettuce leaves, with sliced vegetables, star fruit, and fresh herbs and dipped in *nuoc cham*.

1. Combine the beef, garlic, shallot, peanuts, coconut milk, 2 tablespoons oil, fish sauce, sugar, and pepper in a bowl and mix thoroughly. Form the meat into 24 equal meatballs, then flatten each into a ¼-inch-thick small patty.

2. Heat the remaining oil in a grill pan or nonstick skillet over high heat and sear the patties until crisp on the outside, about 1 minute on each side for medium-rare. To eat, wrap a grilled patty in a lettuce leaf with some fresh herbs and dip in *nuoc cham*.

Bo Vien
Beef Meatballs

Makes 2 dozen

2 tablespoons fish sauce
2 tablespoons vegetable oil
1 teaspoon sesame oil
1 tablespoon sugar
1 small clove garlic, peeled
   and minced
Freshly ground black or white
   pepper to taste
1 pound sirloin round, thinly
   sliced
2 tablespoons potato starch
1 teaspoon baking powder

ABOUT THE SIZE of marbles, these meatballs are most often eaten as a snack or in *pho bo* (page 88). Sometimes they are made with pork skin, which adds a chewy texture; other times they are made smooth, as in this recipe. The trick to getting *bo vien* properly smooth and firm is the addition of the potato starch when grinding the meat into a fine paste. The baking powder gives the meatballs volume as they cook. *Bo vien* can be made in advance, boiled, drained, and kept frozen up to a month. Whether the meatballs are grilled or boiled and served in *pho*, I prefer, like many Vietnamese, to dip them in a mixture of chili and garlic sauce and hoisin sauce.

1. Whisk together the fish sauce, vegetable and sesame oils, and sugar until the sugar is completely dissolved. Stir in the garlic and season with pepper. Add the beef and pound it into the marinade until evenly coated. Allow to marinate, refrigerated, for 1 hour. Then transfer the meat to the freezer for 1 hour.

2. Place the partially frozen beef in a food processor and pulse until ground. Add the potato starch and continue pulsing until you have a smooth and firm paste, about 5 minutes. Add the baking powder and process for 1 minute more.

3. Bring a pot filled with water to a boil over high heat. Pinch off a well-rounded teaspoon of the beef and form it into a ball. Then carefully lower it into the boiling water. Repeat this process until you have used up all of the paste. Cook the meatballs until they float to the surface, about 5 minutes. Drain on paper towels.

4. Heat 1 tablespoon vegetable oil in a nonstick skillet over medium-high heat and lightly brown the meatballs until slightly crisp all over, about 3 minutes. Serve as an appetizer or snack with chili and garlic sauce and hoisin sauce on the side.

Bo Kho Ca Rot
Spicy Beef and Carrot Stew

Serves 4 to 6

¼ cup fish sauce

¼ teaspoon five-spice powder

2 tablespoons sugar

4 pounds short ribs on the bone, halved through the bone, or oxtail cut into 1-inch-thick pieces

1 tablespoon vegetable oil

4 to 6 small yellow onions, peeled

3 large cloves garlic, peeled and lightly crushed

3 ounces fresh ginger, cut into 3 slices and lightly crushed

2 cups young coconut juice or beef stock (page 64)

2 stalks lemongrass, outer leaves and tough green tops removed, root ends trimmed, and bulbs halved crosswise and lightly crushed

4 to 5 star anise

1 cinnamon stick, about 2½ to 3 inches long

3 to 4 dried chilies or 2 to 3 fresh bird's eye or Thai chilies

1 teaspoon annatto seeds

2 to 3 large carrots, peeled and sliced diagonally ¼ inch thick

T HE CLASSIC FRENCH DISH *bœuf aux carottes*, French beef and carrot stew, is the inspiration for this Vietnamese favorite. Although *bo kho ca rot* is commonly made with stew beef, I especially like to use short ribs (the underpart of the prime rib, often used as a roasting rack for prime rib during cooking) or oxtail, both of which are tender and incredibly flavorful and sweet. When buying short ribs, ask your butcher to cut them 2½ to 3 inches across, through the bone, and calculate at least 8 ounces per person, as a lot of the cut is bone and fat.

1. Combine the fish sauce, five-spice powder, and sugar in a dish. Add the short ribs or oxtail, coating well, and allow to marinate, refrigerated, for 4 to 6 hours.

2. Heat together the oil, onions, garlic, and ginger in a sand pot or heavy-bottomed pot over medium-low heat. Cook the ingredients, stirring often, until fragrant and golden, about 10 minutes. Add the marinated meat, scraping the marinade from the dish into the pot. Add the coconut juice or beef stock and cover the pot. Bring to a boil over medium heat. Add the lemongrass, star anise, cinnamon stick, chilies, and annatto seeds and simmer covered (occasionally turning the meat) over medium-low heat for 2 hours. Add carrots and continue braising until the meat

falls off the bones, 1½ to 2 hours more. Skim off the fat and serve with rice on the side.

N O T E : To simplify the task of skimming fat, I carefully remove the onions, carrots, and meat from the pot. Then I place a double or triple layer of paper towels in a sieve set over a bowl and strain the cooking liquid through the paper towels. About 90 percent of the fat clings to the paper towels, while a clear and rich colored stock seeps through. Then, divide the meat and vegetables among 4 to 6 plates containing rice, and drizzle a generous amount of the braising liquid over each serving.

(CLOCKWISE, FROM TOP LEFT) DRIED CHILIES, CINNAMON STICK, STAR ANISE, AND ANNATTO SEEDS

BO SATE
Beef Sate

Serves 4 to 6

2 tablespoons *sate*
  (page 49)
1 tablespoon vegetable oil
1 pound beef sirloin, thinly
  sliced into bite-size pieces
Bamboo skewers, soaked for
  20 minutes and drained
  (optional)
1 medium yellow onion, peeled
  and sliced into thin wedges
  (optional)

ANOTHER POPULAR VIETNAMESE barbecue dish is beef *sate*. Although many Westerners associate it primarily with Thailand, it is possibly derived from Indian cuisine. Widely eaten all over Southeast Asia, it has many national and regional variations. The Vietnamese version is more commonly served in the South, where its spicy flavors are more widely appreciated. The *sate* paste is primarily hot chili pepper, roasted peanuts, and Indian curry powder. I always use a marbled cut of meat such as sirloin, and I slice it against the grain to ensure that the steak is tender when cooked.

1. Mix the *sate* paste and oil in a bowl and add the beef. Mix well so all the pieces are evenly coated. Depending on how long the skewers are, slide 2 to 4 slices of meat onto each skewer, alternating with onion wedges if using. Grill over a barbecue (make sure flames have subsided and the coals are red with white ashes) until the meat is cooked through and crisp at the edges, about 3 minutes per side.

VARIATION: *Bo sate* can also be stir-fried. Heat the oil in a nonstick skillet over medium heat, add the *sate,* and stir until fragrant, about 3 minutes. Increase the heat to high, add the onion and beef, and cook, stirring occasionally, until cooked through, 5 to 7 minutes.

VARIATION: Substitute 1 pound thinly sliced (against the grain) pork tenderloin or chicken breast for the beef sirloin and stir-fry. The chicken will cook in 3 to 5 minutes total.

Bo Xao
Stir-Fried Beef

Serves 4 to 6

1 tablespoon vegetable oil
1 medium yellow onion,
    peeled and sliced into thin
    wedges (optional)
1 pound beef sirloin, thinly
    sliced against the grain into
    bite-size pieces
1 tablespoon fish sauce
Freshly ground black pepper

THE SOUTH of Vietnam has many light, stir-fried dishes, and this beef-with-onion dish is typical. It is served with rice vermicelli (page 111); however, it is just as wonderful served over rice. Often I also add about 6 ounces of yard-long beans or cauliflower florets (stir-fried about 15 minutes prior to adding the beef), or mung bean sprouts (added to the stir-fry about 2 minutes after the beef), two vegetables commonly used in combination with beef. I like using marbled sirloin, but filet mignon is also good if you prefer a leaner cut of beef.

1. Heat the oil in a wok or non-stick skillet over high heat, add the onion, and cook until translucent but firm, 5 to 7 minutes. Add the beef and fish sauce, season to taste with pepper, and stir-fry until beef is cooked through, 2 to 3 minutes.

EXOTIC MEATS

"YOU WANT TO EAT DOG?" asked my guide, Tuan, in Hanoi on a recent trip to Vietnam. He was pointing to a small, golden, crisp-skinned roasted dog—very much in the style of Peking duck—in a bustling indoor food market. A common sight in Hanoi, roast dog is seasonal (best in winter), and eating it is derived from southern Chinese traditions. Halved, it is sold cut into its preferred parts for eating: head with fangs, rump with back legs, and front legs with ribs. (Although Tuan may have been showing off a bit, I was not particularly surprised. I had eaten dog before and would gladly have had some if I had not been in a hurry.) The Vietnamese do not eat just any dog but use only a few, very specific breeds—the preferred one being called "yellow dog." (I have also heard of "black dog" being eaten.) Despite any squeamishness non-Asians may have about eating canines, dog actually tastes somewhat gamy, rather like goat. Not only dog, but also bat, armadillo, bear, porcupine, monkey, field rat, snake, and other exotics are found throughout Vietnam, and it is not uncommon to find specialty restaurants featuring these items. "Only men eat that," expressed my guide during another exotics excursion, this time in Saigon, implying a kind of macho rite.

In specialty restaurants the animals are usually presented live, then killed and cooked immediately. Certain animals, such as the snake, also have the blood drained out and presented as a drink, this followed by a dish of cooked snake meat. Monkey can cost up to three hundred U.S. dollars. So not only is the consumption of exotics macho; it also shows status and wealth. For those who see only cruelty in these preparations, it is important to remember that these traditions are part of a complex and sophisticated culture evolved over centuries, and that many of these meats are believed to have medicinal qualities, and some are valued as aphrodisiacs. The machismo angle may be one of simple exclusion: Vietnamese women, for whatever reason, are happy to leave most of these items to the men.

Although I have described here the strangest exotic meats imaginable, there are others that are considered exotic but are merely the offal of certain barnyard animals, such as chicken, ducks, pigs, and cows. If I have not lost you yet, and if you feel the urge, stir-fry poultry hearts and gizzards with some *sate* paste (page 49). Eating spiced giblets in Vietnam is not dissimilar to eating *giblets à la bourguignonne*, giblets braised in wine, in France, or eating them in a traditional American Thanksgiving corn bread stuffing.

VIETNAMESE COFFEE WITH SWEET CONDENSED MILK

CHAPTER SEVEN

SWEETS & DRINKS

 IN VIETNAM food is often prepared with sweet, savory, and citrus-based ingredients mixed together. Most of the recipes in this book include sugar, fish sauce, and a lemony herb such as lemongrass, holy basil, or cilantro, for example. Accordingly, sweets are rarely eaten at the end of a meal, with fresh fruits being offered instead. ◆ When my family gets together for dinner, we often have sliced oranges or grapefruit for dessert. They are excellent palate cleansers and particularly refreshing, aiding the digestion of any fats eaten during the meal. When we invite guests, we try to find special exotic fruits to serve, such as fresh litchi (also spelled "lychee"), longan, rambutan, and arbutus. The first three fruits have a firm white flesh and a flowery fragrance; the arbutus is red and also powerfully fragrant. These and other exotics are also available canned, and we tend to treat these products as something different entirely. We like to invent cocktails, for example, mixing their sweet syrups with a spirit, a wine, or champagne. Topped with a single arbutus, for example, a simple arbutus vodka cocktail (page 240) becomes something memorable, perfect for a special celebration.

Fruits such as star fruit (also known as carambola), papaya, and mango are eaten as dessert when they are ripe and sweet and are also used when unripe and green. Sliced unripe star fruit makes a beautiful accent in the traditional table salad (page 52) eaten with grilled meats. Similarly, green unripe papayas and mangoes are shredded and dressed with a sweet, tangy dressing made with fish sauce and are also served as salads.

Root vegetables are also used in making desserts. Taro and sweet potato, for example, are often added to a coconut tapioca-based soup. My mother used to make a clear curative soup, steeping chunks of sweet potato and crushed ginger for an hour. When I was feeling a little under the weather, this fragrant infusion was just what I needed.

The Chinese and French have greatly influenced the Vietnamese in their preparation of the desserts they do offer. From the Chinese the Vietnamese have adopted sweet soups like *che chuoi*, banana and coconut soup (page 226). Inspired by the French, they have transformed traditional Gallic desserts into their very own, creating such dishes as as *banh gan*, crème caramel (page 232) made with coconut milk rather than cow's milk, and *chuoi chien*, banana fritters (page 231) usually flambéed with rum.

Several of my aunts living in Paris have developed a Western sweet tooth. Their days often consist of calling friends and making plans to drink tea and indulge in sweets. They like to reminisce about their former lives in Saigon or talk about how their grown-up children are faring today. On my last trip to Paris, I joined the group. They had planned to make *dau xanh vung*, deep-fried glutinous rice flour balls (page 233). While some formed the balls, others deep-fried them. My aunt Loan turned to me at one point and said, "You see, you can fill them with mung bean paste, banana, pork, or taro. You can use any filling; it's like having many recipes." Taking her advice to heart, I have included a sweet version here.

Sweet drinks can be considered drinks or dessert; one such is *che ba mau*, rainbow drink (page 239), which consists of shaved ice, coconut milk, and a layer each of mung beans, red beans, and jelly. It is usually served in a large ice cream soda glass with a long ice cream spoon and straw, in the American diner style.

Still, there are not nearly as many desserts as there are savory dishes in Vietnamese cooking. When entertaining at home, I am often faced with a dilemma. Although I know the traditional desserts, serving my guests a hot sweet soup after a curry, for example, just doesn't work. Sometime ago, I decided to expand the "Trang dessert cart" with refreshing sweets, but I wanted to stay within the bounds of authenticity. I thought of ice cream as the perfect solution, a dessert that was introduced to Vietnam by the French and remains enormously popular there.

"I am in the ballpark," I thought, "if I can create Vietnamese *glaces*." I have included three ice creams, *kem*, made with toasted coconut, or infused with citrusy lemongrass or spicy star anise. These desserts reflect the cross-cultural influences, balanced textures, and complex flavors of the fusion cuisine that has evolved in Vietnam over the centuries.

CHE CHUOI
Sweet Banana and Coconut Milk Soup

Serves 8

2 cups canned unsweetened
   coconut milk
½ cup tapioca pearls
½ to ¾ cup sugar
Pinch coarse sea salt
3 ripe bananas, peeled and
   diced, or 2 cups fresh sweet
   yellow corn kernels
Toasted sesame seeds

O F CHINESE ORIGIN, *che chuoi* is made with coconut milk, tapioca, and chunks of ripe banana. It can be served hot, at room temperature, or chilled. It can also be made with corn, or root vegetables such as sweet potato or taro. In Vietnam sweetness is always counterbalanced with saltiness, and desserts are no exception. Accordingly, I add just a pinch of salt to balance the sweetness.

1. Bring the coconut milk and 2 cups water to a boil in a pot over high heat. Reduce the heat to medium-low, stir in the tapioca pearls, sugar, and salt, and cook until tapioca pearls are translucent, about 30 minutes. Add banana or fresh corn kernels and cook for 10 minutes more.

2. Divide among 8 dessert bowls, garnish each with a sprinkle or two of sesame seeds, and serve hot, at room temperature, or chilled.

VARIATION: For the taro root or sweet potato variation, omit the banana. Follow step 1, but add 1 pound peeled and diced taro root or sweet potato at the same time as the tapioca pearls and cook for 35 minutes.

One day a friend who is allergic to coconut came to my house for dinner. That night I served this tapioca dessert made with 4 cups cow's milk as a substitution for the traditional coconut and water combination. I used ripe bananas for a stronger, more pronounced flavor, and to my surprise, the soup was a big hit not only with him but with everyone else at the table. I recommend it as a variation.

CHE DAU XANH
Sweet Mung Bean Soup

Serves 4 to 6

1 cup peeled split mung beans
2 cups canned unsweetened
   coconut milk
¼ to ⅓ cup sugar

ALTHOUGH THIS RECIPE is usually made as a soup, some cooks prefer *che dau xanh* as a pudding. In my family we find the pudding version to be a bit too heavy. We prefer a more liquid consistency; it is more subtle and easier to digest. Mung beans are sold whole with their green husks on, or split with the husks removed. I recommend the split variety, which will save you many hours of tedious preparation. If whole mung beans are the only ones available, or if you feel adventurous, soak them overnight to soften. This will facilitate removing the husks.

1. Soak the mung beans for 3 hours and drain. Bring 2 cups water to a simmer in a pot over medium heat. Add the mung beans and cook, stirring constantly, until the water is completely absorbed, about 20 minutes.

2. Transfer the beans to a fine sieve set over a heatproof bowl. With the back of a spoon or ladle, press the beans through the sieve. Bring a pot of water to a boil and place the bowl with the mung bean purée over the pot. Add the coconut milk and sugar to the purée, and stir constantly until the mung bean soup is heated through. Serve hot.

PEELED SPLIT MUNG BEANS

Kem Canh Hoi
Star Anise Ice Cream

Makes about 1½ pints

4 cups plus 2 tablespoons
   half-and-half
1 vanilla bean or 2 teaspoons
   vanilla extract
12 whole star anise
¾ cup sugar or more
4 egg yolks
1½ tablespoons tapioca starch
1 teaspoon ground star anise

I N T H I S I C E C R E A M, a vanilla custard is infused with star anise, a dry spice used in many Asian cuisines. The vanilla bean can be reused 2 to 3 times, so do not discard it after making the custard. (Blot it dry prior to putting it away.) If you feel up to it, try infusing the custard with fresh lemongrass (see Variation). Both versions are interesting, refreshing, and bound to be conversation starters after an elaborate meal.

1. Pour 4 cups half-and-half into the top of a double boiler over medium heat. Add the vanilla bean (or vanilla extract) and star anise and simmer for 30 minutes.

2. Meanwhile, whisk together the sugar and egg yolks in a mixing bowl until the yolks turn thick and pale. Strain the half-and-half through a fine sieve to remove vanilla bean, and discard star anise. Temper the yolks by gradually adding the hot half-and-half (a cup at a time) while whisking vigorously so as not to scramble the eggs.

3. Return the mixture to the top part of the double boiler and whisk over simmering water until slightly thickened and heated through, 10 to 15 minutes. Dilute the tapioca starch with the remaining 2 tablespoons half-and-half and add it to the mixture. Continue whisking to a custard

consistency that coats the back of a spoon, about 2 minutes. Refrigerate overnight (or at least 12 hours). Transfer the custard to a heatproof bowl set over an ice bath and refrigerate overnight (or at least 12 hours).

4. The next day, pour the custard into an ice cream maker and process

TAPIOCA STARCH

the custard according to the manufacturer's instructions, 30 to 35 minutes. Transfer the ice cream to a container and freeze until ready to serve. Lightly dust each portion with ground star anise before serving.

VARIATION: Substitute 12 fresh lemongrass stalks for the star anise. Remove the outer leaves and tough green tops from each stalk. Trim the root ends, and with a cleaver lightly crush the white to light green part of the stalks. Finely grind 1 lemongrass stalk and reserve for the garnish. Use the remaining stalks in place of the star anise in step 1 (remove in step 2). For the garnish, make a caramel with ¼ cup sugar and 2 tablespoons water in a nonstick skillet over medium heat. When the sugar starts to bubble and becomes light golden, add finely ground lemongrass and stir until evenly coated. Remove from the heat, transfer to an oiled baking sheet, and crush the candied lemongrass with the handle of a cleaver if necessary. Sprinkle candied lemongrass on top of each serving of ice cream.

KEM DUA
Toasted Coconut Ice Cream

Makes about 1½ pints

¾ cup finely ground
   unsweetened fresh coconut

3 cups canned unsweetened
   coconut milk

1 cup plus 2 tablespoons
   half-and-half

Pinch coarse sea salt

¾ cup sugar

4 egg yolks

1½ tablespoons tapioca starch

THIS COCONUT ICE CREAM is rich and really tasty. As with many Southeast Asian coconut-based desserts, a pinch of salt is added to cut the fat and balance the natural sweetness of the coconut. Here, to add more texture and vary the flavor, I toast the coconut before adding it to the custard. Some cooks are satisfied to chill their custard in an ice bath for 4 hours, but I get better results from keeping it refrigerated overnight. Hint: Many homemade ice creams tend to melt quickly. To prevent this, a small amount of diluted tapioca starch is added to the custard.

1. In a nonstick skillet, toast the fresh coconut over medium heat, stirring to brown evenly, 3 to 5 minutes. Transfer the toasted coconut to a dish and allow to cool.

2. Pour the coconut milk, 1 cup half-and-half, and salt into the top of a double boiler and bring to a simmer over medium heat. Meanwhile, whisk together the sugar and egg yolks in a mixing bowl until the yolks turn thick and pale. Temper the yolks by gradually adding hot coconut milk mixture (a cup at a time) while whisking vigorously, so as not to scramble the eggs.

3. Return the mixture to the top part of the double boiler and whisk over simmering water until slightly thickened and heated through,

10 to 15 minutes. Dilute tapioca starch with remaining 2 tablespoons half-and-half and add it to the mixture. Continue whisking to a custard consistency that coats the back of a spoon, about 2 minutes. Transfer the custard to a heatproof bowl set over an ice bath. Whisk in ½ cup toasted ground coconut and refrigerate overnight (or at least 12 hours).

4. The next day, pour the custard into an ice cream maker and process the custard according to the manufacturer's instructions, 30 to 35 minutes. Transfer the ice cream to a container and freeze until ready to serve. Garnish each serving with some toasted coconut.

CHUOI CHIEN
Banana Fritters

Serves 4 to 6

1½ cups canned unsweetened
   coconut milk
1 large egg
3 tablespoons sugar
Pinch of coarse sea salt
1 cup all-purpose flour
3 ripe bananas, peeled and
   halved lengthwise and
   halved again crosswise
Vegetable oil for deep-frying
¼ cup rum or rice alcohol

BASED ON THE FRENCH dessert *banane flambée*, *chuoi chien* is a battered, deep-fried banana drizzled with rum or rice alcohol and ignited to crisp the fritter further. In Paris, almost all Vietnamese restaurants offer this popular dessert. In a charming ritual, the waiter comes to the table with the banana fritters, then sets them aflame in front of you. If you do this at home and feel unsure about igniting the alcohol, have a pot cover handy to smother the flames.

1. Whisk together the coconut milk, egg, 2 tablespoons sugar, and salt in a bowl until the sugar and salt have completely dissolved. Whisk in the flour until you have a smooth batter. Add banana pieces and mix to coat pieces evenly.

2. Heat the oil in a wok over medium heat to 360° to 375°F. Working in batches, with chopsticks or tongs, pick up the banana pieces one at a time, shaking off the excess batter. Carefully lower them into the hot oil and fry until golden and crisp, about 2 to 3 minutes per side. Drain the bananas on paper towels, then transfer to a heatproof platter. Sprinkle the remaining sugar over the fritters, drizzle with the spirit, and light with a match. With a spoon, baste the bananas with the burning spirit until the fritters start to darken slightly. Serve hot.

BANH GAN
Coconut Crème Caramel

Serves 8

1 cup sugar
2 cups canned unsweetened
   coconut milk
1 cup whole milk
6 large eggs
8 fresh mint leaves of equal size

BANH GAN IS BASED on the French dessert crème caramel, an egg custard baked in a water bath and dressed with a caramel syrup. Although the French use cow's milk for their version, the Vietnamese prefer coconut milk, which is the only significant difference between the two recipes. *Banh gan* is rich but perfectly balanced by the sweet caramel.

1. Melt ½ cup sugar with 3 tablespoons water in a saucepan over medium-low heat, occasionally swirling the pan, until the sugar starts to bubble and turn golden brown, about 7 minutes. Remove from the heat and divide the syrup among 8 ½-cup soufflé ramekins. Tilt the ramekins so the bottoms and sides are covered with the syrup.

2. Preheat the oven to 275°F. Meanwhile, whisk the remaining sugar, coconut milk, whole milk, and eggs in a bowl until the sugar is completely dissolved. Divide the mixture among the ramekins. Create a water bath by filling a baking dish halfway with water. Place the ramekins in it and bake until the custards set, about 35 minutes. Remove from the oven and allow to cool in the water bath. Cover with plastic wrap and refrigerate at least 12 hours. To serve, loosen and turn *banh gan* onto plates so the caramel is on top, drizzling any remaining caramel on the plates around the custard. Serve chilled, garnished with a mint leaf.

Dau Xanh Vung
Sesame Rice Dumplings

Makes 30

¾ cup skinless split mung
  beans, soaked for 3 hours and
  drained
¾ cup sugar
2½ cups glutinous rice flour
½ cup rice flour
1 medium baking potato,
  boiled, peeled, and mashed
½ cup raw sesame seeds
Vegetable oil for deep-frying

FOR THIS POPULAR treat, glutinous rice flour dumplings are filled with mung bean paste, rolled in sesame seeds, and deep-fried. You can eliminate the sesame seeds, steam the dumplings, and serve them in a light homemade syrup sprinkled with toasted sesame seeds. Both versions are delicious. Fried, these dumplings, can also be filled with red bean paste or sweetened taro root for a sweet snack, or stuffed with pork for a savory appetizer. This type of dumpling was adopted from the Chinese, who stuff it with sweet red bean or lotus paste. The mung beans, however, give the recipe its distinctive Vietnamese character.

1. Bring 2 cups water to a simmer in a pot over medium heat. Add the mung beans and ¼ cup sugar. Cook, stirring constantly, until the water is completely absorbed, about 20 minutes. (If the beans are still firm, add a little water and continue cooking until tender.) Remove from the heat and allow to cool, and crush the beans to form a fairly smooth paste.

2. Mix together the glutinous rice flour, rice flour, potato, and remaining sugar in a bowl. Add 1 cup water and mix until all the ingredients are well combined and your dough detaches from the side of the bowl. Knead slightly, 2 to 3 times (the dough should feel moist and slightly sticky). Roll the dough into a long rope, cut into 30 pieces, roll each to form a ball, and flatten each into a disc. Cover with plastic wrap.

3. Divide and shape the cooked mung beans into 30 balls. Enclose each mung bean ball in a rice flour disc and shape into a ball. Scatter sesame seeds on a plate and gently roll the balls until they are evenly coated.

4. Heat the oil in a wok or pot over medium heat to 360° to 375°F. Working in batches, carefully lower the dumplings into the hot oil. Use chopsticks to roll them around, while keeping them apart, so they crisp and turn golden evenly, 3 to 5 minutes. Drain on paper towels and serve with jasmine tea.

BANH KHOAI MI
Cassava Cake

Serves 8

1½ cups canned unsweetened
   coconut milk
Pinch salt
1 cup palm sugar or sugar
1½ pounds cassava root, bark
   removed, shredded (about
   4 cups shredded)
Butter for greasing dish

THE BASIS OF THIS CAKE is cassava, also referred to as manioc or yuca. It is a large root, shaped something like a sweet potato but longer, found in Asian and Hispanic markets. When choosing cassava, be sure that it is firm and light to medium brown in color. Although your instinct may be to peel the root, you will have to take a slightly different approach. The "skin" is actually a bark consisting of the brown skin and a pinkish layer beneath it, about one-sixteenth of an inch thick. The only way to remove it is to run a knife along the length of the root and lift the bark up with the blade. *Banh khoai mi* is pasty and sticky and is very filling. For this reason, it is often served with jasmine tea.

1. Preheat the oven to 375°F. Whisk together coconut milk, salt, and sugar in a bowl until the sugar is completely dissolved. Add the shredded cassava and mix to combine thoroughly. Transfer and evenly spread the cassava mixture in a generously buttered baking dish, 12 by 9 inches. Bake until golden brown, about 1 hour. Allow to cool completely before slicing.

REMOVING THE HUSK
FROM THE CASSAVA ROOT

Xoi Dua
Coconut Sticky Rice

Serves 4

½ cup red azuki beans, soaked
    for 4 hours and drained
½ cup sugar
1½ cups canned unsweetened
    coconut milk
Pinch salt
2 cups steamed sticky rice
    (page 102), prepared just
    before using and kept warm

XOI DUA is a sticky rice–based dessert enjoyed throughout Southeast Asia. The Thai serve it at room temperature with mango, while the Vietnamese like it with red beans or mung beans and a coconut milk sauce. The trick to preparing the sticky rice is to soak it overnight, drain it, and then steam it in a bamboo steamer. This ensures that every grain of rice will be consistently tender but firm. I'm not too much of a dessert person, but whenever I go to a Vietnamese grocer in Chinatown, I am tempted by one version or another of these marvelously varied treats. I usually come home with one of each!

1. Bring 2 cups of water just to a boil in a pot over medium heat. Reduce the heat to low, add the azuki beans and ¼ cup sugar. Cover and simmer until the beans are cooked through, about 3 hours. Remove from the heat and allow to cool.

2. Meanwhile, bring the coconut milk to a boil in a pot over high heat. Reduce the heat to low, add the remaining sugar, the salt, and stir until the sugar is completely dissolved. Remove from the heat and add the warm sticky rice. Cover and allow the rice to soak up most of the coconut milk. Divide the rice among 4 dessert plates and place about 2 tablespoons cooked azuki beans on each serving.

VARIATION: Substitute ¾ cup skinless split mung beans (soaked for 2 hours and drained) for the red azuki beans. In step 1, cook the mung beans with 2 cups water until the water is absorbed, about 20 minutes.

Coffees, Teas, Sweet Drinks, and Cocktails

COFFEE WAS INTRODUCED to the Vietnamese by the French during their early colonization. The Vietnamese, however, like much of French Indochina—including Cambodia, Thailand, and Laos—transformed the traditional *café au lait* into their own special brew. Mixed with sweetened condensed milk, this Vietnamese coffee—or *café vietnamien,* as it is referred to by many Vietnamese, even in the United States—is still enormously popular today.

Tea is drunk black or in a sweetened version mimicking *café vietnamien.* If you are a tea drinker and feel like having an unusual sweet tea drink, try *thé vietnamien,* strong black tea mixed with sweetened condensed milk.

The rainbow drink, *che ba mau* (page 239), layers shaved ice with coconut milk, tapioca, mung beans, and red beans. It is a classic sweet drink or dessert, roughly akin to the idea of a layered liquid *parfait.* It can be topped with canned litchi or longan to give it a crunchy texture and floral note. This version is a favorite among all the kids in my family. Sweet, crunchy, and filling, it allows you to eat the fruit and at the same time enjoy the varied textures and blended flavors. It's a perfect drink for hot summer days.

Another simple drink popular in Vietnam and in Southeast Asia in general is young green coconut juice drunk right out of its shell. Unlike the hard, dark brown coconuts available in most supermarkets, a young coconut is recognized by its bright green skin; thick, ivory-white, fibrous inner core; and a very thin inner layer of coconut meat. A green coconut contains an average of 14 fluid ounces of clear juice. It can be drunk as is or used to make *thit heo kho nuoc dua*, braised pork shank in coconut juice (page 206). For those of you who like young coconut juice sweeter, add some corn syrup.

The cocktails in this chapter are improvisations inspired by drinks I have seen in restaurants in Vietnam, France, and the United States. They all follow a similar pattern: Exotic fruits and their syrups are mixed with vodka, white wine, or champagne. They are meant to be amusing and can act as lubricants for conversation, as the curious and unfamiliar fruits will surely intrigue your guests. There is nothing quite like being able to confidently utter the words *rambutan* or *arbutus* when presented with the innocent query, "Hey, what's in this drink?"

CA PHE
Vietnamese Coffee

Serves 1

1 heaping teaspoon French
   roast coffee
1 tablespoon sweetened
   condensed milk, or more
   to taste

THE FRENCH BROUGHT coffee and their famous *café au lait*—the hot-coffee-and-milk morning drink usually served in big bowls—to Vietnam. From this idea the Vietnamese version was created, combining strong coffee with sweet condensed milk. This sweet coffee drink is consumed not only in Vietnam but also in Thailand, where it is referred to as Thai coffee. *Ca phe* is made by placing ground coffee in a specially made metal coffee filter that sits directly on top of an individual coffee cup. Hot water is then poured over the grounds. If you cannot find this special coffee filter in French, Italian, or Asian markets, make a double espresso and stir in the condensed milk for a slightly stronger but still delicious Vietnamese-style coffee.

1. Place the coffee in the filter set over a cup containing the condensed milk. Screw in the flat plunger so it is tight against the coffee. Pour boiling water to the rim (about ¾ cup) and loosen the plunger to allow the water through. When the coffee has dripped into the cup, stir well and drink hot, or pour into a large glass containing ice for iced coffee.

VARIATION: Make ¾ cup strong black tea and stir in the condensed milk.

CHE BA MAU
Rainbow Drink

Serves 6

¾ cup skinless split mung
beans, soaked for 3 hours
and drained
¾ cup sugar
½ cup red azuki beans, soaked
for 4 hours and drained
1½ cups coconut milk
¼ cup tapioca pearls
1 can longan, drained

THE RAINBOW DRINK is fun and filling, so much so that it can make a perfect afternoon snack on a hot summer's day. It used to be one of my favorite drinks to get in Chinatown, where shops typically sell all sorts of Vietnamese snacks. *Che ba mau* is always colorful, with textures ranging from crunchy agar jelly sticks (available in Asian markets) to starchy beans and creamy coconut milk.

1. Bring 2 cups water to a simmer in a pot over medium heat. Add the mung beans and ¼ cup sugar. Cook, stirring constantly, until the water is completely absorbed, about 20 minutes. Remove from the heat and allow to cool. Refrigerate until ready to use.

2. Bring 2 cups of water just to a boil in a pot over medium heat. Reduce the heat to low, add the azuki beans and ¼ cup sugar. Cover and simmer until the beans are cooked through, about 3 hours. Remove from the heat and allow to cool. Refrigerate until ready to use.

3. Meanwhile, bring the coconut milk and 1½ cups water to a boil. Reduce the heat to low, add the remaining sugar and tapioca pearls, and simmer until the tapioca pearls have become completely transparent. Remove from the heat and allow to cool. Refrigerate until ready to use.

4. In an ice cream soda glass, working in layers, place 2 tablespoons shaved ice in between 3 tablespoons each of everything else starting with shaved ice, coconut tapioca, shaved ice (again), mung beans, shaved ice (again), azuki beans, shaved ice (again), coconut tapioca (again), and a few longans on top. Use ice cream spoons to eat and a straw to sip.

RUOU
Cocktails

THE FOLLOWING are methods for creating great-tasting exotic cocktails. Take a trip to your Asian market and get a can each of rambutan, litchi, arbutus, longan, and loquats. On your way home, stop by your liquor store and get a good bottle each of vodka, white wine, and brut champagne. Follow the simple instructions below, and you will be pleasantly surprised at the results.

Litchi or Longan Vodka: **Mix 1 cup** litchi syrup with 2 cups vodka. Serve in a martini glass and garnish with a single litchi or longan held by a decorative toothpick. Serve chilled.

Loquat or Rambutan Wine: **Mix 1** cup loquat syrup with 2 cups semi-dry white wine. Serve in a martini glass and garnish with a single loquat held by a decorative toothpick. Serve chilled.

Arbutus Champagne: **Mix 1 (or more)** cup arbutus syrup with 4 cups brut champagne. Serve in a champagne coupe with three red arbutus fruit. Served chilled.

Wandering in a small residential area in Paris, my husband and I stumbled upon a tiny Vietnamese restaurant with no more than a dozen tables. A lot about the place was French, but the lacquered scenes of Vietnam life and the small shrine to Buddha gave it an Asian flair. We struck up a conversation with the owner about food and family, and our host delighted us with her cocktail *maison.* It was white wine with syrup from canned arbutus, a fuzzy-looking exotic red fruit the size of a marble, served in a cognac snifter. Madame had created a great aperitif! Inspired, my husband and I have since experimented with canned exotic fruits and white wine, champagne, and vodka. These drinks are conversation starters, perfect as aperitifs before any Vietnamese meal.

RAMBUTAN, LYCHEE, LONGAN, ARBUTUS, AND LOQUATS

Seasonal Menus

The Vietnamese enjoy their food served continuously throughout the meal, and the idea of starting and stopping between courses is something quite foreign to them. This can be rather daunting to a Western cook who wants to spend time with guests, as it requires you to be in the kitchen almost full-time during the meal!

I have developed an alternative approach. These "seasonal" menus—so called because they vary according to the appropriateness of the dishes for each season—are modeled on the standard Western cocktail and three courses. With them, you can cook authentic Vietnamese and enjoy your guests as well as the food.

NOTE: For each seasonal menu, the recipes listed as main courses, with the exception of the soup, should be plated together as one main course. For example, in the Winter menu, the pork shank would be spooned over the jasmine rice, with the water spinach on the side or on top. The tofu soup, as for all soups listed as main courses, would be served individually for sipping and cleansing the palate. The menus serve 4 to 6.

WINTER MENU

COCKTAIL
Litchi Vodka (page 240)

◆

APPETIZER
Stuffed Crab Shells (page 158)

◆

MAIN COURSE
Braised Pork Shank in Coconut Juice (page 206)
Stir-Fried Water Spinach (page 125)
Cooked Jasmine Rice (page 100)
Tofu Soup (page 72)

◆

DESSERT
Coconut Crème Caramel (page 232)

SPRING MENU

COCKTAIL
Loquat Wine (page 240)

◆

APPETIZER
Spring Rolls (page 198)

◆

MAIN COURSE
Ginger and Garlic Rice with Chicken (page 103)
Stir-Fried Mung Bean Sprouts (page 128)
Braised Eggplant (page 134)
Fish and Pineapple Soup (page 75)

◆

DESSERT
Sweet Banana and Coconut Soup (page 226)

Summer Menu

COCKTAIL
Arbutus Champagne (page 240)

◆

APPETIZER
Sizzling "Sound" Crêpes (page 114)

◆

MAIN COURSE
Grilled Shrimp Quenelles on Sugar Cane (page 154)
Grilled Lemongrass Pork Tenderloin Skewers (page 202)
Pickled Vegetables (page 48)
Cooked Rice Vermicelli (page 24)
Scallion Oil (page 50)

◆

DESSERT
Toasted Coconut Ice Cream (page 230)

Fall Menu

COCKTAIL
Longan Vodka (page 240)

◆

APPETIZER
Crab and Asparagus Soup (page 80)

◆

MAIN COURSE
Garlic-Roasted Baby Chickens (page 186)
Stir-Fried Yard-Long Beans (page 126)
Stir-Fried Bamboo Shoots and Shiitakes (page 130)
Cooked Jasmine Rice (page 100)

◆

DESSERT
Banana Fritters (page 231)

GREEN PAPAYA

MAIL-ORDER SOURCES

 Wonderful Asian communities can be found throughout the country, and they are well worth venturing off the beaten path to visit. They not only offer most of the exotic ingredients used in Asian cuisines, but are also windows into the cultures. Some of the best-known Asian communities are Anaheim's Little Saigon and San Francisco's Chinatown, both in California; Manhattan's and Brooklyn's Chinatowns, both in New York City; and Vancouver's Chinatown in British Columbia. There you will find merchants who specialize not only in Chinese and Vietnamese products, but also in Indonesian and Thai foods and, to a lesser extent, Japanese and Korean items. If you live near such a community, take this cookbook with you as a guide when selecting both packaged and fresh ingredients. If you do not live near one, try the following mail-order sources—some of which have catalogs—to find the ingredients you will need to prepare the recipes.

For Asian vegetables and exotic fruit
Diamond Organics
P.O. Box 2159
Freedom, CA 95019
TEL: 888-ORGANIC (674-2642)
FAX: 888-888-6777
WEBSITE: www.diamondorganics.com

Melissa's World Variety Produce, Inc.
P.O. Box 21127
Los Angeles, CA 90021
TEL: 800-588-0151
FAX: 323-588-9774
WEBSITE: www.melissas.com

*For dried or fresh ingredients
and cooking equipment*
Pacific Mercantile Company
1925 Lawrence Street
Denver, CO 80202
TEL: 303-295-0293
FAX: 303-295-2753

For Thai basil, lemongrass, and rau ram
Shepherd's Garden Seeds
30 Irene Street
Torrington, CT 06790
TEL: 860-482-3638
FAX: 860-626-0865

*For dried shiitakes, dried shrimp,
sauces, rice, and flour*
The CMC Company
P.O. Box 322
Avalon, NJ 08202
TEL: 800-CMC-2780
FAX: 609-861-3065
WEBSITE: clever.net/wwwmall/cmc

The Oriental Pantry
423 Great Road
Acton, MA 01720
TEL: 800-828-0368
FAX: 617-275-4506

For dry spices
Penzey's Spices
P. O. Box 933
W19362 Apollo Drive
Muskego, WI 53150
TEL: 414-679-7207
FAX: 414-679-7878
WEBSITE: www.penzeys.com

Kalustyan's
123 Lexington Avenue
New York, NY 10016
TEL: 212-685-3451
FAX: 212-683-8458
WEBSITE: www.kalustyans.com

For squab, baby chickens, and quail
D'Artagnan, Inc.
280 Wilson Avenue
Newark, NJ 07105
TEL: 800-327-8246
TEL: 973-344-0565
FAX: 973-465-1870
WEBSITE: www.dartagnan.com

*For frog's legs, Dungeness crabs, razor
clams, and other special seafood*
Farm 2 Market
P.O. Box 124
Roscoe, NY 12776
TEL: 800-477-2967
FAX: 607-498-5275

WATER SPINACH

Index

NOTE: *Page numbers in* **boldface** *refer to illustrations.*

INDEX OF ILLUSTRATIONS

TABLE OF EQUIVALENTS[*]

LIQUID AND DRY MEASURES

U.S.	METRIC
¼ teaspoon	1.25 milliliters
½ teaspoon	2.5 milliliters
1 teaspoon	5 milliliters
1 tablespoon (3 teaspoons)	15 milliliters
1 fluid ounce (2 tablespoons)	30 milliliters
¼ cup	65 milliliters
⅓ cup	80 milliliters
1 cup	235 milliliters
1 pint (2 cups)	480 milliliters
1 quart (4 cups, 32 ounces)	950 milliliters
1 gallon (4 quarts)	3.8 liters
1 ounce (by weight)	28 grams
1 pound	454 grams
2.2 pounds	1 kilogram

LENGTH MEASURES

U.S.	METRIC
⅛ inch	3 millimeters
¼ inch	6 millimeters
½ inch	12 millimeters
1 inch	2.5 centimeters

OVEN TEMPERATURES

FAHRENHEIT	CELSIUS	GAS
250	120	½
275	140	1
300	150	2
325	160	3
350	180	4
375	190	5
400	200	6
425	220	7
450	230	8
475	240	9
500	260	10

[*] *The exact equivalents in the above tables have been rounded off for convenience.*

Corinne Trang is an author, food writer, and consultant. She has traveled extensively and studied culture and cuisine throughout the United States, Europe, and Asia. She was Producing Editor as well as Director of the Kitchen at award-winning culinary magazine *Saveur*. Trang has cooked privately for the Casa Malaparte Foundation in Florence and Capri, Italy; been a guest critic at California College of Arts & Crafts (CCAC) in San Francisco; and lectured at the University of Applied Sciences in Cologne, Germany. A member of the James Beard Foundation and the International Association of Culinary Professionals, she writes and consults for such publications as *Moneysworth, Bottom Line Personal, City NY, Saveur,* and *Food & Wine*. She lives in New York City.